HYSTERIA: THE HISTORY OF A DISEASE

Detail from "Procession of the Possessed of Molenbeek" from an original engraving by Pieter Brueghel the Elder (1520?–69).

HYSTERIA

THE HISTORY OF A DISEASE

by Ilza Veith

PHOENIX BOOKS

THE UNIVERSITY OF CHICAGO PRESS
Chicago & London

SBN: 226-85252-0 (clothbound); 226-85253-9 (paperbound)
Library of Congress Catalog Card Number: 65-24429

The University of Chicago Press, Chicago 60637
The University of Chicago Press, Ltd., London

To the memory of
HENRY E. SIGERIST
Teacher and Friend

Preface

HYSTERIA, of all mental diseases, has occupied the interest of medical writers since medical writing began. Throughout these millennia, the concepts of its nature, origin, symptoms, and management have undergone many and radical changes.

Despite the dramatic evolution and the importance of this disease in the domain of psychiatry, its history has been largely ignored. Apart from a small number of articles and of brief references in general histories of psychiatry, the only books devoted to this subject were written in French and are no longer readily available.[1] This volume is an attempt to remedy this strange omission.

In the assessment of the vast material of the past which Daniel Hack Tuke described in 1892 as "excessively plentiful,"[2] it becomes evident that much of what has been called hysteria at various periods would now no longer be so described, and much of what is now recognized as symptomatic of hysteria was earlier attributed to other diseases.

In recording this history, I have endeavored to present the disease as the various authors, and other people of the periods in which they lived, understood it, with little or no intent to reconcile their concepts with those of today. Incidentally, among these writers one encounters a great predominance of physicians, clergymen, and philosophers over

---

[1] G. Abricossoff, *L'hystérie aux XVIIe et XVIIIe siècles* (Paris, 1897); Henry Cesbron, *Histoire critique de l'hystérie* (Paris, 1909).

[2] Daniel Hack Tuke, *A Dictionary of Psychological Medicine*, Vol. I, (J. & A. Churchill, 1892), p. 627.

psychiatrists—greater than in the story of any other mental disease.

What actually is hysteria? The term is a familiar part of our general as well as medical vocabulary and evokes similar images in most minds. Its current definition, however, is much more complex than older definitions. The word no longer appears in the *Standard Nomenclature of Diseases*, and it was eliminated in 1952 from the *Mental Disorders Diagnostic Manual* of the American Psychiatric Association, being replaced by the term "conversion symptom."

This expression is a reflection of Freud's theory that neurotic patients generally suffer from a marked emotional tension which arises from an unconscious source, and that this tension may undergo many alterations, i.e., it may be converted from its emotional manifestation into a physical ailment.[3] As Freud said: "It is this characteristic of hysteria which has so long stood in the way of its being recognized as a psychical disorder."[4]

It is often stated by psychiatrists and other physicians that the disease has ceased to exist. Yet no modern textbook of psychiatry in any part of the Western world would be complete without a lengthy chapter on this ailment.

Throughout the tangled skein of its history runs the scarlet thread of sexuality, and in the early recognition of this essential relationship we perceive the roots of Freudian thinking, even in the medical papyri of ancient Egypt. Freud's principal contribution to the treatment of behavioral disturbances in fact took as its starting point the centuries-old effort to understand and cure hysteria.

Despite their apparently superficial dissimilarities, the manifestations of disordered minds have displayed an amazing resemblance in all cultures and throughout the span of observed human conduct. Hysteria in particular has adapted its symptoms to the ideas and mores current in each society; yet its predispositions and its basic features have remained more or less unchanged. In ancient Egypt the conduct of

[3] Poul Bjerre, *The History and Practice of Psychoanalysis* (Boston: Richard G. Badger, 1920), pp. 95–96.

[4] Josef Breuer and Sigmund Freud, *Studies on Hysteria*, Vol. II of *The Standard Edition of the Complete Psychological Works of Sigmund Freud* (London: Hogarth Press, 1957), p. 86.

certain unstable females was attributed to peregrinations of a discontented womb, and the Greeks, who retained this association, gave the disorder its name by calling it hysteria derived from *hystera*, the Greek word for womb. Pierre Janet, the great French philosopher and psychologist, justified the continued usage of this term long after the concepts which had given rise to it had become obsolete. He wrote: "The word 'hysteria' should be preserved, although its primitive meaning has much changed. It would be very difficult to modify it nowadays, and truly it has so great and beautiful a history that it would be painful to give it up."[5] This "great and beautiful history" may give validity to the present effort to trace the evolution of concepts about this extraordinary disease.

In a running story covering many millennia and exciting the interest of innumerable writers and investigators, it is beyond human capacity to encompass all that has been written; and undoubtedly this account of hysteria may omit mention of some jewels of wisdom and understanding yet to be brought to light. Even among the well-known figures of the past there are many who, in the interest of readable brevity, must be left unquoted. The selection is necessarily arbitrary and remains the privilege as well as the responsibility of the historian.

This review of the writings that constitute the history of hysteria has brought to the author's attention an amazing amount of anticipation, and actual formulation of many of the ideas traditionally believed to have originated in the mind of Sigmund Freud. Indeed Freud himself had become quite aware of the many threads, often not very tenuous, that linked not only the thinking of the early nineteenth century with his own but even that of Plato.[6] Freud was complacent about his own lack of depth in philosophy and literature; in fact, he felt that this contributed to his originality and absolved him from the onus of plagiarism.[7] Perhaps this was so.

[5] Pierre Janet, *The Mental State of Hystericals: A Study of Mental Stigmata and Mental Accidents,* trans. C. R. Carson (New York: Putnam & Sons, 1901), p. 527.

[6] Sigmund Freud, *An Autobiographical Study,* trans. James Strachey (London: Hogarth Press, 1946), p. 42.

[7] *Ibid.,* pp. 109–10.

On the other hand, however, if he could have adduced the support of such hallowed authorities as Plato, Galen, and Sydenham, he might have encountered somewhat less opposition in gaining acceptance of his ideas.

The deletion of hysteria from the official roster of mental diseases elicits the question whether a condition so obvious and so concrete to the observers of the past has actually disappeared in modern life. Considering that it took nearly two thousand years to discover the hysterical basis of "conversion symptoms," might it not be possible that other disorders, now less clearly recognized, may be found to be etiologically related to the complex of hysteria?

It is a pleasant obligation to express my gratitude to all who have been of help to me in the completion of this book. Drs. Walter Riese, Henry von Witzleben, Leo M. Zimmerman, and Marjorie Hayes, Mrs. Elizabeth Munger, and my husband have read the manuscript in part or in its entirety. They have made critical suggestions and contributed stimulating and enriching ideas, which have helped to broaden the scope of my undertaking. If any inaccuracies or shortcomings remain, they are of course solely my responsibility. For informal discussion of my work, I am grateful to Drs. J. B. de C. M. Saunders, Richard B. Richter, Sidney Schulman, Lester King, and Lawrence Z. Freedman. I am also grateful to the director and faculty members of the Chicago Institute for Psychoanalysis who invited me to speak to them on the history of hysteria and whose pronounced interest and warm reaction to my lecture awakened in me the realization that a book on the subject might be welcome to professionals in the mental sciences. My gratitude further extends to the medical librarians of the University of Chicago, where the book was begun, and to those of the University of California, San Francisco Medical Center, where it was completed. Both universities are to be thanked for providing me with the academic atmosphere and the time necessary to devote myself to the research for the writing of the book. And, finally, I wish to acknowledge my obligation for the assistance of the United States Public Health Service, National Institute of Mental Health, whose grant No. MHO1563 provided the financial means for the necessary studies and research.

Contents

Contents   xiii

Illustrations

Conceptions from the past blind us to facts which almost slap us in the face.—*William Stuart Halsted*

CHAPTER 1

The
Beginnings

Hysteria is an extraordinarily interesting disease, and a strange one. It is encountered in the earliest pages of recorded medicine and is dealt with in current psychiatric literature. Throughout all the intervening years it has been known and accepted as though it were a readily recognizable entity. And yet, except for the fact that it is a "functional" disorder, without concomitant organic pathological change, it defies definition and any attempt to portray it concretely. Like a globule of mercury, it escapes the grasp. Whenever it appears it takes on the colors of the ambient culture and mores; and thus throughout the ages it presents itself as a shifting, changing, mist-enshrouded phenomenon that must, nevertheless, be dealt with as though it were definite and tangible. To trace the evolution of this disorder it will be necessary to follow its forms as well as the concepts of its origin and the methods of its treatment. The experiences of the past may cast some light on the present.

INTRODUCTION

The term "hysteria" is obviously derived from the Greek word *hystera*, which means "uterus." Inherent in this simple etymological fact is the meaning of the earliest views on the nature and cause of the disease. It was formerly believed to be solely a disorder of women, caused by altera-

tions of the womb. The association of hysteria with the
female generative system was in essence an expression of
awareness of the malign effect of disordered sexual activity
on emotional stability. But these concepts go back to man's
earliest speculations about health and disease, long before
the term "hysteria" had been coined, and they indicate the
prominent role that sexual life played in general well-being
even in remote antiquity. They are documented in the first
recorded medical literature of ancient Egypt, two thousand
years before Christ. And, as will become evident, they persisted with minor modifications in all Western cultures and
throughout all periods well into the nineteenth century.

ANCIENT EGYPT—THE WANDERING WOMB

The earliest sources of recorded medicine emanated from the
two great centers of culture—the Egyptian and the Mesopo-
tamian. Of these the Egyptian records play an important
part in the story of the evolution of the concepts of hysteria.
Knowledge of Egyptian medicine is derived chiefly from a
small number of surviving papyri. The oldest of these, in
fact, deals specifically with the subject of hysteria. This
document is known as the *Kahun Papyrus*, after the ancient
Egyptian city in the ruins of which it was found, and dates
from about 1900 B.C. It is lamentably incomplete; only fragments have survived.[1] They were evidently part of a small
treatise describing a series of morbid states, all attributed to
displacement of the uterus. Each brief enumeration of symptoms is followed by the physician's pronouncement on the
nature of the case and his recommendations for appropriate
treatment.

Of the diseases mentioned in this document, most of
those that are defined clearly enough to be recognizable
would be classed today as hysterical disorders. Significantly,
however, even the ancient Egyptian physicians suspected the
"hysterical" basis for the complaints. This is not specifically

[1] The Petri Papyri, *Hieratic Papyri from Kahun and Gurob (Prin-
cipally of the Middle Kingdom)*, ed. F. Ll. I. Griffith (2 vols.; London:
Bernard Quaritch, 1897); Vol. I: *Literary, Medical and Mathematical
Papyri from Kahun*, pp. 5–11.

stated in the text but is implied by the fact that they are listed under the heading of disorders of the uterus and, furthermore, that the treatment recommended was directed towards that organ. For at that early time, it was taken for granted that certain behavioral disorders were associated with the generative organs, and specifically with aberrations in the *position* of the womb. This was so firmly established that no other explanation for the symptoms was so much as suggested. A few illustrative cases are cited: "a woman who loves bed; she does not rise and does not shake it," another woman "who is ill in seeing" and who has a pain in her neck, a third "woman pained in her teeth and jaws; she knows not how to open her mouth," and, finally, "a woman aching in all her limbs with pain in the sockets of her eyes." These and similar disturbances were believed to be caused by "starvation"[2] of the uterus or by its upward dislocation with a consequent crowding of the other organs. The physician's efforts were therefore quite logically directed towards nourishing the hungry organ or returning it to the place from which it had strayed.

Observations of patients with prolapse may have lent credibility to the uterine-displacement theory, although it is noteworthy that this easily recognized anomaly was never associated with the bizarre phenomena characteristic of hysteria. In the absence of any systematic knowledge of anatomy in general, and of the female generative organs in particular, the notion of a mobile and migratory uterus would not be as absurd as it might sound. Yet, despite the unshakable belief in the role of the wandering uterus, there is no mention in the *Kahun Papyrus* of direct manipulation to restore it to its normal position. Instead, attempts were made to lure or drive the organ back as if it were a living, independent organism. The parts were fumigated with precious and sweet-smelling substances to attract the womb; or evil-tasting and foul-smelling substances were ingested or inhaled to repel the organ and drive it away from the upper part of the body where it was thought to have wandered. So deeply

[2] The nature of the uterine abnormality sometimes was interpreted as a "starvation" of the organ. Much more frequently, however, were displacements in various directions, producing their effects by pressing on contiguous structures, adduced as explanations.

ingrained did these methods become that they were carried over into recent times, long after their original rationale had been forgotten. Thus, strong-smelling herbs such as valerian and asafetida in the form of aromatics, sedatives, and anti-spasmodics were still recommended as specific antihystericals in medical pharmacological textbooks as late as the early twentieth century.[3]

The preoccupation with hysterical manifestations in the *Kahun Papyrus* was not an isolated phenomenon in the medical literature of ancient Egypt. This is suggested by the fact that at least one other and even more important specimen among the small number of known medical papyri deals extensively with this subject. Known after the German Egyptologist Georg Ebers, who first published its facsimile, the *Papyrus Ebers* dates back to the sixteenth century B.C. It has been called "the greatest Egyptian medical document,"[4] and it is most certainly the largest of the antique Egyptian medical texts to have been discovered; moreover, it is complete and well preserved.[5] Unlike other papyri, the *Papyrus Ebers* is a composite of many monographs and may have served as a textbook of general medicine.[6] Apart from fractures and luxations, surgical conditions are not mentioned, but it does touch upon many kinds of diseases, including those in the fields of gynecology and obstetrics.

The chapter entitled "Diseases of Women," dealing largely with hysteria, goes far beyond the therapeutic suggestions in the *Kahun Papyrus*. Among the elaborations are the de-

[3] Adolf Strumpell, *A Textbook of Medicine for Students and Practitioners* (New York, 1911); Torald Sollmann, *A Manual of Pharmacology* (Philadephia, 1918).

[4] *The Papyrus Ebers, the Greatest Egyptian Medical Document,* trans. B. Ebbell (Copenhagen: Levin & Munksgaard, 1937).

[5] The others are the *Edwin Smith Papyrus,* which deals with surgery and which was composed around 1600 B.C.; the *Hearst Papyrus,* which contains prescriptions similar to those in the *Papyrus Ebers;* the *Berlin Medical Papyrus,* which is assumed to have been written about 1250 B.C. and which also contained prescriptions in an unsystematic arrangement; and finally the *London Medical Papyrus,* which was probably written about 1350 B.C. and which, although containing a few prescriptions, consists chiefly of incantations against a variety of diseases.

[6] For a most instructive discussion of the medical papyri, see Henry E. Sigerist, *A History of Medicine,* Vol. I of *Primitive and Archaic Medicine* (New York: Oxford University Press, 1951).

tailed prescriptions "to cause a woman's womb to go to its place." The remedies and their modes of application show the highly imaginative approaches by which control of hysterical symptoms was attempted. One prescription, a potion composed of tar from the wood of a ship and the dregs of beer, was supposed, by its evil taste, to induce the descent of the uterus. Other recipes listed ointments, compounded from a variety of unpleasant ingredients, that were used to rub the affected parts of the body in order to drive down the uterus. One such ointment was composed of dry excrement moistened with beer: "The fingers of the woman are rubbed with it; thou shalt apply it to all her limbs and to her diseased place."[7]

The *Papyrus Ebers*, in agreement with the methods of the earlier *Kahun Papyrus*, also recommended applying a variety of fragrant and aromatic substances to attract the uterus from below. The patient, for instance, was to sit on a roll of cloth that had been moistened with the dregs of an infusion of pine sawdust. Another prescription recommended placing yellow ochre on fresh myrrh and applying it to the patient's pudenda, while at the same time a cloth moistened with liquid myrrh was applied "to the upper part thereof." Further modes of treatment are described wherein fumigation by means of fragrant and powerful substances is used. Among these, "dry excrement of men is placed on frankincense, and the woman is fumigated therewith; let the fume thereof enter into her vulva." Although the medicinal use of highly unappetizing substances was far from uncommon in ancient Egypt, this particular prescription suggests a deliberate choice. The implication of gratifying the uterus with discharges from the opposite sex cannot be disregarded.

As a final measure ". . . to cause the womb to go back to its place: an ibis of wax is placed on charcoal, and let the fumes thereof enter into her vulva."[8] This merits special comment, since it alone of the remedies mentioned in the papyri introduces a magico-religious element to the otherwise entirely rational basis of treatment. For, bizarre as these therapeutic measures may seem to us, they are entirely

[7] The quotations are taken from the *Papyrus Ebers*, pp. 108–9.
[8] *Ibid.*

reasonable within the framework of the then existing concepts of the pathogenesis of hysterical disorders. As pointed
out above, fumigation with pleasing scents could with reason
be expected to entice a wandering uterus back to its normal
seat deep in the pelvis. But to incorporate the aromatic
agents into a waxen bird appears to go beyond reason: it
becomes comprehensive only upon the realization that the
ibis was the symbol of the god Thoth. This male deity
ranked among the most powerful in the Egyptian pantheon.
He personified the moon and was related to the sun; as the
inventor of the art of writing he became the scribe of all the
other gods and partook of their work; and since he was also
believed to be the owner of secret books, he was considered
the god of wisdom.[9] He was revered as an author of books
on medicine and functioned as physician to the gods and the
protector of all who were ill.[10] In the favoring of the patient's pudenda with the fumes of the waxen image of Thoth
we see a combination of rational medical treatment with
symbolism in its appeal to the powers of the god.

This specific instance of the ibis used for vulvar insuffla-
tion inevitably gives rise to further speculations that bear on
modern psychological theories. The employment of the
image of a powerful male deity to lure back a wandering
female organ is highly suggestive of the nature of the underlying ideas concerning hysteria even if they are nowhere
spelled out in detail.

Despite the often fantastic manifestations of hysteria, the
physicians of ancient Egypt tended to regard it as an organi-
cally induced affliction and therefore rarely invoked the
supernatural in its treatment by prayers or incantations. This
is in contrast to the treatment in other medical papyri, for
medicine in ancient Egypt was very largely deistic, and
prayers, incantations, amulets, and exorcisms constituted
important adjuvants to a very extensive polypharmacy. The
general reliance upon rational methods in the *Kahun Papyrus*

[9] Henri Frankfort, *Kingship and the Gods: A Study of Ancient Near Eastern Religion as the Integration of Society and Nature* (Chicago: University of Chicago Press, 1948).

[10] G. Roeder, *Urkunden zur Religion des alten Ägyptens* (Jena, 1916), p. 91.

may be due to the fact that this papyrus stems from the earlier Egyptian period during which medicine was relatively free from considerations of the supernatural. Later there was a definite decline into a world dominated by magic and superstition.

This is not to say that religion was entirely absent in the early medicine of ancient Egypt. The *Papyrus Ebers* itself begins with an invocation that the physician was to recite before commencing treatment: "I will save him from his enemies, and Thoth shall be his guide, he who lets writing speak and has composed the books; he gives to the physicians who accompany him, skill to cure. The one whom the god loves, him he shall keep alive."[11] According to Ebbel[12] this and other spells were not intended to replace the ordinary medical treatment but simply to strengthen it. They should be interpreted as prayers to the gods to intensify the healing virtue of the remedy, much as might be offered today; and as such they were doubtless helpful since faith in the effect of treatment surely contributed to recovery.

Although the role of the priestly caste and the religio-medical character of medical practice in later centuries increased, as mentioned above, it was specifically the earlier ideas that found their way into Greece, where they were incorporated in the foundations of the traditionally rational medicine of that country.[13] Indeed, the most convincing evidence of the continuity of Egyptian and Greek medical thought is perhaps the transmission of views on hysteria. Statements in the Hippocratic work *De morbis mulierum* ("On the Diseases of Women") are almost identical with those in the papyri ascribing hysteria to morbid states, or wanderings of the uterus. But it is in the words of Plato's *Timaeus* that this concept finds its most graphic expression:

The womb is an animal which longs to generate children. When it remains barren too long after puberty, it is distressed and sorely disturbed, and straying about in the body and cutting off the passages of the breath, it impedes respiration and brings

[11] *Papyrus Ebers*, p. 29.

[12] *Ibid.*, p. 25.

[13] For an extremely interesting discussion of this subject, see J. B. de C. M. Saunders, *The Transitions from Ancient Egyptian to Greek Medicine* (Lawrence: University of Kansas Press, 1963).

the sufferer into the extremest anguish and provokes all manner of diseases besides.[14]

This disturbance continues until the womb is appeased by passion and love. "Such is the nature of women and all that is female."

[14] 91c.

CHAPTER II

Graeco-Roman Thought

THE ART of healing in ancient Greece is intimately involved with the name of Hippocrates, and because of his
eminent place in the history of medicine, it might be well to
mention the few known facts about his life and works. The
scanty information that we have must be pieced together
from the Platonic dialogues and some later biographical
studies which reveal that Hippocrates was born in 460 B.C.
on the island of Cos. Tradition holds that he died at 104 years
of age—a tradition that may have been simply a compliment
to the great physician and cannot be accepted as historical
fact. All biographical references agree, however, that Hippocrates traveled over much of Greece, and that he was the
outstanding representative of the Coan school of medicine
which flourished at the same time as the neighboring school
of Knidos. This is all that is known about the "Father of
Medicine," and how many of the seventy-two books contained in the *Corpus Hippocraticum* were written by Hippocrates himself remains equally doubtful. It is quite certain,
however, that they all came into being during or after his
lifetime and bear his stamp in varying degrees. Nevertheless
it was inevitable that some traces of older and even foreign
medical theories found their way into Greek medicine, and
it was probably by this route that the Egyptian notions on
the nature of the uterus and its migratory propensities were
perpetuated in the *Corpus Hippocraticum*.

THE NAME

In the Egyptian papyri the disturbances resulting from the movement of the womb were described, but they had not yet been given a specific appellation. This step was taken in the Hippocratic writings where the connection of the uterus (*hystera*) with the disease resulting from its disturbances is first expressed by the term "hysteria." It appears in the thirty-fifth aphorism, which reads: "When a woman suffers from hysteria or difficult labour an attack of sneezing is beneficial." In light of the Egyptian prescriptions this might mean that the spasm of sneezing would push the uterus back in place.

In Greek literature the term "hysteria" is more frequently used in its adjectival form and is applied to such conditions as certain forms of respiratory difficulty in which the choking sensation was believed to be due to the pressure of the displaced uterus. Similarly, the *globus hystericus* could be explained on the basis of such organic malposition. This phenomenon was thought to occur primarily in mature women who were deprived of sexual relations; prolonged continence was believed to result in demonstrable organic changes in the womb. The thinking ran that in such situations the uterus dries up and loses weight and, in its search for moisture, rises toward the hypochondrium, thus impeding the flow of breath which was supposed normally to descend into the abdominal cavity. If the organ comes to rest in this position it causes convulsions similar to those of epilepsy. If it mounts higher and attaches itself to the heart the patient feels anxiety and oppression and begins to vomit. When it fastens itself to the liver the patient loses her voice and grits her teeth, and her complexion turns ashen. If the uterus lodges in the loins, the woman feels a hard ball, or lump, in her side. But when it mounts as high as the head, it causes pains around the eyes and the nose, the head feels heavy, and drowsiness and lethargy set in. Beyond these specific symptoms, the movement of the womb generally produces palpitations and excessive perspiration and convulsions similar to those observed in epilepsy.[1] The anatomical difficulties in the way of such free and extensive migrations were apparently of no concern to these writers. This may in part be due to an overwhelming ignorance of bodily structure and particularly that of the female generative system.

Such conditions were to be treated in the following manner. The physician was to undertake a manual examination to search for the dislodged uterus taking special care to avoid touching the liver; also a bandage was to be applied below the hypochondria to prevent further ascension of the womb. Into the forcibly opened mouth of the patient the physician was to pour strongly perfumed wine. Fetid fumigations for the nose and aromatic ones for the uterus were to help return the organ to its normal abode.

Although all symptoms were thought to appear in both widows and spinsters, the after-treatment of both types of patients was different. Immediately following the attack, all patients were to be given a strong purgative and subsequently a draught of ass's milk. Afterwards one applies aromatic fumigations to the uterus: a pessary with buprested[2] and in the morning one with bitter almonds. After two days' interval, one gives an aromatic injection into the uterus, and on the following morning applies a pessary (soaked in) mint. After one day's interval (there will again be) aromatic fumigations. This is what one should do for the widow, but the best is for her to remarry and to become pregnant. So far as the spinster is concerned, the physician advises her to take a husband; he applies nothing to the uterus nor does he administer any purgatives; instead he gives fleabane[3] and castor oil to drink in wine on an empty stomach. The woman is not to inhale or anoint her head with perfumes.

In another Hippocratic treatise entitled *On the Nature of Woman*[4] the following conditions and remedies are de-

[1] This discussion is primarily based on the Hippocratic text *On the Diseases of Women*, i.e., *Des maladies des femmes* in *Oeuvres complètes d'Hippocrate*, trans. E. Littré (Paris: Baillière, 1851), Vol. VIII: Book I, paragraphs 7 and 32; Book II, paragraphs 123–27.

[2] Any of a large family of (Buprestidae) poisonous beetles with short notched antennae and long bodies tapering at the rear.

[3] A member of the Aster family.

[4] *De la nature de la femme*, in the Littré edition of *Oeuvres complètes d'Hippocrate*, Vol. VII, paragraphs 73, 75, and 87.

scribed. If the uterus is turned towards the viscera and causes choking, the woman is to drink juniper wine and Ethiopian cumin.[5] She is to wash herself with hot water and is to drink after the bath. If the uterus is displaced and moved too far aside, one crushes some barley in the husk and some tamarisk,[6] also some deer horn, and mixes it all with wine and prepares a fumigation of the womb.

The doubt whether *On the Diseases of Women* and *On the Nature of Woman* belong among the genuine works of Hippocrates has never been satisfactorily resolved and the question of the authenticity or spuriousness of these treatises will not be dicussed here. For our purposes, it should suffice that the ancient world considered both to be parts of the *Corpus Hippocraticum*. But beyond these simple and somewhat crude descriptions of hysterical manifestations and their treatment, the book on *Epidemics*[7] presents the earliest known case histories of hysterical neuropathy. The first, dealing with hysterical mutism, reads as follows: "The wife of Polemarchus felt a sudden pain in her groin; her menses having failed to set in. . . . She was without voice through the entire night until the middle of the next day . . . [and only able] to indicate with her hand that the pain was in her groin." Another, dealing with a woman obviously suffering from hysterical loss of motor function, relates: "Following a short and insignificant cough she experienced a paralysis of the right upper limb and the left lower limb, nothing [no paralysis] in the face, nothing [affected] her intelligence. This woman began to improve on the twentieth day."

Further manifestations believed to be of hysterical origin are described in the therapeutic section of *On the Nature of Women*. Most explicit is the case of crural and sciatic neuralgia. Here it is stated "If the uterus approaches the legs and the feet, you will recognize it by the following sign: the woman has spasms of the big toes, pain under the nails, which is also felt in the legs and thighs. If matters are like

[5] A dwarf plant of the carrot family, native to Egypt and Syria, and cultivated for its aromatic seeds.

[6] Any of a genus of shrubs or trees, typical of the tamarisk family chiefly of desert shrubs and trees having narrow entire leaves and flowers with stamens and a one so-called ovary.

[7] *Oeuvres complètes d'Hippocrate*, Book V.

this, the patient should be washed in a great deal of hot water, then she should be given a steam bath; afterwards one applies fetid fumigations and finally one annoints the pubes with perfume of roses."

The Hippocratic physician was aware of the importance of a careful differentiation between hysterical symptoms and those of organic disease. With reference to convulsions the differential diagnosis between hysteria and epilepsy was essential in order to indicate appropriate treatment. This was accomplished by the application of digital pressure to the patient's abdomen. If she could feel this pressure, her ailment was of hysterical origin; if not, she was probably suffering from epilepsy.[8]

The treatments of hysterical disorders in the Hippocratic texts are similar to those in the Egyptian papyri and were directed toward achieving the same purpose. In disturbances that were diagnosed as "suffocation of the womb" two types of fumigation were used to induce the uterus to move downward, namely, those with malodorous substances which were to be inhaled or sweet-scented aromas which were applied below. In cases where the uterus was assumed to be pressing upon the intestines, caraway-flavored wine was prescribed, to be followed by a hot bath and subsequent cooling drinks. And if the uterine dislocation was believed to be the sequel to amenorrhea, medicated pessaries made of strips of linen or wool were inserted into the vagina. The latter treatment, however, was not recommended for virgins. Elderly virgins as well as widows, including those who had had children, were thought to be particularly vulnerable to hysterical afflictions caused by irregular menses; marriage was recommended to them as the speediest way of achieving a cure.[9] It is this recommendation that translates the sexual element, initially implied in the earliest concepts of hysteria, into tangible terms and that, as will be seen in subsequent chapters, continued to be among the standard prescriptions for more than two thousand years.

Because of the surpassing authority of Hippocrates and his

[8] Regimen in Acute Diseases 35. *Oeuvres complètes d'Hippocrate,* VII.

[9] On the Nature of Woman 26, 73–75, 87. *Oeuvres complètes d'Hippocrate,* VII.

works, his teachings prevailed not only throughout antiquity
but almost until our own time. This is true for the views on
hysteria in particular and of the large part of the *corpus* in
general.

The doctrine of supreme importance in the *Corpus Hippocraticum* is the all-pervading concept of the natural origin
of disease and the vigorous denial of superhuman, divine, or
demonic causation. This is most explicitly stated in connection with epilepsy. For reasons not entirely clear, this malady
had been so generally accepted as being of divine origin that
it was called the "sacred disease."[10] In his book bearing the
same title, Hippocrates utterly demolishes all claim for
supernatural origin beyond that of any other disease. Epilepsy is also of particular interest in the study of hysteria because the two diseases bear so much resemblance to each
other that they are frequently discussed together. Despite the
efforts described above to differentiate between the two,
confusion occasionally occurred. The Hippocratic treatise on
epilepsy begins as follows:

I am about to discuss the disease called "sacred." It is not in
my opinion, any more divine or more sacred than other diseases,
but has a natural cause, and its supposed divine origin is due
to men's inexperience, and to their wonder at its peculiar character. Now while men continue to believe in its divine origin
because they are at a loss to understand it, they really disprove
its divinity by the facile method of healing which they adopt,
consisting as it does of purifications and incantations. But if it
is to be considered divine just because it is wonderful, there
will be not one sacred disease but many, for I will show that
other diseases are no less wonderful and portentous, and yet
nobody considers them sacred.[11]

Hippocrates then discusses other diseases which would
seem no less sacred or god-sent than epilepsy, "but nobody
wonders at them." Here he particularly refers to madness
"from no obvious cause" making men commit many strange
acts from which they return to apparent sanity, only to relapse at another time into states of similar disturbance. He
believes that those writers of the distant past, who first

[10] For a detailed study on the history of epilepsy see Owsei Temkin,
The Falling Sickness (Baltimore: Johns Hopkins Press, 1945).

[11] *Hippocrates,* trans. W. H. S. Jones (Loeb Classical Library), II,
139–41.

attributed a sacred character to epilepsy, were like the magicians, charlatans, and quacks of his own day. "Being at a loss, and having no treatment which would help, they concealed and sheltered themselves behind superstition, and called this illness sacred, in order that their utter ignorance might not be manifest."

In seeking the cause of epilepsy Hippocrates was the first in the history of medicine to arrive at the conclusion that the seat of the disease is in the brain. Amplifying this statement he presents a superb description of the functions of the brain which had hitherto been neglected or ignored:

Men ought to know that from the brain, and from the brain only, arise our pleasures, joys, laughter and jests, as well as our sorrows, pains, griefs and tears. Through it, in particular, we think, see, hear, and distinguish the ugly from the beautiful, the bad from the good, the pleasant from the unpleasant, in some cases using custom as a test, in others perceiving them from their utility. It is the same thing which makes us mad or delirious, inspires us with dread and fear, whether by night or by day, brings sleeplessness, inopportune mistakes, aimless anxieties, absent-mindedness, and acts that are contrary to habit.[12]

Hippocrates concluded that the brain was the most important organ of the human body and that the eyes, the ears, tongue, hands, and feet, indeed the entire body, act in accordance with the discernment of the brain; and arrived finally at the classic definition in which he characterized the brain as "the interpreter of consciousness." Despite the very close similarities between the manifestations described above and those of hysteria, Hippocrates surprisingly maintained the uterine origin of the latter condition and strictly excluded it from the category of mental disease.

TEMPLE HEALING

The scientists of the Hippocratic period, and even the philosophers, accepted the rational explanation of epilepsy and of medicine in general because it was thoroughly compatible with their all-inclusive concept of nature. But this rationalism did not reach the majority of the general population of

[12] *Ibid.,* p. 175.

ancient Greece—a people still close to their gods. They saw
that rational medicine was effective in many instances but
that it failed to serve the needs of a great number of patients
who suffered from obscure or chronic diseases. Medical care
for these persons was sought from other sources and by
other means. The Greek world was dream-conscious; political and personal decisions were based on dreams. A healing
cult, utilizing dreams and dedicated to a healing god, combined the two elements dearest to all. The source of such
healing was provided by the temples which were dedicated
to Aesculapius, the god of medicine.

Like many of the Greek gods, Aesculapius had a worldly
career prior to his deification. Nothing, however, is known
about his earthly existence beyond the conjecture that he
may have been a highly respected priest-physician who so
won the esteem and affection of the people that he was accorded the role of a god. The exact time of his deification is
not known, but it is believed that his cult had existed many
centuries before it reached Athens in the fifth century B.C.
The principal centers of the cult were in Epidaurus, Cos,
Pergamon, and Tricca. During the reign of Alexander the
Great (336–323 B.C.) it is estimated that there were at least
three hundred Aesculapian temples in Greece.

The paucity of historical facts is amply made up by a great
many legends. The mythological story of Aesculapius begins
even before his birth. It tells us that he was the son of
Apollo, who, in a fashion not unusual among Greek gods,
had become enamored of an earthly maiden, Coronis. When
Coronis was forced by her unsuspecting parents to marry an
Arcadian youth, Apollo's wrath knew no bounds and he slew
Coronis with a thunderbolt. Only when she was about to be
consumed by the lightning flash did Apollo realize that she
was carrying his child. At the last moment he snatched the
child from its dying mother and took him to Chiron the
Centaur, who was famous as a physician and herbalist. Under
Chiron's tutelage, Aesculapius studied the healing art and
soon surpassed his teacher, for his patients never died and he
even succeeded in recalling the dead. Eventually, the guard-
ian of Hades began to fear that the underworld would become depopulated through the efforts of so effective a
physician, and he complained to the great Zeus, who found

it necessary to destroy Aesculapius. When Apollo interceded for his son, however, Zeus relented somewhat and elevated him to the heavens, thus making him the god of healing.

The temples of Aesculapius were generally situated in localities of natural beauty, which provided a pleasing environment to the patient. After an initial period of sacrifices, ablutions, and fasting, he was placed on a couch in one of many small rooms and was told to rest; cure was to be wrought by the god Aesculapius, who would appear in a dream. A number of votive tablets found at the temple sites tell of the dreams and the visions the patients experienced during their temple sleep. In most cases, it seems, Aesculapius appeared to them and brought about their recovery by words alone or by manipulation at the site of the malady. The god carried a staff and was often accompanied by one or more of the large snakes which abounded in the temples. Sometimes the patients felt that they were touched or licked by these snakes. According to the tablets, cure was the almost invariable result of these dreams. It was a distinctly psychotherapeutic atmosphere in which these cures were undertaken with rudiments of many of the procedures that were to endure through the millennia to the present day. Even the couch, of a fame then scarcely foreseeable, was in evidence.

A great deal of speculation has arisen about the mechanism by which these salutary effects were achieved. Suggestion, undoubtedly, played an enormous part. There is good evidence that in many cases the temple priests impersonated Aesculapius in speaking to the half-dreaming patients; there is the further hypothesis that the priests went through the ritual of sham surgery. It has also been thought that the priests may have used hypnosis, and a strong probability exists that they used a judicious mixture of all three approaches. The effectiveness of these ministrations is all the more plausible because a great many of the patients appear to have suffered from hysterical afflictions and hence were receptive to the mystical and ritualistic procedures of temple healing. The following cases taken from inscriptions that were excavated at the site of the great Aesculapian temple in Epidaurus are examples that would seem to confirm this impression:

Inscription 3. A man, whose fingers with the exception of one were paralyzed, came as a suppliant to the god. While looking at the tablets in the temple, he expressed incredulity regarding the cures and scoffed at the inscriptions. But in his sleep he saw a vision. It seemed to him that he was playing at dice below the Temple, and was about to cast the dice, [when] the god appeared, sprang upon his hand, and stretched out his [the patient's] fingers. When the god had stepped aside it seemed to the patient that he could bend his hand and [he] stretched out all his fingers one by one. When he had straightened them all the god asked him if he would still be incredulous of the inscriptions on the tablets in the Temple. He answered that he would not, [and the god said to him:] "Since, then, formerly you did not believe in the cures, though they were not incredible, for the future your name shall be 'Incredulous.'" When day dawned, he walked out sound.

Inscription 4. Ambrosia of Athens, blind of one eye. She came as a suppliant to the god. As she walked about in the Temple, she laughed at some of the cures as incredible and impossible that the lame and the blind should be healed by merely seeing a dream. In her sleep she had a vision. It seemed to her that the god stood by her, and said that he would cure her, but that in payment he would ask her to dedicate to the Temple a silver pig, as a memorial of her ignorance. After saying this, he cut the diseased eyeball, and poured in some drug.

Inscription 5. A voiceless boy. He came as a suppliant to the Temple for his voice. When he had performed the preliminary sacrifices, and fulfilled the usual rites, the temple servant who brings in the fire for the god, looking at the boy's father, demanded he should promise to bring within a year the thank-offering for the cure if he obtained that for which he had come. The boy suddenly said, "I promise." His father was startled at this, and asked him to repeat it. The boy repeated the words and after that became well.[13]

The subject of fees is frequently mentioned in these inscriptions; and it appears that thank-offerings of sacrificial animals, objects of art, votive tablets, or precious metals were usually expected. That they were essential in the healing ritual is confirmed by the inscriptions recording the histories of two blind men whose sight was restored but who lost it again after refusing to make the prearranged donation to the temple. The size of the fees varied according to the patients'

[13] Emma J. and Ludwig Edelstein, *Asclepios: A Collection and Interpretation of the Testimonies* (Baltimore: Johns Hopkins Press, 1945), I, 230-31, 233-235.

means and from the poor even the smallest and most insignificant offerings were graciously accepted. Large fees, however, were expected from wealthy patients and some were encouraged to donate buildings, baths, or add other structures to the temples. Among the largest recorded gifts was that of Phalysios of Naupaktos, who donated two thousand gold pieces in return for the recovery of his vision.

Apparently, many patients suffering from transitory blindness, probably of hysterical origin, sought help at the temples. The following inscription deals with another case of this nature:

Inscription 18. Alketas of Haleis. This blind man had a dream. It seemed to him that the god came up to him and opened his eyes with his fingers. And that he first saw the trees of the Temple. At daybreak he walked out restored to health.[14]

Also of special interest is the following case where the expectation of recovery was so strong that a cure was effected by rather crude means and without recourse to temple sleep or other more elaborate preparation:

Inscription 16. Nikanor, a lame man. While he was sitting wide-awake, a boy snatched his crutch from him and ran away. But Nikanor got up, pursued him, and so was cured.[15]

These illustrations are sufficient to indicate the peculiar character of Aesculapian medicine and its differences from religious healing in the traditional sense. Prayer as such was not used. Furthermore, although the healing was primarily by suggestion, certain of the patients came to the temple with avowed skepticism, despite which they were cured. This would indicate a most effective use of visual, auditory, and other stimuli of such convincing power as to overcome the previous disbelief. It is of course also possible that the inscription writers exaggerated the element of disbelief in order to make the cures appear all the more miraculous and to overcome the skepticism in later suppliants who read the inscriptions.

But if it was true that persons with grave afflictions came to an Aesculapian temple with unconcealed doubt, why then did they come at all? Why did they not go to one of the profane healers who abounded in ancient Greece? This ques-

14 *Ibid.*, p. 233.   15 *Ibid.*

tion is difficult to answer and yet various suppositions come
to mind. They may have expressed doubts in order to forestall any later disappointment. It is further possible that the
patients had visited other healers without being cured by
them and had become thoroughly discouraged. And, finally,
it is conceivable that the non-religious doctor had declined to
undertake the treatment, for the Greek physician could
select the cases he wished to treat and decline those that
appeared hazardous or unpromising. This was doubtless one
of the reasons for the apparently complete absence of professional antagonism between the temporal and the religious
healers of antiquity.

However, the skeptics were infrequent. The vast majority
of the population came imbued with hope and faith, not
only the sick but also the healthy who wished to preserve
their well-being. So successful were the temples that the cult
of Aesculapius flourished well into the Christian era and only
gradually gave way to the veneration of Christ the Physician.
During all this time, however, along with the temple healing
there was an active medical profession in Greece and later in
Rome that pursued its calling in the Hippocratic tradition
and considered disease a natural phenomenon to be treated
by rational means.

THE MALIGN DISEASE OF THE WOMB

The survival of the Hippocratic tradition and the transmission of its doctrine is evidenced in the writings of Aulus
Cornelius Celsus. His work is the first systematic treatise on
medicine which has come down to us. Little is known about
its author except that he lived in the first century A.D. Unlike
the Roman physicians of Greek origin who wrote in their
native language, Celsus was a native Roman and composed
his *De medicina* in patrician Latin. Because of this departure
from current medical usage and because his book on medicine was only part of a large encyclopedic work dealing with
all the knowledge of his day, it has been assumed that Celsus was not himself a practicing physician but a most
erudite layman who had made all knowledge his province. It
is probably for these reasons that his medical work failed to

enter the mainstream of Graeco-Roman and medieval medical thought. After its rediscovery during the Renaissance, however, it was widely read and greatly admired, for the exquisite beauty of its Latin style as well as for its medical content, and earned for Celsus the epithet *"Cicero medicorum."*[16]

Although the doctors of Celsus' day largely ignored his writings, the educated laity read them with avidity, as may indeed have been the author's intention. Thus, they became an important part of contemporary thought.[17] As an encyclopedist, Celsus was necessarily familiar with the medical writings of all who had preceded him, but it was Hippocrates in particular whom he admired. In his passages on hysteria he reveals a greater dependence upon the ideas of the Master than in many of his other descriptions, although he does not quote him directly, as he does in other passages of his work. Celsus does not refer to hysteria by name but discusses it under the heading "On Diseases of the Womb"; in fact, he describes it as *the* disease of the womb.

Females are subject to a malignant disease of the womb; and next to the stomach, this organ is highly susceptible of being affected either in itself, or by sympathy affects the rest of the body. Sometimes this affection deprives the patient of all sensibility, in the same manner as if she had fallen in epilepsia. Yet with this difference, that neither the eyes are turned, nor does foam flow from the mouth, nor are there any convulsions: there is only a profound sleep. This disease returning frequently to some females at last becomes habitual.[18]

In the Hippocratic fashion, the treatment was designed to draw the uterus back in place. As an elaboration of the traditional regimen, Celsus recommended that the therapy be extended an entire year in order to avoid recurrence and that wine be proscribed for the same length of time. He observed that hysterical patients tended to void frequent and copious quantities of limpid urine, and he advocated exercise and massage as a remedy. Another therapeutic innovation was

[16] Clifford Albutt, *Greek Medicine in Rome* (London: Macmillan & Co., 1921), pp. 202 ff.

[17] Max Neuburger, *History of Medicine*, trans. Ernest Playfair (London: Oxford University Press, 1910), pp. 213–19.

[18] L. Targa (ed.), *Aul[us] Cor[nelius] Celsus on Medicine, in Eight Books*, trans. Alexander Lee (London: E. Cox, 1831), I, chap. iv, 20, 307.

the use of blood-letting during the attack, a form of treatment which in later centuries became universal and unquestionably often injurious. If the patient did not seem sufficiently strong to withstand such a seriously depleting measure, Celsus recommended as an alternative the application of
suction cups at the groins.

THE WOMB IS AN ANIMAL

Although, in general, the original text of *De medicina* seems
to have been preserved intact, there is distinct evidence that
portions of the section dealing with hysteria are missing.
Much of the material not found in Celsus emerges in the
writings of Aretaeus of Cappadocia. This younger contemporary was even more single-minded in his adherence to
Hippocrates than was Celsus, although the latter became
known as the "Latin Hippocrates." Aretaeus, a physician
who wrote in Greek, is thought to have lived in the second
half of the first century or in the second century A.D. Nothing is known about him, and the incomplete but sizable portion of his superb medical works is his only legacy. Fortunately, his discussion of hysteria is among the chapters that
have been preserved almost intact and from their study it becomes evident that he incorporated in them the thoughts of
Hippocrates and Plato as well as his own experiences. That
his powers of observation were extraordinarily keen is
proved by his assertion that there was a form of hysteria un-
connected with the uterus which could also affect men. This
statement, as well as a similar one in the writings of Galen of
Pergamon, was ignored by his contemporaries and did not
reappear for nearly a millennium and a half, at which time it
was again disregarded.

Apart from the brief reference to male hysteria, however,
the value of Aretaeus' description serves chiefly to transmit
a summary exposition of all preceding thought. He divided
his entire medical material into acute or chronic diseases and
listed hysteria, or rather "Hysterical suffocation," as he
called it, among the former. He begins this chapter with a
description of the uterus which closely resembles that of
Plato: "In the middle of the flanks of women lies the womb,

a female viscus, closely resembling an animal; for it is moved of itself hither and thither in the flanks, also upwards in a direct line to below the cartilage of the thorax, and also obliquely to the right or to the left, either to the liver or spleen; and it likewise is subject to prolapsus downwards, and, in a word, it is altogether erratic."[19]

This statement reveals either ignorance or conscious disregard of actuality of the structure of the female generative organs. However, the last part of the sentence confirms the hypothesis put forth in connection with the Egyptian papyri, namely, that it was the observation of uterine prolapse that suggested the possibility of a migratory organ. Subsequently, Aretaeus explains that the womb "delights, also in fragrant smells, and advances towards them; and it has an aversion to fetid smells, and flees from them; and, on the whole, the womb is like an animal within an animal." He continues, "When, therefore, it is suddenly carried upwards, and remains above for a considerable time, and violently compresses the intestines, the woman experiences a choking, after the form of epilepsy, but without convulsions." This occurs, he believes, because the liver, diaphragm, lungs, and heart are squeezed together, impeding breath and causing loss of speech. The accompanying heaviness of the head, loss of sensibility and, finally, deep sleep he attributed to the fact that the carotids were compressed "from sympathy with the heart."

It is here that Aretaeus makes his significant observation that "in women there also arises another affection resembling this form, with sense of choking and loss of speech, but not proceeding from the womb; for it also happens to men, in the manner of *catochus*."[20] Apart from this brief statement, however, there is no further conjecture on the origin of this type of disturbance, and he returns to a discussion of the erratic behavior of the womb during attacks of hysterical suffocation. From this he infers that "the affection occurs in young women, but not in old. For in those in whom the age,

[19] Francis Adams (ed. and trans.), *The Extant Works of Aretaeus, the Cappadocian* (London: Sydenham Society, 1856), pp. 285–87.

[20] From the Greek: *katochē*, i.e., epilepsy; from *kat-echō*, hold fast. The trancelike phase of catalepsy in which the patient is conscious but cannot move or speak.

mode of life, and understanding is more mobile, the uterus also is of a wandering nature; but in those more advanced in life, the age, mode of living, understanding, and the uterus are of a steady character." This statement departs from the earlier texts which include widows and elderly virgins as being predominantly susceptible to this ailment.

In a later chapter, dealing with the "Therapeutics of Acute Diseases" Aretaeus treats of the "Cure of the Hysterical Convulsion."[21] This, too, is largely based on earlier writings. Of special interest here is his effort to add some anatomical knowledge to his etiological notions of hysteria and his explanation of the cause and cure of uterine prolapse.

The uterus in women has membranes extended on both sides of the flanks, and also is subject to the affections of an animal in smelling; for it follows after fragrant things as if for pleasure, and flees from fetid and disagreeable things as if for dislike. If, therefore, anything annoy it from above, it protrudes even beyond the genital organs. But if any of these things be applied to the os, it retreats backwards and upwards. Sometimes it will go to this side or to that,—to the spleen and liver, while the membranes yield to the distension and contraction like the sails of a ship.[22]

He describes the condition of prolapse as "a troublesome, painful and unseemly complaint, rendering it difficult to walk," but he considers it definitely a part of the general picture of "hysterical convulsion," for its alternative is the ascent of the womb. This, he maintains, can happen so suddenly that "it very speedily suffocates the woman, and stops the respiration as if with a cord, before she feels pain or can scream aloud, or can call upon the spectators, for in many cases the respiration is first stopped, and in others the speech." This description bears a strong resemblance to those states later termed "hysterical paroxysm" which for centuries seem to have been the most salient characteristic of hysteria.

In such cases, Aretaeus advises, it is essential that a physician be called quickly to prevent the patient's death. Among the measures recommended to the doctor by Aretaeus are many that have been previously described. Interestingly, he

21 *Works of Aretaeus*, pp. 449–51.

22 *Ibid.*, p. 449.

also furnishes the rationale for the Hippocratic aphorism concerning the favorable portent of sneezing, in the following manner: "Having produced sneezing, you must compress the nostrils; for by the sneezing and straining, in certain cases, the uterus has returned to its place." Reminiscent of the least appetizing of Egyptian prescriptions is the suggestion that "old urine [applied to the nose] greatly rouses the sense of one in a deathlike state and drives the uterus downwards."

A DISEASE OF CONSTRICTION

From what has been said, it is apparent that the Graeco-Roman writers were generally unoriginal and derivative in their approach to the problem of hysteria. A notable exception, however, is Soranus of Ephesus, known to his contemporaries and immediate successors as "Prince of the Physicians" (*Medicorum princeps*) and revered well into the Middle Ages. In spite of his great reputation, little is known about his personal life beyond that he was born in the second half of the first century at Ephesus in Asia Minor. He is said to have studied in Alexandria, which, since its founding in the third century B.C., continued to be the leading center of scientific medicine. Upon completion of his studies he followed the example of many of his Greek colleagues and settled in Rome, where he engaged in practice during the reigns of the emperors Trajan and Hadrian (A.D. 98–138).[23]

Although he is known to have written voluminously—the extant fragments of his writings contain references to numerous books—most of his writings "are only to be appreciated through the more or less dim medium of translations and compilations."[24] Fortunately, the only work that is almost completely preserved is also Soranus' most valuable—the highly original treatise on gynecology. This book reveals him to be the most eminent obstetrician and gynecologist of antiquity and for many subsequent centuries. Since these specialties were rarely the concern of physicians, his instruc-

[23] *Soranus' Gynecology*, trans. (and with an introduction by) Owsei Temkin (Baltimore: Johns Hopkins Press, 1956), p. xxiii.

[24] Max Neuburger, *op. cit.*, I, 234.

tions are largely directed to the midwife, for whom he
establishes standards of discipline and sobriety. He further
demands that she be without greed for money "lest she give
an abortive wickedly for payment,"[25] and that she be "free
from superstition so as not to overlook salutary measures on
account of a dream or an omen."[26]

The latter strictures interestingly reflect the moral and social atmosphere of Soranus' day. Some additional ancillary
observations are also of interest because they bear indirectly
on the subject of hysteria. The question of the age until
which females should remain virgins occupies a separate
chapter in the *Gynecology*[27] and throws some light on the
concept of the onset of maturity in the society of that time.

In introducing the problems relative to virginity, Soranus
compares both sexes and observes that "since the male merely discharges seed he does not run any risk from the first
intercourse." The female, however, because of the possibility
of conception, is endangered by premature defloration. He
is critical of those who advocate that women should remain
virgins only until they feel an urge to copulate, and who
reason that "nature herself, in dumb animals and humans
alike, has implanted certain torments and has set in motion
appetites with regard to the proper time for intercourse, so
that the body itself urges the approach to the pleasure of
copulation." This comparison seemed invalid to Soranus. In
animals, he believes, the age for mating is physiologically
fixed, while human beings are stirred by their senses and
imagination, as is the case in such "virgins who have not been
brought up wisely and lack education [and who] arouse in
themselves premature desires." He therefore urges that the
state of virginity be maintained until about the fourteenth
year, when the beginning of menstruation indicates the
maturity of the womb and its readiness to conceive. On the
other hand, he warns that lengthy postponement of defloration carries its own dangers since "the neck of the uterus remains collapsed in the same manner as the genitals of men
who have no sexual relations."[28]

The contributions of Soranus, in general, can be under-

[25] *Soranus' Gynecology*, p. 7.   [27] *Ibid.*, I, chap. viii.
[26] *Ibid.*   [28] *Ibid.*, I, chap. viii, 31.

stood only in the context of the medical philosophy he professed. He belonged to the "Methodist" school of medicine. This sect had evolved at about the beginning of the Christian era in opposition to two older schools, the "Dogmatists" and the "Empiricists." The Dogmatists, also known as Rationalists, emphasized theoretical principles and believed that it was imperative for the physician to study the structure and function of the body in order to know the *cause* of disease. The Empiricists had their philosophical roots in the doctrine of skepticism; they held that all knowledge was uncertain, that causes could not be investigated, and that the only valid reasoning in medicine was by experience, experiment, and analogy.

The Methodists, like the Empiricists, rejected the study of anatomy and physiology as having no bearing on the practice of medicine. In contrast to the humoral doctrine, which formed the basis of the other schools of thought, they advanced the concept of "atomic" structure. The body was believed to be composed of minute and indivisible particles which, of course, bore no relation to atomic bodies in their modern context. The atoms were supposed to be in constant and regular motion in states of health. Disease arose when the normal flow of atoms was either accelerated or retarded. As in many early systems of natural philosophy all aberrations were considered due to an imbalance, a disequilibrium between certain forces; and diagnosis required only the recognition of the specific inequality to account for all diseases. Thus, the Methodists limited their diagnostic criteria to the recognition of either an abnormally dry, tense, and constricted state (*status strictus*); or, conversely, of an excessively moist, relaxed, or fluid state (*status laxus*). Since certain conditions could not be easily classified in this manner, allowance was made for a "mixed state" if neither alternative was sufficiently pronounced. The attractiveness of so simple a classification to account for all diseases is immediately evident. Therapy based on this pathological system was equally uncomplicated inasmuch as it required only the giving of astringent or tonic substances in cases of *status laxus* and relaxing drugs in states of stricture. It is also obvious that adherents of this school of thought could easily dispense with the study of anatomy and physiology.

Soranus, the most prominent of the Methodists, however, was too good a physician to ignore these sciences altogether; in fact, he was well acquainted with human anatomy and particularly with that of the female reproductive organs. This deviation from the basic tenets of Methodism appears in his discussion of gynecological hygiene, which required an explanation of the nature of the female organs. Some of this, he says, can be learned directly from dissection. It is presumed he made anatomical studies, which practice he justifies most cleverly: "And since dissection, although useless, is nevertheless studied for the sake of profound learning, we shall also teach what has been discovered by it. For we shall easily be believed when we say that dissection is useless, if we are first found to be acquainted with it, and we shall not arouse the suspicion that we reject through ignorance something which is accepted as useful."[29]

Having thus established his reasons for digression into the field of anatomy, Soranus presents a detailed discussion of the structure and function of the female generative organs which, while far from complete and entirely clear, is still vastly superior to all others of his day. Although he speaks at length of the structural differences between virgins and those women who have borne children, it is interesting that he emphatically denies the existence of the hymen. Whether this is an oversight or, as Neuburger stated, "a fact which throws a curious light upon the conditions of life in Rome"[30] is open to conjecture.

Of major importance, however, in connection with hysteria is Soranus' contention that the uterus is *not* an animal even though it may resemble one in certain respects.[31] This long-held belief, which he denies, was probably figurative rather than literal, although he chooses to treat it as a bald statement of fact. In his emphatic rejection, however, he introduces new thought on the discussion of hysteria. He never doubts that the disease is related to the uterus, but he refuses to accept the idea that the uterus is able to wander about. In conformity with the tenets of the Methodist School,

[29] *Ibid.*, I, chap. ii, 7.   [30] *Neuburger, op. cit.*, p. 236.

[31] *Soranus' Gynecology*, I, chap. iii ("What Is the Nature of the Uterus and the Vagina"), 9.

he offered the explanation that hysteria was a *disease of stricture* emanating from the uterus but affecting the whole body. This rationale clearly influenced his therapeutic regimen. In his chapter on the subject, Soranus explains that "hysterical suffocation" had received its name from the stricken organ and from its predominant manifestation, suffocation. He defines the seizure as "obstructed respiration together with aphonia and a seizure of the senses caused by some condition of the uterus."[32] According to his observations the disease is generally preceded by "recurrent miscarriages, premature birth, long widowhood, retention of menses and the end of ordinary childbearing."[33] He describes the actual attack as a generalized convulsion from which the patient recovers quickly and is usually able to remember what happened. This presumed ability to recall the hysterical attack is an important factor used by Soranus to differentiate it from similar conditions, including epilepsy.

Since hysteria is a disease of violent "constriction" and appears in acute as well as in chronic form, Soranus suggests a regimen for the management of each type of manifestation. At the time of the attack the patient is to be put to bed in a comfortably warm and moderately light room and to be aroused from her unconscious state by gentle manipulations and warming compresses. If speech does not return, vacuum cups and sweet olive oil are to be applied to the groins, the pubes, and the adjacent regions. These and other soothing and warming applications are intended to lessen the stricture and to bring about relaxation. Once achieved, it is maintained by a suitably gentle regimen.

In chronic hysteria advantage should be taken of the intervals between paroxysms to restore the patient's equilibrium by "various passive exercises and promenades, reading aloud, vocal exercise, anointing, gymnastics, baths, and varied food." Other and more vigorous countermeasures follow later, if the gentler methods fail to bring about a cure. If, however, the condition still remains intractable, additional measures are indicated. These include a rather drastic procedure: after having brought about vomiting by feeding

---

[32] *Ibid.*, III, chap. iv ("On Hysterical Suffocation"), 149.
[33] *Ibid.*

radishes to the patients, "one also must make the patient
choke by means of white hellebore." This treatment by
similia similibus was unusual at the time but many centuries
later assumed importance because of the therapeutic maxims
of Paracelsus; it was in diametric opposition to the Methodist
approach, which generally advocated *contraria contrariis*. Its
use in this disease implies not only the recalcitrance of the
condition but again gives evidence of the broad-minded and
basically eclectic attitude of Soranus. When the desired
effect had been attained, the patient was sent on travels by
land and sea and was advised to take "natural waters."

Among the most interesting aspects of Soranus' discussion
of the treatment of hysteria is his critique of all previous
therapeutic measures, in which he states:

> the majority of the ancients and almost all followers of the other
> sects have made use of ill-smelling odors (such as burnt hair,
> extinguished lamp wicks, charred deer's horn, burnt wool, burnt
> flock, skins, and rags, castoreum with which they anoint the
> nose and ears, pitch, cedar resin, bitumen, squashed bed bugs,
> and all substances which are supposed to have an oppressive
> smell) in the opinion that the uterus flees from evil smells. Where-
> fore they have also fumigated with fragrant substances from
> below, and have approved of suppositories of spikenard [and]
> storax, so that the uterus fleeing the first-mentioned odors, but
> pursuing the last-mentioned, might move from the upper to the
> lower parts.[34]

His criticism also extends to Hippocrates,[35] who, he stated,
"made some of his patients drink a decoction of cabbage,[36]
others asses' milk."[37] In another context Hippocrates wrote,
according to Soranus, that the uterus is twisted as the intestines are in intestinal obstruction and that he inserted a
small pipe and blew air into the vagina by means of a blacksmith's bellows, thus causing dilatation.[38] Says Soranus,
". . . the uterus does not issue forth like a wild animal from
the lair, delighted by fragrant odors and fleeing bad odors;

[34] *Ibid.*, p. 152.   [35] *Ibid.*, p. 153.

[36] Cf. *On Women's Diseases:* Loeb ed., II, 123; Littré ed., VIII, 266.

[37] Cf. *On the Nature of Women:* Loeb ed., chap. 3; Littré ed., VII,
314–15; and *On Women's Diseases:* Loeb ed., II, 131; Littré ed., VII, 278.

[38] Cf. *On the Nature of Women:* Loeb ed., chap. 14: Littré ed., VII,
332. Hippocrates does not, however, mention blacksmith's bellows here.

rather it is drawn together because of stricture caused by inflammation."[39] It is difficult to discern what Soranus meant by inflammation, a term that is encountered in the literature of the period but without any intimation of its meaning.

Other forms of treatment censored by Soranus included those of Diocles of Charystos, who pushed the uterus toward the lower parts by pressing upon the hypochondriac region; those of Xenophon, who employed loud noises by beating metal plates together; and those of Asclepiades, who besides compressing the hypochondriac region with bandages and strings of gut, "shouts loudly, blows vinegar into the nose [and] allows sexual intercourse during remissions."[40] Soranus found the latter treatment entirely contraindicated, since he believed that coitus caused atony and thus affected the patient adversely, a reason difficult to reconcile with the Methodist point of view.

ABSTINENCE AND RETENTION

The great Galen of Pergamon (A.D. 129–99) also denied the ability of the uterus to wander about.[41] He too related hysteria to the womb; yet he developed his own etiological theories, which drastically diverged from all other current opinions, although they were in fact rooted in ancient physiological concepts.

Because Galen's fame was second only to that of Hippocrates and his influence on the subsequent ages was greater than that of any other Graeco-Roman medical writer, his thoughts and personality require special attention. Fortunately, there are ample sources for the study of both. Unlike the "Father of Medicine" and all subsequent writers mentioned above, of whose lives and personalities almost nothing is known, Galen revealed himself by interspersing his medical writings with much detailed autobiographical information. It

[39] *Soranus' Gynecology*, p. 153.

[40] *Ibid.*

[41] Although Galen was familiar with the writings of Soranus, his reasoning concerning hysteria differed radically from that of Soranus. See George Sarton, *Galen of Pergamon* (Lawrence: University of Kansas Press, 1954), p. 97.

is an irresistible temptation, therefore, to digress somewhat and to present the character of this famous physician, even beyond those aspects which relate to hysteria.

Galen's enduring stature arises from his manifold contributions not only to all phases of medical thought, but to philosophy and religion as well. He wrote voluminously and, in contrast to the questions of authenticity of many of the Hippocratic writings, there is little doubt that the writings that bear Galen's name are actually from his pen. His interests knew no bounds; his writings covered all aspects of medicine and surgery, and extended scientific thinking far beyond the vision of his contemporaries. He prepared an anatomical treatise more complete than any previously attempted, together with observations and speculations regarding function. His physiological views were based in significant part upon actual animal experimentation, on which rests Galen's additional fame as the founder of experimental physiology. Yet, with all his great intellectual curiosity and independence, he recognized greatness in others and had an abiding admiration for his father's mental aptitude and the work of Hippocrates. Throughout his life he strove with varying success to live up to the pattern of these men.

Galen was born in Greek Asia Minor in the city of Pergamon, which was famous for its temple to Aesculapius, its medical teachers, and its gladiators. In this setting he was brought up by an erudite and kindly father, who shared his rich knowledge of logic, grammar, and arithmetic with him and who planned to interest his son in dialectic theory so that he would become a philosopher. When Galen reached his seventeenth year, however, his father had a vivid dream which impelled him to turn his son's attention to the study of medicine. As mentioned above, dreams at that time often served as guides to human destiny. Beyond academic instruction, his father taught him to despise reputation and honor and to revere truth alone. A scholar trained in geometry, arithmetic, architecture, and astronomy, he instructed his son not to affiliate himself hurriedly with any one school but to "go on for a long time, learning and testing . . . striving after justice, moderation, courage and intelligence."

Galen was most impressed, however, by his father's personal qualities, which sharply contrasted with his mother's:

Now, personally I cannot say how I got my nature (*physis*). It was however, my great fortune to have as my father a most good-tempered, just, efficient, and benevolent man. My mother, on the other hand, was so irascible that she would sometimes bite her serving-maids, and she was constantly shouting at my father and quarrelling with him, worse than Xantippe with Socrates. When I saw, then, the nobility of my father's conduct side by side with the shameful passions of my mother, I made up my mind to love and cleave to the former behaviour, and to hate and flee from the latter. And besides this enormous difference between my parents, I observed that he was never depressed over any affliction, while my mother became annoyed at the merest bagatelle. You yourself doubtless know that boys imitate what they are fond of, and avoid what they do not like to see.[42]

But in spite of the father's magnificent example, and the name given his son "Galenos" (the Peaceful One), Galen's writings reveal a man contentious, argumentative, competitive, and proud. Galen, however, had ample justification for pride. His superior intelligence had enabled him to absorb the best general and medical education possible in his day. Following his studies with the medical teachers of Pergamon, he traveled for nine years over much of Asia Minor and the Greek mainland, observing the diseases peculiar to each region. His final goal was Alexandria, in Egypt, where the great scientific tradition of Herophilus and Erasistratus lingered on and where "the physicians . . . accompany the instruction they give to their students with opportunities for personal inspection [*autopsia*]."

He returned to Pergamon in A.D. 157 to accept an appointment as surgeon to the gladiators. Four years of this work gave him wide opportunity to observe human anatomy and physiology and to practice orthopedic and restorative surgery as well as general medicine. Galen then sought the culmination of his career in Rome, the focal point of the Graeco-Roman world. The fortunate recovery of a distinguished patient established his name almost at once. He was sought out by patients of high social rank and was generously remunerated; he held public anatomical demonstrations, dissecting dogs and apes, which served to teach medical stu-

[42] Arthur J. Brock (tran.), *Greek Medicine: Being Abstracts Illustrative of Medical Writers from Hippocrates to Galen* (London & Toronto: J. M. Dent & Sons, Ltd., 1929), p. 171.

dents and to entertain members of the aristocracy, who attended this new diversion in large numbers. This sudden success was to render him indifferent towards his medical colleagues from whom he had so quickly taken their most prominent patients and the limelight almost overnight.

Except for one lengthy absence, Galen lived in Rome for the remainder of his life. The reason for his one absence cast a shadow on his character, suggesting that personal courage was not among his strongest attributes. He had been in Rome but four years when the city was stricken by a severe epidemic of plague. Galen hurriedly left the capital and took up practice in his native city, Pergamon. When he was called back to the imperial court at Rome three years later, however, he accepted the invitation with avidity.

That he matured during his absence is borne out by his own words:

Then somehow, when I went to Rome the second time at the command of the Emperor . . . I determined to do no more public teaching or demonstrating, as I had success greater than I could have hoped for in my practice. I knew how, when any doctor gets a reputation, his rivals envy him and call him a quack, and I would have liked to stitch up their spiteful tongues. In the presence of patients, however, I said nothing more than necessary. Nor did I teach or demonstrate to crowds as before; I merely showed by my practice how well acquainted I was with the science of medicine.[43]

His personal courage, however, changed little in his mature years. The emperor Antoninus was involved in a campaign with the Germans and, in Galen's own words, "he was extremely anxious to get me to go, but was persuaded to excuse me on being told that my family god Aesculapius commanded otherwise—he whose worshipper I declared myself to be since the time when he had saved me from a dangerous suppurative condition." Upon hearing this, the emperor worshipped the god and ordered Galen to remain in Rome until his own victorious return and entrusted his young son Commodus to Galen's medical care.

As it happened, however, the military campaign proved to be a lengthy one, and Galen used the emperor's absence to complete his works *On the Utility of Parts* and *On the*

---

[43] *Greek Medicine*, p. 176.

Principles of Hippocrates and Plato. The latter treatise attested to his devout admiration for the work of these men, although in general Galen was proud of his own independent thought. He did not belong to a particular school and considered himself an eclectic. With this freedom from cultism, Galen selected from among the works of all his medical and philosophical predecessors but was most deeply influenced by Aristotle's teleological principles. His treatise *On the Utility of Parts* even carried this belief into dogma, explaining that only a thoughtful creator could have designed each part of the human body for the very function for which it was intended. The tremendous posthumous influence of Galen, which dominated medicine for more than fourteen centuries can be ascribed in large part to this treatise. Although Galen was not a Christian, his belief in one supreme creative power was highly acceptable to the early Church Fathers. It thus came to pass that the medieval world received uncritically, as dogma, almost all of the surviving works of Galen. Unfortunately, this blind and unquestioning faith prohibited any changes, with the result that the great scientist and innovator inadvertently became an obstacle to further medical progress for centuries.

In addition to his scientific studies, Galen's writings give us insight into the life of a successful Roman physician. His relationship with his colleagues was a rather strange one. He admits that he was not liked by other physicians, but the great popular esteem in which he was held compelled them frequently to make use of him as a consultant. Nor does he conceal his delight, on such occasions, in dazzling the patients and their families by the brilliance and accuracy of his diagnoses, which certainly must have added to the discomfiture of the attending physicians.

The breadth of his grasp of the interdependency of body and mind is revealed by his appreciation of psychosomatic disturbances. A case in point concerned a lady who suffered from sleeplessness, listlessness, and general malaise. Thorough examination failed to produce evidences of physical illness and Galen concluded that she was suffering either "from melancholy, or else was troubled about something she was unwilling to confess." He required further observation to establish the cause and adopted an expectant attitude. A few days later, and quite by chance, the actual basis for her illness was discovered. He relates:

After I had diagnosed that there was no bodily trouble, and that the woman was suffering from some mental uneasiness, it happened that, at the very time I was examining her, this was confirmed. Somebody came from the theatre and said he had seen Pylades dancing. Then both her expression and the colour of her face changed. Seeing this, I applied my hand to her wrist, and noticed that her pulse had suddenly become extremely irregular. This kind of pulse indicates that the mind is disturbed; thus it occurs also in people who are disputing over any subject. So on the next day I said to one of my followers, that, when I paid my visit to the woman, he was to come a little later and announce to me, "Morphus is dancing to-day." When he said this, I found that the pulse was unaffected. Similarly also on the next day, when I had an announcement made about the third member of the troupe, the pulse remained unchanged as before. On the fourth evening I kept very careful watch when it was announced that Pylades was dancing, and I noticed that the pulse was very much disturbed. Thus I found out that the woman was in love with Pylades, and by careful watch on the succeeding days my discovery was confirmed.[44]

As was his custom, he added a final discussion to this case history in which he chides other physicians for having been unable to detect the psychic elements in this and similar illnesses; and he exclaims with apparent annoyance; "I suppose it is because they have no clear conception of how the body tends to be affected by mental conditions. Possibly they do not know that the pulse is altered by quarrels and alarms which suddenly disturb the mind."

The depth of Galen's awareness of the importance of psychogenic factors is brought out in his treatise entitled *That the Mental Faculties Follow the Bodily Constitution*. Here he analyzes the meaning, function, and seat of the soul, weighing this interrelationship in the light of Platonic and Aristotelian thinking. The influences of mind and body upon each other were reciprocal. Mental influences could engender physical ailments; but also mental disturbances as such could often be the result of organic derangements.

Despite Galen's realization of the intimate association of body and soul in general, he did not extend it to his ideas on hysteria. So firmly rooted was the belief that this disease was

---

[44] *Greek Medicine,* pp. 213–14.

a manifestation of somatic derangement of the uterus that Galen accepted it without question. He agreed with Soranus, however, in denying the ability of this organ to wander about, but, from here on, his ideas are his own.

According to Galen, a secretion analogous to the semen of the male, and actually so designated, was produced in the uterus. Retention of this substance, like retained menses, could lead to a corruption of the blood, a cooling of the body, and eventually an irritation of the nerves which produced the hysterical fit. He compared this "poisoning" to the venom active in a rabid dog. Galen based his theories concerning seminal retention as the cause of hysteria on the basis of his protracted observation of one patient and found them confirmed by subsequent case histories. This patient was a widow who suffered from repeated hysterical paroxysms; these ceased immediately after her second marriage. Soon afterward she was again widowed and again was beset by her previous disturbances. From this apparent relationship of hysterical manifestations with sexual abstinence he concluded that the cause was "seminal retention."[45]

Galen said that he had seen many hysterical women, "for it is in these words that they describe themselves," whose symptoms fell into three clinical categories. Those in the first group lost both consciousness and the ability to move, presenting at the same time a pulse which was so weak and small that it was scarcely perceptible. The hysterical patients of the second group remained conscious, able to move and lucid of mind, but tended to collapse from weakness and respiratory difficulties. The predominant manifestation of the third group was contractures of the limbs. The common factor was that they all suffered from uterine affections, although they differed from one another in severity and in the form of their complaints. The mechanism by which these variegated disturbances are produced is explained in considerable detail by Galen: "It is recognized that this malady occurs particularly among widows, and above all in those who have been regular in their menses prior to their widowhood, fertile and receptive and eager to the advances of their

[45] Galen, *De locis affectis*, Lib. VI (Venice, *apud* Junta, 1541), II, 39, as quoted in Henri Cesbron, *Histoire critique de l'hystérie* (Paris: Asselin et Houzean, 1909), p. 42.

husbands." On the basis of these observations, Galen concluded that the hysterical manifestations in such women occurred either because of the suppression of the menses or of the outflow of the semen, no matter what the symptoms were.

In pursuing this theory, Galen offered the following further hypothesis: if repressed semen, i.e., abstinence or lack of sexual relations, gave rise to troubles in women it was logical that a similar cause would lead to analogous disorders in men. Thus ran his explanation of the existence of male hysteria. His recognition of a syndrome resembling hysteria in males was a most significant contribution. He noted that such states also followed sexual abstinence, and he therefore assumed that they were caused by retention of sperm. From this he derived his frequently reiterated conviction that failure of spermatic emission was more deleterious even than failure of the menstrual flow.

So far as men are concerned one also finds considerable differences. I have known individuals who out of modesty abstained from venereal pleasures and fell into torpor; others, similar to melancholics, were seized by despair and sadness without reason; and because of their distaste for food they develop poor digestion. In reflecting upon these events, for my part it seemed to me that the retention of sperm has a much more noxious influence upon the body than the retention of the menses. This is particularly evident in those persons whose sperm is by nature . . . abundant and who lead an idle life.[46]

Galen found further corroboration of this belief in the response of a widowed patient to his treatment, which involved the application of warm substances and digital manipulation.

Following the warmth of the remedies and arising from the touch of the genital organs required by the treatment there followed twitchings accompanied at the same time by pain and pleasure after which she emitted turbid and abundant sperm. From that time on she was freed of all the evil she felt. From all this it seems to me that the retention of sperm impregnated with evil essences had—in causing damage throughout the body—a much greater power than that of the retention of the menses.[47]

[46] *Ibid.*, p. 44.   [47] *Ibid.*

Having established this to his satisfaction, Galen then points out the fallacies in the theories of uterine migration: "Those who are experienced in anatomy will recognize, even without my help, the weakness of their reasoning"; and, on this basis, he indicated the absurdity of the assumption that the uterus can rise towards the stomach and even more so that it is able to jump over the stomach and touch the diaphragm. He concluded that "we must consider as totally preposterous the opinion of those who, by means of this reasoning, make the womb into an animal."

Galen anticipated that physicians and particularly midwives would reject his conclusions, since they claimed that the womb was often observed to have ascended or to have turned to one side or the other. He challenged them to admit that in most hysterical patients the womb maintained its normal position. This, he asserted, was invariably true in widows who were afflicted by hysteria and yet had no retention of the menses. In these patients, he argued, their disease must surely stem from the retention of the semen.

It is important to observe that, as often occurred with Galen's writings, some of his more bizarre conclusions regarding hysteria gained credence and adherence in the succeeding ages, while many of his scientific and well-reasoned observations were eclipsed and forgotten. Thus, for centuries to come, medicine clung to the theory of congested sperm, but made little use of his insight into the protean manifestations of hysteria, which he expressed so cogently: *"passio hysterica unum nomen est, varia tamen et innumera accidentia sub se comprehendit"* ("hysterical passion is just one name; varied and innumerable, however, are the forms which it encompasses").

CHAPTER III

The End of Antiquity

With Galen of Pergamon the development of Graeco-Roman medicine had reached its acme and its end. Galen's expressed contempt for the understanding and knowledge of his colleagues was not merely a manifestation of undue pride and arrogance—it was doubtless frequently justified. In originality, breadth, and depth, his work immeasurably surpassed that of his contemporaries; and, even more, that of his successors who were content merely to compile and annotate the medical writings of antiquity. Even during his lifetime, in the second century A.D., an irreversible decline of intellectual endeavor had begun, which gained momentum in the succeeeding centuries. The deterioration of medicine was but one aspect of a general decay of the arts and sciences. Galen's attempts to enlarge existing knowledge by adding the fruits of his own investigations, although retaining full reverence for the Hippocratic spirit, were not shared by his fellow physicians who found security in blind adherence to the tenets of the current medical sects. Like the writers, builders, and artists who were satisfied in trying to re-create the masterpieces of classical antiquity, the physicians clung to the letter of ancient writings with no effort to go beyond them to attain new insights.

THE RETURN OF THE SUPERNATURAL

Strangely enough, there was a coincident growth of popular interest in medicine which paralleled the decline of science. The Methodist doctrine, which flourished in Galen's time and with which he contended on many occasions, had so simplified the study and practice of medicine that all of it could be taught in six months. Some intellectuals even advocated that educated laymen be instructed in patient care so that they might treat themselves and their households. This medical preoccupation by the laity resulted in self-medication, to which the less scrupulous physicians catered avidly.

The most important factor in the decline of medicine was the growing influence of mysticism, not only upon the population at large but also upon the educated. In the second and third centuries A.D., successive waves of severe epidemics brought chaos to the Roman Empire with which medicine was unable to cope. Human misery was further aggravated by famine and injuries resulting from a series of natural disasters. Even the sophisticated and the educated in large numbers turned to the Aesculapian temples for comfort and healing. If Galen and his father could revere their family god, Aesculapius, and bow to the portents of his dream commands, how much more susceptible was the population in general!

The rising religious intensity and its expression in growing submission to temple healing helped prepare the way for the acceptance of monotheism. An ardent devotion to the healing god, however, implied belief in opposing supernatural powers that caused diseases. In the pantheon of ancient Greece, certain deities had supposedly been endowed with the punitive power of inflicting illness and it was against this belief that Hippocrates had directed his treatise, *Sacred Disease*. But in this later period, with the world veering towards monotheism, multiple gods with specific disease-producing powers were no longer acceptable. In their place, evil spirits were blamed—a return to a much older concept, which is latent in all cultures and rarely entirely absent in popular imagination. Thus, belief in demons as conveyers of disease and disaster, long denied by the educated and the prominent, again came to the fore and eventually penetrated all classes of late Hellenistic society. These newly reawakened superstitious fears, plus the increasingly fervent veneration of Aesculapius as healer of physical and spiritual ills, created an emotional climate that was receptive to Christianity with its inherent promises of salvation. Like Aesculapius, Christ was revered as the physician of the body and soul; and the reports of His miraculous cures struck a responsive chord among the worshippers of Aesculapius. Many were further attracted to the new faith because of its emphasis on charity and philanthropy, its compassion for the sick, and the spiritual solace it offered to all mankind.

Christianity, in its turn, had to contend with many tenacious pagan concepts, some of which were gradually adapted to and eventually became part of Christian thought. That this amalgamation had taken place in the fifth century A.D. is borne out by the writings of St. Augustine (A.D. 354–430), whose teachings prevailed in Europe for more than a thousand years.[1] The confluence of Christian and pagan ideas extended to the beliefs regarding hysteria; and, strangely enough, from the fall of the Roman Empire through the Renaissance, Augustine and his writings were closely involved in shaping European thought.

THE VIRTUES OF ABSTINENCE

The ideas so far traced about hysteria reveal that increasing emphasis was placed upon sexual factors as the predominant cause of hysteria. This culminated in Galen's emphasis upon enforced sexual abstinence as the principal etiology. The sex act was looked upon as a purely physical phenomenon; and its suppression was thought to lead to entirely somatic consequences, of which hysteria was one manifestation. Thus, as has been repeatedly stated, hysteria in antiquity was viewed as a tangible, concrete, and logical reaction to a temporary organic imbalance of the body. This was made clearly manifest by Galen's description of the achievement of release induced by digital manipulation in one of his widowed patients, in which treatment was purely mechanical and erotic undertones were apparently entirely lacking. Medically, at least, antiquity seems to have made a clear distinction between sexual function and eroticism. The sexual

[1] Hugh Pope, O.P., *Saint Augustine of Hippo* (London: Sands & Co., 1937), p. xv.

urge was a physical one like hunger and thirst and as such was of concern to the physician and freely discussed in the medical literature. Although sexual factors were the cause of hysteria, eroticism played a small part.

This pagan concept of sex as a natural function without relation to social stigma or morality encountered opposition when Christianity took hold. With the early ecclesiastical writers, questions of lust, sensuality, carnal pleasure, sin, and guilt began to pervade all thinking about sex and differentiations were introduced between physical union for procreation and the evil of erotic pleasure. Therefore, sexual abstinence was considered a virtue and to ascribe to it deleterious effects was unthinkable. Nor could indulgence as a therapeutic measure be countenanced. Despite all this, the association of hysteria and sex was so deeply ingrained that it could not be ignored.

The pattern for the resolution of this dilemma was most clearly formulated by Augustine. A study of his writings discloses that he considered sexuality odious and, by its very nature, infused with lust. Sexual union thus became justified only as a means of procreation and should be untainted by any vestiges of sensual pleasure. The writings of Augustine further suggest that carnal pleasures are the work of unholy spirits which were formerly personified by pagan gods and for which he substituted powers that fitted into the framework of Christianity, such as incubi, succubi, witches, and demons.

For an understanding of Augustine's views as they pertain to the development of our study, it is necessary to reflect briefly upon his life—an easy task, for his *Confessions* are really a detailed autobiography—and to quote pertinent passages from his voluminous writings. He was born in 354 in Tagaste, a small Numidian town in North Africa, the son of Patricius, a pagan official, and Monica, a Christian. Among his early, recurring impressions were his mother's persistent efforts to win her husband to Christianity, which were eventually successful, just a year before Patricius' death. Her missionary zeal also extended to Augustine—initially, however, without success. He devoted himself instead to acquiring a thorough classical education in Madauros and Carthage and to the carefree enjoyment of a pagan life of pleasure, which, as might be expected, was sternly censored and deplored by his devout mother. With an extraordinarily vivid memory, he recorded this period in his *Confessions:*

> To Carthage I came, where there rang all around me in my ears a cauldron of unholy loves. I loved not yet, yet I loved to love. . . . I sought what I might love, in love with loving, and safety I hated, and a way without snares.

> To love then, and to be loved was sweet to me; but more when I obtained to enjoy the person I loved. I defiled, therefore, the spring of friendship with the filth of concupiscence, and I beclouded its brightness with the hell of lustfulness. . . .

> I fell headlong then in to the love, wherein I longed to be ensnared. For I was both beloved, and secretly at the bond of enjoying; and was with joy fettered with sorrow-bringing bonds, that I might be scourged with the iron burning rods of jealousy, and suspicions, and fears, and angers and quarrels.[2]

Thus his many temporary dalliances gave way to a deep attachment to a young African who bore his illegitimate son Adeodatus, the "God-given," when Augustine was only eighteen years of age. It has been suggested[3] that his later regret for having taken this mistress caused him to suppress her name but not his guilt. Although their attachment was a close and lengthy one, he never appears to have considered marrying her; nor did his mother urge him to take this step, even though she refused to receive him in her house so long as he lived in this "unlawful marriage." Augustine had a great and lasting love for his son Adeodatus.

Augustine was greatly attracted to the study of philosophy after reading Cicero's *Hortensius,* a work now lost. Somewhat later he adopted Manichaeism—a religious philosophy compounded of Zoroastrian dualism and Christian theology—which greatly displeased his mother and which he later renounced. After completing his studies, he earned his livelihood as a teacher of rhetoric in Carthage, Rome, and finally in Milan.

During this time his mother made great efforts to have him married. In Milan a maiden was found who was of good

[2] St. Augustine, *The Confessions of St. Augustine,* trans. E. B. Pusey (rev. ed.; Oxford: John Henry Parker, 1843), Book III, p. 29.

[3] *St. Augustine, The City of God against the Pagans,* trans. George E. McCracken (Cambridge, Mass.: Harvard University Press, 1957), pp. viii ff.

family and so pleasing that although she was "two years under fit age" Augustine decided to wait for her. Upon his
mother's insistence he dismissed his concubine, leaving his
"heart which clave unto her . . . torn and wounded and
bleeding." Vowing never to know another man, she returned
to Africa, leaving her son with his father. Augustine did not
match his mistress' vow. Impatient of two years' delay until
marriage, "not being so much a lover of marriage, as a slave
to lust," he took another mistress.[4]

Eventually he came under the spiritual influence of Ambrosius, Bishop of Milan, under whose guidance he resigned
his teaching position, separated himself from his mistress, and
went with his son to live with his mother on the estate of
friends near Milan. His baptism a year later, when he was
thirty-three was one of the great joys of his mother's life.
She died soon thereafter. In time Augustine returned to
Africa, where he was ordained as a priest and later conse-
crated as the Bishop of Hippo. It was here that he fulfilled
his destiny. His ecclesiastical studies and writings, which
emanated from this otherwise insignificant See, made him
one of the most influential of the Church Fathers. So voluminous was his literary output that, in Karl Jaspers' words,
"The study of the complete works is a task of a lifetime for
scholars, or of meditation for monks. Augustine had apparently written every day, and it now seems that an equally
long life would be required for the perusal of his works, as
the author had in composing them."[5] His best known books
are his *Confessions*, written around A.D. 400, and *The City of
God*, written during A.D. 413–26.

Describing his conversion, Augustine implies that he was
guided by divine command. On that important day he
turned to the writings of Paul and, opening the book at random, he found the following passage: ". . . put ye on the
Lord Jesus Christ, and make not provision for the flesh, to
fulfil the lusts thereof."[6] The Augustine who, as a pagan
youth, had begged of the Lord "Give me chastity and con-

[4] *The Confessions,* pp. 103–5.

[5] Karl Jaspers, *Plato, Augustin, Kant: Drei Gründer des Philosophierens* (Munich: R. Piper & Co., 1957), p. 101. (Translation mine.)

[6] Rom. 13:14.

tinence, only not yet,"[7] now found himself ready to obey the exhortation of Paul; he elected the life of a recluse.

Perhaps one should agree with the author of "A sketch of the life and character of St. Augustine"[8] that there might be more merit in dwelling on "the complete and harmonious Augustine in his mature years than in retelling the often-told tale of his youth." But it is "in the erratic career of the young and passionate man" that one finds the key to his later views, which exerted so overwhelming and lasting an influence.

Augustine's interests and concerns covered every aspect of contemporary thought, including medicine and the natural sciences, since all had bearing on his envisioned City of God. Because his words gave direction to the intellectual endeavor of the Middle Ages and beyond, his thoughts on health and disease and on miraculous healing and demonic possession are particularly significant for our purposes. Despite his dedication to the tenets of Christianity, he recognized that the multiple gods of other beliefs were so deeply rooted in popular consciousness that to deny them would only arouse opposition among those whom he wished to convert. Skilfully, he gave them designations compatible with the Christian doctrine, modified their actions and characters as experience demanded, and wove them into the fabric of the Church. Thus it was possible to populate his world with such supernatural figures as demons, witches, incubi, and succubi.

DEMONS AND POSSESSION

Although Augustine's delineation of the sphere and activities of these evil forces was wisely tentative and circumspect, he, nonetheless, infused into the Western world such a strong and lasting preoccupation with demonology and witchcraft that it persisted long after his spiritual leadership had waned. His own rationalizations on these subjects are of extraordinary interest. Through them we can comprehend the changing intellectual climate which is generally associated with medievalism. Specifically, they altered the social atti-

[7] *The Confessions*, Book VIII, p. 146.

[8] C. C. Martindale, S.J., in *St. Augustine*, by M. C. D'Arcy, S.J., *et al.* (New York: Meridian books, 1957), pp. 81–119.

tude towards the hysteric and changed him from a sick human being beset with emotional needs and physical distress into someone more or less wilfully possessed, bewitched, in league with the devil, and even heretical.

In Augustine's own reflections, however, only the seeds of these developments can be detected. He was not unaware of the difference between natural illness and demonic possession.[9] Of the former, he said: "There is no pain of body driving out pleasure, that may not befall the wise man; no anxiety that may not banish calm. A man's physical integrity is ended by the amputation or crippling of his limbs; his beauty is spoiled by deformity, his health by sickness, his vigor by weariness, his agility by torpor and sluggishness." All that is beautiful in man's countenance and movement is ruined when "sickness bring on palsy or, still worse, a spinal deformity so severe that a man's hands touch the ground as though he were a four-footed beast." Even more deplorable does he consider the affections of the "primary endowments of the soul," such as deafness and blindness, and, worse than that, when illness unsettles the mind! Where is it then, Augustine ponders, that reason and intelligence go, and into what strange sleep? "We can hardly hold back our tears when mad men say or do extravagant things—things wholly unlike their customary behavior and normal goodness." But, without elaborating on the nature of the difference between madness and demonic possession, other, perhaps, than of degree, he continues: "Still worse is the case of those possessed by demons. Their intelligence seems driven away, not to say destroyed, when an evil spirit according to its will makes use of their body and their soul."

Although Augustine does not reveal how he distinguishes possession from madness, he makes it clear in a later chapter devoted to miraculous healing[10] that demonic seizures can be cured only by miracles, whereas diseases, though amenable to supernatural cure, may also be overcome by human medical effort. Indeed, in order to prove that even in his day miracles were still being wrought in the name of Christ—

[9] St. Augustine, *The City of God*, Book XIX, chap. 4, in *Writings of Saint Augustine*, trans. Gerald J. Walsh and Daniel J. Honan (New York: Fathers of the Church, 1954), VIII, 195–96.

[10] *Ibid.* (Book XXII, chap. 8), pp. 431–50.

sometimes through His name, and sometimes through the intercession of relics—Augustine listed a great number of miraculous cures, many of which he himself had witnessed. Among these were diseases of an obviously somatic nature, such as cancer of the breast, hernia of the scrotum, rectal fistula and gout, the cures of which were related with the sole purpose of demonstrating the superiority of prayer over medical treatment and surgical intervention. Other patients suffering from paralysis or blindness, without any taint of demonic involvement, are described as rapidly and completely restored to health after being exposed to prayer or touched by relics. It is obvious that many of these persons were suffering from functional rather than organic disturbances—a distinction neither Augustine nor his contemporary physicians were able to make.

Some of the most striking of the miraculous cures occurred in patients whom Augustine considered to be demoniacs:

There is an estate in the country less than thirty miles from Hippo Regius, called Victoriana. The shrine there is dedicated to the martyrs of Milan, Protasius and Gervasius. To this shrine there was brought a youth who had become possessed by a devil, one summer's day at noon, when he was cooling his horse in the flowing waters of a river. This demoniac was lying near the altar of the shrine as though he were as dead as a corpse, when the lady of the villa came to vespers and evening prayers, as was her wont, along with her maids and some nuns. As soon as they began to sing, the demoniac, as though struck by the sound, came to and, trembling all over, took hold of the altar. Unable or not daring to move, there he remained, as though he had been tied or fastened to the altar. The demon, crying out at the top of his voice, began to beg for mercy, and to confess where and when he had taken possession of the young man. Finally, the demon declared that he would depart. He did so, but not before threatening to work havoc with certain parts of the young man's body. These parts the demon named. Thereupon, an eye was found torn from its socket, resting on the cheek and hanging by a tiny vein as by a root. The pupil, which was black, turned white.

Those who had witnessed all this, and others who had been attracted by the screaming, prostrated themselves in prayer. They were overjoyed by the youth's return to sanity, but grieved by the dislocation of the eye. Some insisted that a doctor be called, but the youth's brother-in-law, who had brought him to the shrine, said simply: "God who put this demon to flight is able, through the prayers of His saints, to restore the sight of this eye." Thereupon, as best he could, he pushed the eye back into its socket, bandaged it with his handkerchief, and said that the bandage must not be removed for at least a week. A week later, the bandage was removed. The eye was found to be in perfect condition. Many other miracles occurred at that shrine, but I need not mention them here.

I know of another demoniac, a young girl of Hippo, who was freed from possession as soon as she anointed herself with some oil into which the tears of a priest who was praying for her had fallen. I also know of a bishop who prayed for a demoniac, a young man whom he had never seen, but who was at once delivered from the devil.[11]

From these and similar histories it is evident that possession by demons and devils was thought to express itself predominantly in violent behavioral disorders rather than in physical illness. It is fundamental, however, in Augustine's thought that he considered all human suffering, including organic disease, as manifestations of innate evil, consequent upon original sin. As he repeatedly noted, evil is not to be found in the bodily substance or any natural substance per se, but in the will.[12] Although he did not refrain from making sarcastic remarks at the futility and ignorance of physicians, he did not entirely reject the practice of medicine. Actually, his description of miraculous cures reveals a degree of familiarity with medicine and even with the great medical writings of antiquity; but he clearly placed greater faith in divine intercession than in medicine or surgery.

Tales of miraculous cures similar to those cited by Augustine became legion during the Middle Ages,[13] and gradually all attempts to distinguish between mental illness and spirit obsession ceased. Eventually, churchmen even attributed the origin of physical disease to the workings of evil powers, a view not shared by the concurrent medical writers. As mentioned earlier, in the days of Augustine these powers consisted largely of demons and devils. Later, as the result of the rising misogyny among the clergy, witches in

---

[11] *Ibid.* (Book XXII, chap. 8), pp. 440–41.

[12] *Ibid.* (Book XVI, chaps. 5–9), see especially VII, 252–62.

[13] Loren MacKinney, *Early Medieval Medicine; with Special Reference to France and Chartres* (Baltimore: Johns Hopkins Press, 1937), pp. 60 ff.

large numbers came upon the scene of the supernatural. Augustine had no such leanings, possibly because of his great admiration for his mother. He denied the belief of many of his contemporaries that in the resurrection all human beings would be men, regardless of their former earthly existence.[14] That view, he felt, sprang from the misinter-

Fig. 1. Expulsion of the Devil by exorcism. (From Kurt Selig-mann, *The History of Magic* [New York: Pantheon Books, n.d.].)

pretation of two passages of scripture, which read: "Till we all come . . . unto a perfect man";[15] and "conformed to the image of his Son."[16] He agreed with those who had no doubt that both sexes would be resurrected.

In order to prove that conjugality and procreation are compatible with the absence of lust, he re-created the idyl of

[14] *Writings of Saint Augustine* (Book XXII, chap. 17), VIII, 464.
[15] Eph. 4:13.   [16] Rom. 8:29.

the Garden of Eden before concupiscence was released by the eating of the fruit from the tree of knowledge. His somewhat anatomical comments read:

Merely because we have no present experience to prove it, we have no right to reject the possibility that, at a time when there was no unruly lust to excite the organs of generation and when all that was needed was done by deliberate choice, the seminal flow could have reached the womb with as little rupture of the hymen and by the same vaginal ducts as is at present the case, in reverse, with the menstrual flux. And just as the maturity of the fetus could have brought the child to birth without the moanings of the mother in pain, so could connection and conception have occurred by a mutually deliberate union unhurried by the hunger of lust.

Here Augustine deems it necessary to end these deliberations because "as things now are, the demands of delicacy are more imperative than those of discussion." Moreover, he fears, that even the hypothesis of voluntary control cannot be raised "without the imagination being filled with the realities of rebellious lust."

Evidently lust was rampant in Augustine's day and frequently associated with the nefarious tricks of the pagan deities:

And then there is all that talk about those gods in the wilds and the woods commonly called *incubi*, who have been so frequently importunate and successful in seeking to satisfy their lust with women. We have the accounts of a great many victims, or of trustworthy reporters who talked with the victims, of these assaults. There are also the demons whom the Celts called *deuces*. There are so many tales of their attempted or completed impurities that it would be verging on rudeness to deny them all. However, I would not dare to decide on evidence like this, whether or not certain spirits, embodied in the kind of aerial substance, whose force we can feel when it is fanned against our bodies, are subject to the passion of lust and can awake a responsive passion in women.[17]

Augustine's attitude towards the magical arts in general was one of cautious belief and profound condemnation. He felt that many extraordinary phenomena far beyond the limits of human power could be attributed only to magic and

[17] *Writings of Saint Augustine* (Book XV, chap. 23), VII, 470–71.

that the perpetrators thereof should be severely punished. He
wrote:

> Meanwhile, if I say that such stories are not to be credited,
> there are men living today who will solemnly depose that they
> have heard such things from unimpeachable sources or even
> know the "facts" at first hand. When I myself was in Italy, I
> used to hear such tales in connection with a certain district
> where the women innkeepers were imbued with magic arts and
> would give to such wayfarers as they could ensnare a kind of
> cheese concealing something that at once changed them into
> beasts of burden. Only when they transported whatever the land-
> ladies needed would they come to themselves. Meanwhile, I was
> told, they were not mentally reduced to the level of beasts, but
> continued in full possession of their human rationality, as was
> the case real or imagined of Apuleius, who in *The Golden Ass*
> tells how he drank poison and was turned into an ass, preserving
> throughout this experience his rational powers.[18]

Such phenomena were unbelievable to Augustine at first,
because they lacked verification and also because of their
extravagance. Yet when he took into full account the unlimited power of God, he accepted the rationale that His
creatures, even the demons, could exhibit whatever capacities
He permitted them. But, once these satanic bodies were
acknowledged as being angelic by creation and malignant by
corruption only, they could not be endowed with the power
to create substances *de novo*, nor could they transform man's
body, and even less his mind. What they could do, however,
was to make God's creatures *appear* different. Thus, it is
man's imagination and not his body over which the demons
wield power, and it is by this device that Augustine interpreted his own impressions, the stories of his contemporaries,
and the myths and legends of antiquity. Even "Circe, with
songs, transforming Ulysses' companions" became believable
to him, for "with God's righteous permission, these examples of sleight-of-hand could not have been difficult for the
demons."[19]

Augustine, whose intellectual background was founded
upon classical literature and philosophy and whose emotional
orientation was derived entirely from early Christian theology, personifies the transition from Graeco-Roman to medi-

[18] *Ibid*. (Book XVIII, chap. 18), VIII, 107.

[19] *Ibid*., p. 109.

eval thought. In many ways, he marks the end of the Greek tradition. His legacy influenced the succeeding generations so profoundly because it filled both their intellectual and emotional needs. It embraced all considerations of health and disease and by virtue of his deistic orientation brought them within the purview of the clergy. Although he did not speak specifically of hysteria, his writings greatly altered the general views on this disease and particularly the treatment of its

FIG. 2. The Devil in love. (From *The History of Magic* [New York: Pantheon Books, n.d.].)

victims. The nature of this change will become evident in subsequent discussion.

The Roman Empire was crumbling when Augustine died in A.D. 430. Vandal conquerors had reached Africa and were besieging Hippo during the last days of his life. The Natural Law of the Greeks, which placed man under its inescapable dominion, was supplanted by early Christian theological speculations. Remnants of scientific and medical knowledge survived only in the monasteries, which became the centers of intellectual endeavor. Studious monks, concerned with the care of sick brethren, culled from the documents practical advice and information but ignored whatever was not immediately relevant to their task or was objectionable on religious grounds.

CHAPTER IV

Hysteria in the Middle Ages

W HETHER THE DARK AGES were really centuries of "intellectual stagnation of bigotry, pedantry, and cruelty," as described by Fielding H. Garrison, or whether they were, in Loren MacKinney's words, "First rate intelligences worked hard over the crude materials at hand" need not be debated here.[1] It is certain, however, that for eight hundred years, from the fifth century to the thirteenth, the art of healing did not develop. Clerical medicine alone was literate and, according to the records left, concepts of illness and healing actually regressed and sometimes resembled their most primitive stage in the apparently total acceptance of miraculous healing, albeit saints and holy relics took the place of earlier animistic deities. Many churchmen, and the most vocal if not always the most prominent, drew their medical knowledge from the Bible and the writings of the Church Fathers. In the words of Augustine, as their chief source of inspiration, they contrived to find only one message, namely, that "there are no diseases that do not arise from witchery and hence from the mind."

Besides the religious healers, there were at all times a body of lay physicians, but little is known about their methods and theories. It appears that they, as well as some of the clergy, carried on many of the Graeco-Roman practices.

[1] Fielding H. Garrison, *An Introduction to the History of Medicine* (Philadelphia: W. B. Saunders Co., 1929), p. 140. H. Barnes, *The History of Western Civilization* (New York: Harcourt, Brace & Co., 1935), I, 737, as quoted by Loren MacKinney, *Early Medieval Medicine*, p. 12.

This led to a curious dichotomy concerning the etiology and treatment of hysteria. The physicians adhered to the ancient uterine theory, interwoven with Galen's dictum about the role of retained sperm and the dangers of sexual abstinence, and, necessarily, to the traditional physical treatments. These views and methods persisted well into the Renaissance.

The theological explanation of the manifestations of hysteria was that they were caused by the person's alliance with unholy powers that inhabited the shadows of the world. To some degree this belief included all mental diseases; it was held particularly about hysteria, with its bizarre manifestations, its sudden and transient attacks of paralysis and blindness, its striking paroxysms, its fleeting pains, and its myriad of other temporary malfunctions. Hysteria ceased to be a disease—it became the visible token of bewitchment and thus fell within the domain of the Church, the Inquisition, and even the temporal powers, since penalties were inflicted by the lay arm. With the exception of the few who were fortunate enough to come into medical hands, hysterics became victims of the witch craze, that long and dreadful mass delusion that held Europe in its sway for many centuries and constituted one of the darkest chapters in history.

The beginnings of this obsession were insidious. Its roots are probably found within the earliest Judaeo-Christian tradition, in the Mosaic dictum "Thou shalt not suffer a witch to live."[2] But witches were rarely seen and even fewer were put to death. Throughout the dominion of Greek thought, man's rational search for natural causes had little need to blame disembodied spirits and phantoms for events that might yet yield a scientific explanation.

At the beginning of the Christian era, however, when religion dominated once more, aberrations were again attributed to evil spirits that had to be driven out through exorcism and other ritualistic procedures. Christ had done so and had given His disciples the same power. But, as Sigerist points out, "Possession by a demon was in itself an accident and not a crime. Christ had not punished demoniacs but had cured them by driving out the evil spirit. With the belief in witchcraft, however, it was assumed that witches had been se-

2 Exod. 22:18.

duced by the devil or had entered a pact with him: they had become infidels and their crime was heresy. As heretics they were not treated but punished.[3] This change became evident in the sixth and seventh centuries. The historian Mackay aptly speaks of this period as the "early days" of little knowledge."[4] It was characterized by the belief in the power of the devil and his agents to affect human conduct, which relieved the individual from his responsibility for his own failings and defects. A whole train of superstitions arose which went way beyond the powers vested in supernatural beings by Augustine. The most devastating was that certain men and women were given the power to summon evil spirits to help them bring harm to their enemies.

DISEASES ARISE FROM WITCHERY

The lore of demons and witches and the evil they wrought pervades the annals of the various countries in the early Middle Ages; but organized persecution of persons accused of witchcraft was not instituted until the ninth century when Charlemagne banished those suspected of this practice. When this measure fell short of being a sufficient deterrent, he decreed the death penalty for all "who in any way evoked the devil, compounded love-philters, afflicted either man or woman with barrenness, troubled the atmosphere, excited tempests, destroyed the fruits of the earth, dried up the milk of cows, or tormented their fellow-creatures with sores and diseases."[5] That neither these laws nor the tortures of the Inquisition had any but a stimulating effect upon this hideous delusion is amply borne out by the subsequent history of witchcraft. It has been too richly documented and elaborately told by innumerable authors to bear repetition.

Suffice it to say that for centuries thousands of innocent persons were accused, tortured, and murdered on the charge

[3] Henry E. Sigerist, *Civilization and Disease* (Chicago: University of Chicago Press, 1943), pp. 82–83.

[4] Charles Mackay, *Memoirs of Extraordinary Popular Delusions* (London: Richard Bentley, 1841), I, 462.

[5] Jules Garinet, *Histoire de la magie en France* (Paris: Foulon, 1818), p. 29.

of witchcraft. Undoubtedly many mentally deranged persons brought this tragic evil upon themselves as a means of gaining momentary recognition and notoriety despite its grim consequences. The counterpart of this calamitous picture was the terror with which potential victims feared the malign activities of demon-inspired enemies. No man thought himself, his family, or his possessions secure from the machinations of the devil and his agents. Every disaster that befell him was attributed to a witch. Destruction of his house by

FIG. 3. Evocation of the Devil. (From *The History of Magic* [New York: Pantheon Books, n.d.].)

lightning, death of his cattle, accidents and deaths within his family, and his own diseases and failings—all ceased to be heavenly visitations to test his strength and fortitude; they were simply the work of a witch, whose confession and death would undo her harm. France, Italy, Switzerland, Germany, Scandinavia, England, Scotland, and even America were successively beset by this mania, and interest in all other crimes paled beside that in alleged witchcraft.

Hysterics clearly fitted within this atmosphere. They were the patients upon whom a spell had been cast, blinding and paralyzing them, and even making them impotent on their wedding night. Strangely, among the hysterics there were also those who admitted intercourse with the devil and his emissaries, strange sexual habits and wild orgies, and practicing witchcraft upon men who spurned their love or forsook them to marry others. These weird confessions became increasingly complex and progressively more lascivious over the years as more and more refined varieties of torture were applied. It appears that people intentionally tried to surpass each other in enlarging upon the raptures of the imaginary joys of the flesh in response to their inquisitors' eager and cruel persuasion.

In all aspects of the fantastic story of the witch mania, we recognize a crude exaggeration of Augustine's ideas. His tales of miraculous healing, his belief in the existence of demons and demon-engendered disease, his admission of the power of magic and his endorsement of its severe punishment, and, above all, his damnation of lust and sensual pleasures were magnified a hundred-fold. Although based on the scriptures, his writings were the chief sources of reference and confirmation for the inquisitors. They were undoubtedly exalted by a sense of righteousness, feeling secure in using their literal translation of Augustine's words in carrying out the will of the Lord. In only two aspects did they differ from Augustine: their excessive violence and their hatred of women.

MALLEUS MALEFICARUM

The most extraordinary document to emanate from this mania was the *Malleus Maleficarum* (1494), known in English as the "Witches Hammer." It was a remarkable book, incredibly vicious and the cause of countless tortures and deaths.

The Papal Bull of Innocent VIII issued in Rome in 1484, which gave rise to the fearful volume, announced that in various sections of northern Germany as well as in other sections of Europe "many persons of both sexes . . . have abandoned themselves to devils, incubi and succubi" and by a number of unholy means have committed many horrible crimes. "These wretches furthermore afflict and torment men and women . . . with terrible and piteous pains and sore

diseases, both internal and external; they hinder men from
performing the sexual act and women from conceiving,
when husbands cannot know their wives nor wives receive
their husbands."[6] To apprehend these deluded souls, the
Pope commissioned Heinrich Kramer and James Sprenger,
monks of the Dominican Order and professors of theology,
to travel through the affected regions and to act as merciless
inquisitors on behalf of the Church. The *Malleus Maleficarum* was written by them jointly and served them and
their delegates as a textbook of persecution.

Although it was written after the Dark Ages had given
way to the presumed enlightenment of the Renaissance, its
tone and spirit exemplified the former period rather than the
latter as we are wont to visualize it—thus emphasizing the
oversimplification involved in the arbitrary terms used in
designating historical epochs. With this medieval quality as
it appears to us, the *Malleus Maleficarum* throws light on
one facet of the Renaissance that is generally ignored: during
the very time when science was reborn, when the arts blos-
somed as never before, when literature was enriched by the
rediscovery of the writings of classical antiquity, superstition
went on a rampage and lost itself in the wildest flight of
fancy. Indeed, it was the invention of printing, one of the
most dynamic contributions of the Renaissance, that helped
the "Witches Hammer" achieve its inordinate influence.

The impact of this book was immediate and frightful. It
soon became an international "best-seller" throughout
Europe. Thirty editions of it appeared within less than two
hundred years following the original publication.[7] Subsequent to its first appearance, according to Sigerist, thousands
of mentally sick persons suffered torture and death "ad ma-
jorem Dei gloriam."[8] Mackay estimates conservatively that
in many cities in Germany alone "the average number of executions for this pretended crime was six hundred annually,
or two every day, if we leave out the Sundays, when it is to

[6] The Bull of Innocent VIII (1484) in *Malleus Maleficarum*, translated with an introduction, bibliography, and notes by Montague Summers (London: Pushkin Press, 1951), p. xix.

[7] The most recent translation was by J. W. R. Schmidt and was published as *Der Hexenhammer* (Berlin: H. Barsdorf, 1906).

[8] *Civilization and Disease*, p. 83.

be supposed that even this madness refrained from its work."[9]

A careful study of this fantastic document reveals beyond doubt that many, if not most, of the witches as well as a great number of their victims described therein were simply hysterics who suffered from partial anesthesia, mutism, blindness, and convulsions, and, above all, from a variety of sexual delusions. Although a summary of the entire work would go beyond the scope of this study, some of its most pertinent passages will be discussed. The book is divided into three parts. The first gives a definition of witchcraft and its necessary constituents, "which are the devil, a witch and the permission of the Almighty God." The second part deals with the *modus operandi* of the witches and the means of thwarting the perpetrators. The third part describes the judicial proceedings in both the ecclesiastical and the civil courts against witches and, indeed, all heretics.

In the first part the inquisitors set out to prove that belief in witches is an essential part of the Catholic faith and that denial of their existence is heresy. They further state at length that, in order to bring about the effect of magic, the devil has to co-operate, and they quote St. Augustine as their ultimate authority to the effect that the abomination of witchcraft[10] arose from this "foul connexion of mankind" with the devil!

According to these presumably chaste and celibate Dominican monks, this co-operation of devil and witch could take place only by one action: indulgence "in every kind of carnal lust with [his emissaries the] Incubi or Succubi[11] and all manner of filthy delights."[12] Although devils were generally incorporeal they could at times assume human shape and

[9] Mackay, *op. cit.*, p. 463.

[10] It is significant that Augustine spoke of "magicians" rather than of "witches." Kramer and Sprenger blithely amend this by indicating that Augustine *meant* witches whenever he spoke of magicians.

[11] According to the authors of the *Malleus*, the devil appears as "succubus"—i.e., copulative partner to men and as "incubus" to women. Proceeding naïvely and etymologically, Kramer and Sprenger explain: "They are called Incubi from their practice of overlaying, that is debauching, for they often lust lecherously after women and copulate with them." *Malleus*, pp. 24–26.

[12] *Malleus*, p. 21.

copulate directly, but often they resorted to other means.
Agreeing with Augustine,[13] Kramer and Sprenger maintained
that devils were able to collect human semen, which they
could then transfer and inject into the bodies of human
beings. These would then act as vehicles for the devils' nefarious purposes.

In the distorted judgment of the repressed and, possibly,
guilt-ridden authors of the *Malleus*, any kind of sexual rela-

Fɪɢ. 4. Witches' Sabbath. (From *The History of Magic* [New
York: Pantheon Books, n.d.].)

tions, even within the bond of matrimony, that evoked
pleasure, were assumed to be the devil's doings. By tortuous
reasoning based on the works of Augustine, the ability to
experience sexual pleasure derived from involvement with the
devil. A woman's pleasures could have come only from
satanic copulation; the man in turn derived his gratification
from the unholy wiles of his devil-inspired partner. Thus, if
either party was guilty of lust, the blame inevitably fell on
the female. The *Malleus* contains innumerable confessions by
young girls, women of all ages, and even nuns[14] that describe

[13] *On the Trinity* in *Writings of Saint Augustine, III.*
[14] *Malleus*, pp. 165–67.

in detail the sensuous pleasures they experienced in such unholy copulations, after which they were left bereft of their sight, hearing, movements, or other faculties. "At times also women think they have been made pregnant by an Incubus, and their bellies grow to an enormous size; but when the time of parturition comes their swelling is relieved by no more than the expression of a great quantity of wind."[15] This bewitchment is described as occurring in one of three ways: "First, as in the case of witches themselves, when women voluntarily prostitute themselves to Incubus devils. Secondly, when men have connexion with Succubus devils; yet it does not appear that men thus devilishly fornicate with the same full degree of culpability; for men, being by nature intellectually stronger than women, are more apt to abhor such practices. Thirdly, it may happen that men or women are by witchcraft entangled with Incubi or Succubi against their will. This chiefly happens in the case of certain virgins."[16]

It is evident from the foregoing that women were the chief targets in the witch hunts. To justify this obvious bias, the authors of the *Malleus* discussed at length the question "Why is it that women are chiefly addicted to evil superstitions?"[17] Their reasoning is so extraordinary that much of it must be quoted verbatim. The following is their definition of "the fragile sex":

What else is woman but a foe to friendship, an unescapable punishment, a necessary evil, a natural temptation, a desirable calamity, a domestic danger, a delectable detriment, an evil of nature, painted with fair colours! Therefore if it be a sin to divorce her when she ought to be kept, it is indeed a necessary torture; for either we commit adultery by divorcing her, or we must endure daily strife.[18]

Even in grief a woman must not be trusted: "And the tears of a woman are a deception, for they may spring from true grief, or they may be a snare. When a woman thinks alone she thinks evil."[19]

According to the authors, the cause of this wickedness lies in the formation of the first woman from a "rib of the breast which is bent as it were in a contrary direction to a man."

[15] *Ibid.*, p. 167.   [17] *Ibid.*, pp. 41 ff.   [19] *Ibid.*
[16] *Ibid.*, p. 164.   [18] *Ibid.*, p. 43.

Because of this defect, they assert, "She is an imperfect animal; she always deceives." For this reason also a woman "is more carnal than a man as is clear from her many carnal abominations." They further maintain that envy and jealousy are women's chief emotions, that their memories are weak, their intelligence wanting, and affections and passions inordinate.

The *Malleus* contends that it is natural for women with all these traits to form an alliance with the devil, who caters to their whims and fulfils their lust, and that, if thwarted in any way, "they deprive man of his virile member."

We have already shown that they can take away the male organ, not indeed by actually despoiling the human body of it, but by concealing it with some glamour [enchantment], in the manner which we have already declared. And of this we shall instance a few examples.

In the town of Ratisbon, a certain young man who had an intrigue with a girl, wishing to leave her, lost his member; that is to say, some glamour was cast over it so that he could see or touch nothing but his smooth body. In his worry over this he went to a tavern to drink wine; and after he had sat there for a while he got into conversation with another woman who was there, and told her the cause of his sadness, explaining everything, and demonstrating in his body that it was so.[20]

The woman asked him whether he suspected anyone of having wished him evil and advised him not to refrain from violence in order to bring about a cure. He thereupon set out to look for the girl whom he had jilted. At first she maintained her innocence, but when he began to choke her with a towel she promised to lift her curse. "And the young man . . . plainly felt, before he had verified it by looking or touching, that his member had been restored to him by the mere touch of a witch."

The *Malleus* then quotes a similar experience which had been told by a venerable Father from the Dominican House of Spires.

"One day," he says, "while I was hearing confessions, a young man came to me and, in the course of his confession, woefully said that he had lost his member. Being astonished at this, and not being willing to give it easy credence, since in the opinion

20 *Ibid.*, p. 119.

of the wise it is a mark of light-heartedness to believe too easily,
I obtained proof of it when I saw nothing on the young man's
removing his clothes and showing the place. Then, using the
wisest counsel I could, I asked whether he suspected anyone of
having so bewitched him. And the young man said that he did
suspect someone, but that she was absent and living in Worms.
Then I said: 'I advise you to go to her as soon as possible and
try your utmost to soften her with gentle words and promises';
and he did so. For he came back after a few days and thanked
me, saying that he was whole and had recovered everything.
And I believed his words, but again proved them by the evidence
of my eyes."[21]

The alleged power of witches went far beyond curses on
men's sex organs. "They can with God's permission, cause
all other infirmities with no exception." They could send
leprosy and epilepsy,[22] take away reason, and even cause
death in their desire for revenge. One who had been so killed
was "a well-known gentleman, whom his mistress wished to
come to her on one occasion to pass the night; but he sent his
servant to tell her that he could not visit her that night because he was busy. She promptly flew into a rage, and said
to the servant: Go and tell your master that he will not
trouble me for long. On the very next day he was taken ill,
and was buried within a week."[23]

In the last part of the *Malleus* the authors give detailed
instruction in the methods to be followed during an inquisition—ways of humiliating victims presented to the judges,
completely nude and shorn of all hair and the slow, increasingly severe tortures to be applied by officers, who were
instructed to do so "not joyfully [but] rather appearing to
be disturbed by their duty."[24] Interrogation was supple-
mented by actual testing. Pricking the skin for areas of anesthesia was a frequent test; regions of insensitivity were considered satanic stigmata, confirmatory of bewitchment. This
is of particular interest in our study of hysteria, since loss of
cutaneous sensation is one of the well-recognized criteria of
hysterical malfunction. Other cruel and gruesome tests offered the suspect the unhappy choice of dying to prove her
innocence or execution because she was found guilty. Death

21 *Ibid.*, p. 136.

22 *Ibid.*, pp. 136–37.

23 *Ibid.*, p. 139.   24 *Ibid.*, p. 225.

by drowning or by burning was usually the ineluctable fate of these tragic victims.

The immense popularity of the *Witches Hammer* was doubtless due in large part to its prurience. It fanned latent sadism all over Europe and stimulated the output of books in other countries, which added further fury to the witch mania. In England witchcraft was first made a statutory crime in 1541.[25] Ten years later, two further enactments enumerated false prophecies, conjuration, witchcraft, and sorcery as punishable offenses; but the extreme penalty was imposed only upon those who by means of spells, incantations, and contracts with the devil attempted to destroy the lives of their neighbors. Finally, in 1562 a law was passed and sanctioned by Queen Elizabeth that recognized witchcraft as a crime of the greatest magnitude. This was the beginning of organized persecution in that country, which reached its

[25] For a detailed "Chronological Table" of executions, trials, and laws relating to witchcraft until 1701, see Francis Hutchinson, *An Historical Essay concerning Witchcraft* (London: R. Knaplock, 1718), pp. 13–46.

Fig. 5. Execution of witches in England. (From *The History of Magic* [New York: Pantheon Books, n.d.].)

climax in the early part of the seventeenth century, concurrent with the height of the madness all over Europe. No country was exempt from the mania. In Scotland, the Ninth Parliament of Queen Mary in 1563 decreed punishment and death for witches and some of their accusations even involved many of the nobility. The growth of the Puritan movement augmented the fear of witches in England, as it had on the Continent in the movements leading to the Reformation. Once the Calvinists and Lutherans, who themselves had been persecuted as heretics, attained sanction through the Reformation, they in turn persecuted those whom they considered witches with a ferocity that sometimes surpassed that of the Roman Catholics.

In both England and Scotland the detection of witches became a lucrative vocation. Those so employed traveled about testing suspects for anesthetic areas. Pitcairn relates that in the trial of Janet Peaston in 1646 the magistrate of Dalkeith

caused John Kincaid of Tranent, the common pricker, to exercise his craft upon her. He found two marks of the devil's making; for she could not feel the pin when it was put into either of the said marks, nor did the marks bleed when the pin was taken out again. When she was asked where she thought the pins were put in her, she pointed to a part of her body distant from the real place. They were pins of three inches in length.[26]

Although these "common prickers," as they were officially called, aroused a great deal of resentment among the population, their expert testimony was accepted without question. Towards the end of the seventeenth century, however, the fury abated somewhat, the number of witch trials decreased and some of the intellectual leaders even expressed their disbelief of "modern witchcraft." Among the most influential of these writings was John Webster's *The Displaying of Supposed Witchcraft,*[27] in which he flatly stated:

There are Actions in most of those Relations ascribed to Witches, which are ridiculous and impossible in the nature of things; such are (1) their flying out of windows, after they have anointed themselves, to remote places. (2) Their transforma-

[26] Charles Mackay, *Extraordinary Popular Delusions and the Madness of Crowds* (New York: L. C. Page & Co., Inc., 1932), p. 513.

[27] London, 1677.

tion into Cats, Hares, and other Creatures. (3) Their feeling all
the hurts in their own bodies which they have received in those.
(4) Their raising Tempests, by muttering some nonsensical
words, or performing ceremonies alike impertinent as ridiculous.
And (5) their being suck'd in a certain private place of their
bodies by a Familiar. These are presumed to be actions incon-
sistent with the nature of Spirits, and above the powers of those
poor and miserable Agents. And therefore the Objection sup-
poseth them performed onely by the Fancy; and that the whole
mystery of Witchcraft is but an illusion of crasie imagination.[28]

John Webster and his fellow skeptics, "such course-
grain'd Philosophers as those Hobbians and Spinozians,"[29]
were called Sadducees by the adherents of the witch belief.
In answer to Webster's allegations, Joseph Glanvil, late
Chaplain in Ordinary to His Majesty and Fellow of the
Royal Society, wrote a lengthy and lurid tome entitled
*Saducismus Triumphatus, or Full and Plain Evidence con-
cerning Witches and Apparitions.* He discussed and refuted
Webster's proposition that witches and apparitions are but
"Melancholik Dreams or hysterical Imaginings" and presented a large number of well-authenticated cases of modern
witchcraft. At the end, he appended a translation of "An
Account of what happened in the Kingdom of Sweden in
the Years 1669 and 1670 in Relation to the Persons that were
accused for Witches: Tried and Executed by the King's
Command." Here we begin to see the association of bizarre
behavior with the word and the idea of hysteria, a tendency
which we will observe with increasing frequency as sanity
replaces the mania of witch hunting.

Glanvil's efforts at a reasonable and dispassionate inquiry
took the form of admitting the "proud and phantastick pre-
tences" of hysterics who believed themselves in immediate
communion with the Deity; and he termed them "but a
high-flown notion of warm imagination and over-luscious
self-flattery."[30] He further granted that "melancholy and
imagination have very great force, and can beget strange
perswasions, and that many stories of witchcraft and apparitions have been but melancholy fences." And he finally
admitted "that there are many strange and natural diseases

[28] Quoted in Joseph Glanvil, *Saducismus Triumphatus* (London:
J. Collins & S. Lownds, 1681), Part 1, p. 9.

[29] *Ibid.*, p. 16.   [30] *Ibid.*, pp. 48–49.

that have odd symptoms and produce wonderful and astonishing effects beyond the usual course of Nature, and that
such are sometimes falsely ascribed to witchcraft."[31] But in
spite of these very important concessions, he maintained that
most aspects of witchcraft were true, even if they were
strange and uncouth, and he dwelt on them in detail and at
length. The result was that the *Saducismus Triumphatus*
caused a revival of the flagging witch mania as did the publication of many new and increasingly lurid books on the
subject—as many as twenty-five volumes in that number of
years.

But the tide had begun to turn. The Reverend Francis
Hutchinson, Chaplain in Ordinary to His Majesty and Minister of St. James's Parish in Bury St. Edmunds, found in
1718 that "these books and narratives are in the tradesmen's
shops and farmers' houses, and are read with great eagerness
continually levening the minds of the youth who delight in
such subjects." He went on to state with great courage that
"considering what sore evils these notions bring where they
prevail, I hope no man will think but that they must be com-
bated, oppos'd and kept down."[32]

Hutchinson's *An Historical Essay concerning Witchcraft*
was an attempt to dispel notions of witchcraft once and for
all. It was written as a dialogue between a clergyman, a Scottish advocate, and an English juryman, who requested the
guidance of the clergyman about what attitude he was to
take in a forthcoming witch trial. The most pressing question
raised was how to "judge when the confessions of witches
proceed from a sound mind and when from imagination and
vapours."[33] The clergyman expressed his firm conviction
that most phenomena of supposed witchcraft, if not sheer
imposture, were in reality but "Natural Fits and Vapours
[hysteria], for when some sort of Fits which are undoubtedly Natural continue, they alter the Habit of the Body . . .
and then their Fancies and Symptoms are most surprising.
There are marvelous Effects both in their Minds, Eyes, Ears
and Voices."[34] Hutchinson quoted numerous instances to

[31] *Ibid.*, Part II, pp. 7–9.   [32] Hutchinson, *op. cit.*, p. xiv.
[33] *Ibid.*, pp. 4–5. Vapors were synonymous with hysteria at that time.
[34] *Ibid.*, p. 52.

prove his point and, interestingly, he selected the witch trials in New England as his most striking example.[35]

The outbreak of the witch mania in the American colonies lagged somewhat behind. The many stories of devil mischief published in England reached the New World towards the end of the seventeenth century, creating an air of general unrest which, in Salem in 1692, crystallized into suspicion of specific individuals. This movement was accelerated by a dramatic case in which an old Irish woman by the name of Glover was accused by a mason's family named Goodwin of having bewitched their daughter. The accusation was made by a girl who had been "subject to fits" for many years and was confirmed by her two brothers, who were similarly afflicted. Neighbors observed that the three young Goodwins became completely rigid on certain days with joints so stiff that they could not be moved, whereas at other times their bones became so soft that they could not support their bodies. The old woman was questioned and asked to say the Lord's Prayer in support of her innocence. A mistake in her recital was considered proof of her guilt and she was executed as a witch.

This was the beginning of the New England witch hunt. Shortly afterwards the daughter and niece of the Calvinist minister Parris (or Parvis) began to fall to the ground in daily fits. They complained of a tightening of the throat and choking sensations and they maintained that the devil himself had inserted balls in their windpipes to suffocate them. They claimed they were being pricked all over with needles and one of them even vomited needles. Similar experiences were soon related by other women of the community, some of whom had as many as six attacks each day; and all of them claimed to have seen witches or even the devil himself while they were unconscious. In each instance they told of having been tormented by devilish or witchlike persons and threatened that the pains would continue unless they entered into a pact with Satan. "Some of them shewed the Scars of their Wounds, which they said were made to fetch Blood with to sign the Devil's Book; and some said they had Imps

[35] *Ibid.*, pp. 72–94.

to suck them, and showed Sores raw, where they said they were sucked by them."[36] They charged that they recognized the devil's messengers among their neighbors and named more than two hundred suspects. They were imprisoned and brought to trial; and after an inquisitional interrogation they were condemned. At least nineteen persons were executed, one of whom was a five-year-old child.

The mania spread from Salem to Andover and might have gone unchecked there also if a highly respected Boston merchant who found himself suddenly accused of wizardry had not sued the community for £1,000. This effectively stopped the Andover witch hunt.

In Salem, however, it seems to have been the slowly mounting revulsion at the gruesome spectacle that put an end to the prosecutions. Although belief in witchcraft itself did not end, the people began to wonder whether it might not be the judges and the jury themselves who were the victims of a devilish plot rather than those from whom confessions of guilt had been extracted. As suddenly as it had begun, prosecution was stopped and the accused were freed, including eight persons already sentenced to death.

Perhaps the most deplorable role in the New England delusion was played by Cotton Mather (1663–1728), a congregational minister and one of the most celebrated of the American Puritans. Of prominent ancestry—his father, Increase, was the president of Harvard University—Cotton Mather was well educated, receiving both his Bachelor's and Master's degrees from Harvard. From his earliest years, Mather was imbued with the mission of returning New England to its original state of purity. Firmly convinced of the omnipresence of evil supernatural beings and the harm they wrought, he published his *Memorable Providences relating to Witchcraft and Possessions,* in which he indorsed the prosecution of witches. He further elaborated on satanic possession in *Wonders of the Invisible World.*[37]

[36] Cotton Mather, *History of New England* (1702), Book VI, p. 80.

[37] This book was challenged by the Boston merchant Robert Calef (1648–1719), who in his *More Wonders of the Invisible World* (London, 1700) bitterly attacked Cotton Mather for his participation in the witch mania and condemned the belief in witchcraft in New

Mather's powerful presence and the impact of his publications doubtless stimulated the witch craze in New England. Although he strongly approved of and participated in
the trials, he felt that each case should be studied separately
and that the judges should be careful in accepting evidence.[38]
This reservation probably stemmed from Mather's scientific
orientation and training which, early in his career, led him to
consider medicine as a profession before he had overcome
stammering. His scientific contributions were important and
earned him election to the Royal Society in 1713. His greatest achievement was his pioneering effort in introducing
inoculation against smallpox in the Colonies. A further contribution was a book on medicine written in 1720, in which,
paradoxically, he considered persons of the type he had
earlier persecuted for witchery to be victims of a disease,
hysteria. This phase of Mather's activity will be referred to
later. Suffice it to say here that he functioned on two divergent intellectual planes, and in the witch hunt itself he
was anything but a scientific observer. Because of this eccen-
tricity in an otherwise intelligent and scientifically minded
person, and also because of Mather's great renown, extend-
ing even to England, it was particularly towards him that
Hutchinson vented his great anger.

In contrast to Mather, who invariably suspected the work
of evil spirits, in England Hutchinson interpreted the complaints of suffocation experienced by some of the victims, as
a distinct sign of hysteria. He called their paroxysms hysterical rather than demoniac, and spoke of one girl who had
been exorcised by Cotton Mather as suffering from fits of
hysteria rather than from bewitchment. In Hutchinson's
opinion, her journeys and rendezvous with fellow witches
"were not real, but fantastick things like Dreams," which
should have been obvious to Mather, since he and other wit-
nesses were often with the girl when she imagined that she

England. Calef's book was largely instrumental in restoring a rational
view in England. See G. L. Burr, *Narrative of the Witchcraft Cases*
(New York: Barnes and Noble, 1959), which contains a reprint of
Calef's *More Wonders of the Invisible World*.

[38] Cotton Mather, *Diary*, ed. W. C. Ford (1911–12). See also Perry
Miller, *The New England Mind: From Colony to Province* (Cambridge, Mass.: Harvard University Press, 1953).

was attending a witches' meeting. In view of this, Hutchinson felt:

Courts of Justice may as well hang People, upon their Confessions, for the Murders they think they commit in their Dreams, as for what they fancy they do in these Trances. What if this Girl, in this Extasy of Mind, when she had not the Use of her Reason, had made a Compact, and thought she had set her Name to it, and joyned with other Witches in Murders, and confessed them? What wise Man would have turned such a Confession to her Hurt? Physick for Madness would be proper for such a one; but a Stake, or Gallows would be barbarous. It would be harder yet to hang other People for what these Brainsick Persons fancy they see them do.[39]

That this continued, though with diminishing frequency, is borne out by the subsequent history of witchcraft. The last notorious event occurred in 1749 at a convent in Würzburg in Germany. A number of nuns suddenly thought themselves bewitched. They all felt as though they were suffocating and had frequent paroxyms; one of the nuns who had swallowed a handful of needles evacuated them through abscesses at various parts of her body. The suspicion of witchcraft fastened itself upon a young nun, Maria Renata Sänger, who was arrested and charged with sorcery. During her trial the accusers swore to a number of fantastic stories, alleging her ability to change herself into a pig, a cat, and a hare; secretly milking the cows in the meadows; and terrifying the other nuns by appearing in their rooms in animal disguise. These and other accusations led to her being condemned and burned alive in the market place of Würzburg.[40]

Tragic and ludicrous as was this final convulsion of mass hysteria, its aftermath was an apparently total loss of concern with witchcraft throughout Europe. The opinions and attitudes of Hutchinson and others like him suddenly became universal. The whole bizarre structure of witchcraft and wizardry became recognized as a delusion; and both the perpetrators and their victims were seen merely as sick human beings, if not gross imposters. As a corollary the afflicted persons, most of whom were clearly hysterics, required medical rather than religious attention.

[39] Hutchinson, *op. cit.*, p. 77.
[40] Mackay, *Extraordinary Popular Delusions*, pp. 555–56.

CHAPTER V

Magic and the Supernatural in the Far East

THE CENTURIES of witch mania and devil possession have left an indelible imprint on the memory of Western society. The questions arise whether this phenomenon could only develop in cultures based on the Judaeo-Christian background or whether similar manifestations could not also arise among those peoples who are untouched by the tenets of Christian morality; and whether each society might not in the framework of its own supernatural structure find its expression in terms of forces endowed with the power of possessing and corrupting mortals. In fact, the science of anthropology has listed specific examples of types of hysterical reactions encountered exclusively in certain geographical regions. The best-known is the "arctic hysteria," which manifests itself by ecstatic states and a constant and compulsive copying of the movements and words of another individual. Very similar to that is "latah," which occurs among women in Southeast Asia. The victims of these phenomena and latah, like the witches of the West, are predominantly women who are compensated for the discomfort of their illnesses by the attention and through the amusement of the bystanders. This favorable audience reaction is their major

This chapter is a revision of "The Supernatural in Far Eastern Concepts of Mental Disease," which appeared in *Bulletin of the History of Medicine*, XXXVII, No. 2 (1963), 139–58, and is reprinted here by permission of the editor.

reward for their hysterical performances.[1] It is hardly surprising then that in East Asia certain forms of hysteria also attached themselves to specific agents of possession, all of which had their roots in the ancient animistic religions of China and Japan. An important difference between the belief in witches and the belief in the supernatural powers of foxes, badgers, meteors, and other components of nature was that in the West the possessed were invariably persecuted, since possession was thought to be surrounded with sin and guilt, whereas in the Far East no personal responsibility attached itself to the victims of such forces. And although in East Asia occasional records report death by violence of those who were believed to be possessed, it was particularly persons suspected of the act of posessing who were targets of assault and persecution.

China and Japan have shared a common system of medicine since the Chinese concepts and practices were introduced into Japan some fifteen hundred years ago. This commonality includes not only scholarly and philosophical concepts but also much of the folk medicine. The history of psychiatry in the Far East reveals with particular clarity the coexistence of two totally divergent streams of thought, namely, the learned philosophical, or medical approach, and the folk beliefs and practices which dominated the thinking of an overwhelming majority of the population. It is especially the latter that I wish to discuss here.

The long-held *scholarly* explanation for mental disease in China and Japan, as I have brought out in previous publications,[2] was the theory of the dyscrasia of the dual power, Yin and Yang, the negative and the positive, the evil and the good, the female and the male components that activate the human body as well as the universe around it. This dyscrasia or imbalance of the dual power was caused by an infringement upon *Tao*, "The Way," or moral guide to right living. Prevention of disease demanded that the individual follow

[1] Ralph Linton, *Culture and Mental Illness* (Springfield, Ill.: Charles C Thomas, 1956), pp. 115–16.

[2] Ilza Veith, "Psychiatric Thought in Chinese Medicine," *Journal of the History of Medicine and Allied Sciences*, X, No. 3 (1955), 262–63; *Some Philosophical Concepts of Early Chinese Medicine* (Basavangudi: Indian Institute of Culture, 1950), Transaction No. 4.

the precepts of Tao; cure was held to result from return to Tao. Supernàtural elements were totally absent from these moral speculations of the scholarly and social elite.

The *popular* beliefs, on the other hand, are essentially centered upon supernatural causation of disease. These powers bear a superficial, though striking, resemblance to those that haunted the minds of the medieval Western world. They differed in the mental image of the spiritual bodies, endowing them with typically Oriental fantasy, which often attained a complexity and deviousness that is rather baffling to the Western mind. The contrast between these images and those of the more familiar carriers of mental and physical illness in medieval Europe will be clearly revealed in the examples to be given later from Chinese and Japanese sources. Another difference is that the Far Eastern preoccupation with spirits, ghosts, and demons was not terminated by a scientific awakening but continued to flourish in modern times. It is entirely possible that even today, in rural regions of China and Japan, belief in demonic and ghostly causes of mental disease is still as prevalent as that in its natural origin.

Source material concerning these phenomena is not to be found in medical and philosophical treatises. They are revealed in ancient and recent folktales, novels, and short stories, and they have also been described at great length by a multitude of eminent Orientalists of the last century whose observations were made in many different parts of the Far East. From these writings emerges a pattern of thought that is consistent, though—literally—worlds apart from the sober naturalistic philosophy which we generally find in classical Chinese and Japanese literature. The pattern is built around a nether world of witches and wizardry, of animal demons and ancestral spirits, all of which can bring madness as well as cure it.

Before discussing the nature of the sinister powers of the Orient in relation to mental disease, attention must be called to another dichotomy between the popular and the scholarly ideas. The views of the learned held the unshakable assumption of the indivisibility of spirit and substance and of mind and matter. In this they were guided by their concept of the creation and function of the universe and man which were handed down from the earliest Chinese writings, particularly the *Tao Tē Ching*, traditionally attributed to Lao-tzu some five or six centuries B.C.[3] The popular mind, however, saw body and soul as separate entities; and after the introduction and popularization of Buddhism in the third and fourth centuries A.D. in China and, somewhat later, in Japan, the belief in the duality of mind and matter found further corroboration in the doctrine of transmigration and reincarnation. On closer examination, it becomes evident that most Oriental superstitions pertaining to mental disease were predicated on the possibility of separating the soul from the body, and owed their proliferation largely to the importation of Buddhism into the Far East.

The belief in spirits, however, preceded the advent of Buddhism in China and appears to go back to the earliest times. An ancient Chinese proverb reads, "Three measures above our heads lies the beginning of the Spirit World." Yet the spirits were not confined to the upper regions; they were in the water, in caves, in trees, and in graves; they lurked under the earth and under rocks. They swarmed about the homes of men in populated as well as in isolated regions and, according to many tales, their favorite abodes were the privies where man is alone and helpless and flight difficult. Of particular danger were the highways at night, when Yin governs nature and sends forth its specters of darkness. Those encountering the demons often died on the roadside without visible injury, or they developed swellings and ulcers and died upon returning to their homes. Even the imperial harems were not free of demons that bewildered the minds of men as shown in the following story:

The Forbidden City was haunted in the Süen hwo period (1119–1126) by a being known as *lai*, a lumpish thing without head or eyes. Its hands and feet were covered with hair shining as varnish. When at midnight a thundering noise was heard, the people in the Forbidden City all cried: "The *lai* is coming!" and they bolted the doors of all buildings. Sometimes the spectre lay down in the bed of a lady of the harem, which was then felt to be warm; and at daybreak it rolled out of the bed and disappeared, nobody knowing where it had gone. And when the

[3] Arthur Waley, *The Way and Its Power: A Study of the* Tao Tē Ching *and Its Place in Chinese Thought* (New York: Grove Press, 1958).

ladies of the harem dreamed that they were sleeping with somebody, that somebody was the *lai*.[4]

Other apparitions described as hairy, of monstrous height, and intent on violating young maidens were known to cause madness in those who beheld them and for two millennia they were dreaded equally in China and Japan. The fear of these and the numberless other specters which caused accidents and disease was so integral a part of Far Eastern life, that defense measures were taken only at the imminent threat of actual harm. This attitude was particularly evident in regard to health and disease and was in keeping with the Oriental proverb, "Kiss the feet of Buddha when you are sick; when you are well you may forget to burn incense." With the first indication of illness, however, especially if it affected the mind, all the strange rituals came into play that had been evolved for just such occasions. They were carried out by special priests whose function it was to counteract and defeat the noxious powers which had doubtless caused the illness.[5] It is significant that in their totally irrational curative rites we find a strange, though distorted, connecting link between the scholarly and popular view of mental alienation. As priests, even though they used magic influence, they belonged to the realm of Yang representing light and life. They were thus endowed with ascendancy over disease which, no matter what its causation, was governed by Yin, the representative of darkness and death.

This priesthood had its origin in China's primitive animistic religion. Its members were designated by the symbol *Wu,* which first appears in the *Chou Li,*[6] the "Rites of the Chou" dynasty (1122–255 B.C.), and has continued to the present, meaning wizard, witch, medium, and, above all, exorciser of demons. When it became the popular belief that illness was caused by demoniacal possession, the *Wu* eventually became

[4] J. J. M. de Groot, *The Religious System of China* (Leyden: E. J. Brill, 1910), V, Book II, 473.

[5] E. D. Edwards, *Chinese Prose Literature of the T'ang Period* (London: Arthur Probsthain, 1937), I, 53.

[6] The authorship and date of the *Chou Li* is uncertain and has been the subject of much controversy. See Ilza Veith, "Government Control and Medicine in Eleventh Century China," *Bulletin of the History of Medicine,* XIV, No. 2 (1943), 159–72.

PLATE I. St. Ignatius of Loyola exorcising the possessed.
(After a painting by Peter Paul Rubens [1577–1640].)

PLATE II. Aureolus Bombastus Theophrastus von Hohenheim: Paracelsus (1493–1541).

PLATE III. Ambroise Paré (151(

almost synonymous with physician and the combination of *Wu-i*, "magical physician," which appeared in Confucius' *Lun Yü* (XIII, 22), is also still used today.

The ability of the *Wu* to act as a physician was largely due to his exorcising power, which was considered essential in the treatment of mental disease. Many cures wrought by male or female magical physicians were recorded throughout the course of Chinese history. The following incident is a good example. It takes place during the T'ang dynasty (A.D. 618–906) and deals with a female *Wu* in Kiang-su, who was famous for her skill in expelling evil influences. She was called to the house of a peasant, "Ch'en whose daughter was so terribly tortured by a spectre that she had fits of madness, in which she sometimes inflicted injuries on her own self, jumping into fire or running into water; and meanwhile she became pregnant as if by sexual commerce with men."[7] True to her reputation and with tremendous personal exertion, the healer succeeded in inducing a deep slumber in the patient, and the "next day she was released" from her obsession.

The resourcefulness of the priests in coping with the demons of disease was vast. Their procedures were logically related to the cause of the specific disease as they saw it, and they used ruses, decoys, force, or incantations depending on the given situation.[8]

The rites of the priestly healer were not without danger to himself and hazardous occasionally even to the patient. Von der Goltz cites a Peking newspaper report of August 20, 1878, which tells of ministrations that actually caused the patient's death. A *Wu* was called to the bedside of a young girl who appeared to be talking with strange voices and presented the impression of great mental disturbance. To drive out the evil spirits who were responsible for this condition, the priest executed a wild dance, in the course of which he inflicted such severe sword blows upon the body of the girl

[7] De Groot, *op. cit.*, VI, Book II, 1227–28.

[8] M. W. de Visser, "Fire and ignes fatui in China," *Mittheilungen des Seminars für orientalische Sprachen zu Berlin*, Vol. XXVII, Part I (Berlin, 1914); and Henri Doré, *Recherches sur les superstitions en Chine* (Shanghai, 1911).

that she finally died.[9] Although this outcome was rare, the ritual itself was common, but, as a rule, the healer inflicted the wounds upon himself rather than upon the patient. For this purpose he generally had an arsenal of instruments of self-torture including a set of five swords—the number corresponding with the traditional five elements, the five main organs, the five emotions, and all the other five main factors of which, according to Chinese and Japanese scholarly tradition, all things and beings were thought to be composed.

In general, medical priesthood was retained in certain families who jealously guarded their potent magic. Moreover, it was assumed that the power to cure was derived from a greater proportion of Yang than that possessed by ordinary mortals and that this power of Yang was transmitted by heredity. In spite of the prevailing veneration of age, it was believed that the younger *Wu* had greater healing powers than their older colleagues. In view of the tremendous exertions required in the performance of the healing rites, and the considerable self-mutilation, which often led to severe loss of blood, it seems probable that most healing priests could not carry their profession into advanced age. Because the *Wu* was thought to act as an emissary of the higher powers, it was assumed that the effect of priestly healing would be obviated by the demand of fees. He could, however, accept presents when they were offered voluntarily. Thus it became customary for the patients or their families to reward the healer according to their ability and their appraisal of his performance.

As would be expected in a society dominated by the cult of ancestral worship, by far the most dreaded among all the harmful forces were the spirits of the dead. Particularly resentful were the spirits of those whose burial had not been attended by the necessary rites and who felt offended by this neglect, and those who had died by violence. At executions, so frequent in the Far East, the attending crowd burned fireworks to chase away the spirit of the victim, and the presiding official further protected himself by having, in front of his home, a fire over which his attendants carried

[9] Frhr. von der Goltz, "Zauberei und Hexenkünste, Spiritismus und Schamanismus in China," *Mitteilungen der Deutschen Gesellschaft für Natur- und Völkerkunde Ostasiens,* Book II, 51 (Tokyo, 1893–97), p. 17.

him. This practice was based on the belief that fire, the mightiest of all elements, conferred the greatest immunity from the diseases caused by such spirits and, indeed, by all demons and specters. As the source of light and life, fire was the very essence of Yang and therefore in natural opposition to illness and death, which belonged to the realm of Yin. A strange ritual, developed from this belief, was called "walking on a path of fire." It was resorted to whenever man wished to cleanse himself from prior contact with evil or protect himself against its pursuit. For the official ceremony of fire-treading a very thin layer of charcoal was ignited, and the glowing coals were rapidly traversed by a barefoot priest and subsequently by all those who sought safety from spirit persecution. Fire was always treated with considerable reverence so as to safeguard its protective quality. Refuse was never to be thrown into the flames. In Japan this prohibition even extended to the burning of parings of fingernails, toenails, or human hair, and those transgressing this interdict were believed to turn insane. The custom of exploding bamboo cuttings and later of firecrackers developed in connection with the fire ceremonies, and since the explosives combined fire with loud noise they were held doubly effective in the frightening away of evil spirits.[10]

Like those who had died by execution, those who were killed unjustly retained the power of revenge long after death; this was particularly true of children who had fallen prey to the widespread custom of infanticide. Especially vulnerable to ancestral mischief were young girls whose marriageable age had passed without the appearance of a suitable husband. Forever deprived of a proper place in society, they tended to believe themselves haunted and to become emotionally unbalanced. In some the delusion eventually led to insanity. According to one author, the spirits of the dead took particular delight in tormenting these frustrated young women with erotic desires, which by leading to masturbation resulted in madness.[11] The description of this last se-

[10] De Groot, *op. cit.*, pp. 943 ff., 1292 ff.

[11] J. P. Kleiweg de Zwaan, *Völkerkundliches und Geschichtliches über die Heilkunde der Chinesen und Japaner* (*Natuurkundige Verhandelingen van de Hollandsche Maatschappij der Wetenschappen to Haarlem*), Third series, Part 7 (Haarlem: Erven Loosjes, 1917), p. 48.

quence hardly seems plausible in light of the general Chinese theory that female masturbation was not associated with any dire sequelae and therefore was not to be discouraged. This permissive attitude is quite in contrast with that towards masturbation in the male. In men it was believed that semen carried the essential life force and that, at birth, each male was endowed with a specific quantity. Each ejaculation expended a portion of this vital essence which could never be fully replenished. These theories had much deeper roots than mere popular belief. They appear to have been part of the early scholarly Chinese medical writings which are no longer extant in their original form. They were incorporated, however, in a large compendium of Chinese medicine, the *Ishimpo*, which was made in Japan by Yasuyori Tamba in the tenth century A.D. Although this book was not printed until the very end of the Tokugawa period (1854), it was frequently copied by hand and became an important textbook for Japanese physicians.[12] Because of this intense concern with the preservation of semen, an irresistible urge towards masturbation and nocturnal emissions was usually interpreted as the work of vengeful spirits who took the shape of seductive young women and pursued their victims even in dreams. The consequent psychic disturbances were doubtless often due to the fear of the dire effects which followed the irreplaceable loss of vital substance.

Another frequent cause of mental derangement was the ability attributed to the dead to steal the soul of the living. Such catastrophes were believed to happen during sleep, when the soul was occupied with dreams and could easily be lured away. Although all the departed had the power to return to earth and to plague the living, one group of spirits was held to be particularly powerful. This was the *T'ien Ku* in China, known as the "Tengu" in Japan, both of which may be literally translated as the "Celestial Dog." Originally conceived in China as dog-faced comets or meteors, the Tengu later were regarded as mountain demons and as such became known in Japan. There, they were eventually incorporated into Buddhist beliefs and assumed the role of the

12 One of the original manuscript editions is preserved in the Historical Library of the Takeda Pharmaceutical Company in Osaka, Japan.

ghosts of departed priests who had led dissolute lives and had thus become emissaries of the devil. In this capacity the Tengu drove people to madness and, if they found other evil priests, they led them to the "Tengu Road," one of the dreaded punishments of the Buddhist hell for vanity and hypocrisy. Even in the recent past the Tengus' powers were considered limitless and dangerous to all. Guided by sheer whim, they possessed their victims and spoke through them in strange voices, they led them astray and deprived them of their memory, and they caused unending anxiety among the parents whose young sons were thought to be the favorite victims of these evil demons.[13]

With this strong implication of the spirit of the dead in all forms of mental alienation, it was reasonable to attempt restoration to sanity by immediate efforts to propitiate the departed. Ceremonies and gifts at the graves and ancestral altars, and elaborate rituals, were devised to recapture the souls of the demented for their rightful owners. Since the supernatural was involved, failure to produce the desired results was not considered the fault of the medical priest who conducted these rites but was ascribed to the implacable hostility of the dead. Moreover, there was always a chance that other and less easily specified forces might have caused the disease, for, actually, almost any component of the vegetable, mineral, and animal kingdoms was recognized as a potential abode of malign spirits.

The latter belief persisted from China's early religion, animism, which was never completely abandoned, and continued to exist side by side with the realistic sophistication of Confucianism. It is interesting that Confucius confined his teachings to the cultivation of character, the art of governing, and personal ethics and never expressed himself "on extraordinary things, feats of strength, disorders, or spiritual beings." He never even pondered over the mysteries of life and death. Whether by doing so he ignored the myths of his people or accepted them without question is unresolved. His followers preserved silence on these subjects also and did not voice any opposition when Taoist and Buddhist writers made

[13] See M. W. de Visser, "The Tengu," *Transactions of the Asiatic Society of Japan*, XXXVI, Part II (Yokohama, 1908), 25–99.

free use of the old myths and legends to further their own doctrines.[14]

Vestiges of animism were distinctly interwoven into the later more formalized practices of Taoism, and it was absorbed even more completely in the vast pantheon of Buddhism. This complex religious fabric was further modified and adapted to Japanese thought with the adoption of the Chinese language and culture by Japan. The figure of the Tengu exemplifies the animation of an object such as a meteor, its change of identity in China, and, finally, its further transformation in Japanese folklore. Innumerable other animate and inanimate substances have been equally endowed with spectral potency. Although each of them has had a place in the popular thought and beliefs of the Far East, no single figure has had as important a role in Chinese and Japanese fantasy as that played by the fox.

Indeed, so rich is the lore of this animal's protean powers that a complete survey of all the legends and fairy tales devoted to the fox spirit are beyond the powers of one person. Examination of the fox lore is further complicated by the fact that it evolved independently in both China and Japan. Here I propose to cite but a small number of tales, selected from the vast store of such narratives in both Chinese and Japanese literature to illustrate their relation to concepts of mental disease. Collectively, they give an impression of the enormously wide range of attributes and roles of the fox, which has so colored Far Eastern popular thought concerning behavioral aberrations.

In Japan the fox was originally regarded as the messenger of Inari, the rice-goddess who was believed to have had a vulpine shape, and in this context the fox was a benign creature; vestiges of this aspect are still preserved in Japanese fox lore. But, later, even Japan adopted almost wholly the ancient Chinese belief in the animal's demonic traits and its consummate skill in taking human shape for the purpose of haunting and possessing men.

The earliest known reference to the malign role of the fox is found in the *Book of Odes*,[15] where its very appearance

[14] See E. D. Edwards, *op. cit.*, II, 1–5.

[15] *Shih Ching*, a collection of ancient ballads selected and arranged by Confucius. See A. Wylie, *Notes on Chinese Literature* (Shanghai: American Presbyterian Mission Press, 1867).

on the scene was interpreted as having presaged the collapse of a kingdom.[16] Later, during the Han dynasty (206 B.C.–A.D. 220), the fox assumed a more personal role which affected individuals, singly or in groups, and brought disease, insanity, and death as well as economic or political misfortune. It is this capacity which has persisted through the centuries with gradually increasing emphasis on the causation of psychic diseases ranging from minor disturbances to severe psychoses. In achieving these ends, foxes were believed able either to enter human beings and to take possession of their souls or themselves to assume human appearance in order to exert their influence on others.

Confusing to the Western mind is the dual role often played by the fox, wherein he appears as the cause of mental disease and, at the same time, as an imposter who pretends to cure it. A typical example is a story from the *Hsüan-shih-chi* (late eighth century A.D.). It tells of a ten-year-old boy, the son of a minor palace official, who was intelligent, studious, and so well-mannered that he was beloved by all. But illness began to transform his personality completely. When the father was on the point of summoning a doctor of Taoist arts, a man knocked at the door and identified himself as a healer. Offering to dispel the affliction with charms, he said, "This boy suffers from a sickness which is caused by a fox demon." He thereupon applied his arts and suddenly the boy rose from his bed and exclaimed with a normal voice that he was cured; and indeed he seemed restored to his old self. The grateful father generously rewarded the "doctor," who took his leave and promised that henceforth he would call every day because:

though the boy was cured of that disease, still he lacked a sufficient quantity of soul, wherefore he uttered every now and then insane talk, and had fits of laughter and wailing, which they could not suppress. At each call of the doctor, the father

[16] This description of foxes as synonymous with bad omens and associated with noxious spirits was widespread in Han literature (206 B.C.–A.D. 280) and subsequently entered the "Standard Histories," where it is mentioned in the *Book of Tsin* (A.D. 265–419) and is particularly evident in the *History of the South* (A.D. 420–589). According to the latter source even the rulers and their court were beset by fears of foxes, and it is told that a dream of a fox was a sufficient omen of disaster to the empire as to cause an emperor to sell himself as a slave to a Buddhist monastery. *Nan Shih*, 10, Book II, 12–13.

requested him to attend to this matter too, but the other said: "This boy's vital spirits are kept bound by a spectre, and are as yet not restored to him; but in less than ten days he will become quite calm; there is, I am happy to say, no reason to feel concerned about him." And the father believed it.[17]

When the disease dragged on, another doctor was called in, and, finally, a third, and suddenly the three began a noisy fight among each other. When eventually silence ensued the frightened father returned to the sick room. There he was startled to find "three foxes stretched on the ground, panting and motionless." He then realized that one of the three foxes must have been the first "doctor" and that it was he who not only had caused the disease but even had prolonged it wilfully. Enraged, he beat all the foxes until they were dead, and "in the next ten days the boy was cured."[18]

One of the favorite disguises of the "were-foxes," as they were termed by de Groot in his classic work on "Demonology,"[19] was the body of lovely young girls who seduced their male victims into sexual and even marital relationships, causing them forever to lose interest in other women. If the deception was discovered by a priest or relatives of the victim, and the woman, now revealed as a fox, had been exorcised, the young man might soon be cured of his obsession. But when the infatuation was arbitrarily terminated by the demons, there often followed long periods of profound mental disturbance, melancholia, and sometimes death. So well-known was this affliction that it inspired the T'ang poet Po Chü-i[20] to exclaim, "A woman who fawns upon a man like a vixen[21] destroys him at once and forever; for days and months she causes his mind to quiver."

But men were not the only victims of foxes. It was believed that through a series of metamorphoses the same animal could assume successively the images of enchanting females and seductive males in order alternately to plague their male and female prey. In a widely quoted passage of the *Hsüan-chung-chi*, which was composed in the early cen-

[17] De Groot, *op. cit.*, V, Book II, 583–86.

[18] *Ibid*.

[19] *Ibid.*, pp. 582 ff.   [20] A.D. 772–846.

[21] In modern usage the characters for "vixens" are still used to denote seductive, bewitching.

turies of our era, these magic changes are described as follows: "When a fox is fifty years old, it becomes a beautiful female, . . . or a grownup man who has sexual intercourse with women. Such beings are able to know things occurring at more than a thousand miles distant; they can poison men by sorcery, or possess them, and bewilder them, so that they lose their memory and knowledge. And when a fox is a thousand years old, it penetrates to heaven, and becomes a celestial fox."[22]

This is further elaborated by an author of the Ming dynasty,[23] one who exempts women from fox possession:

When a fox is a thousand years old; it goes to heaven for the first time and does not haunt people any longer. The purpose of the foxes in enchanting men is to take the vital spirit away from them in order to transfer it to their own bodies. But why do they not enchant women? Because foxes are animals of *Darkness* [like women they belong to the principle *Yin*], and he who has *Light* [the principle *Yang*] within himself is liable to be enchanted by them. Even male foxes always take the shape of women to seduce men.[24]

The immunity of women to fox possession, so logically expressed in this quotation, was not accepted by many; there are innumerable accounts of females who were so beguiled. The following Japanese story is unusual, since it was told by a minister and involved a princess of the blood.[25] In keeping with an ancient custom, at the time of the emperor's coronation this young virgin had been sent to the imperial shrine at Ise, where she was to stay throughout his reign. After four years in the temple, she was heard to call out with a loud and strange voice, stating that a god was speaking through her. Those who heard her said she appeared insane. This impression was further confirmed when she ordered two Shinto temples to be built in the vicinity of the shrine and summoned a large group of irreverent people to join her there. These she commanded to perform a sacred dance and

[22] De Groot, *op. cit.*, pp. 586–87.

[23] Hsieh Chao-chi, sixteenth century.

[24] M. W. De Visser, "The Fox and Badger in Japanese Folklore," in *Transactions of the Asiatic Society of Japan*, XXXVI, Part 3 (Yokohama: Kelly & Walsh, Ltd., 1908), 10.

[25] It appears in the diary of the minister Ono-no Miya (956–1046) and happened during the tenure of his office.

to continue with other wild dances for many days and
nights. The evil sorcerers of the capital soon realized that the
princess was possessed by a fox and made an image of this
animal, which they established as the chief deity of the
Temple of Ise.

Since further information is lacking, it is of course impossible to arrive at a satisfactory opinion on the cause and
nature of the princess' derangement. It seems reasonable to
assume that among the contributing factors was her exalted
yet exceedingly lonely life as a temple virgin and her not
knowing how long it would continue. The absence of any
attempt at exorcism or treatment and the freedom given to
the patient in permitting her to act out her delusions were
probably due to the deference accorded to her noble birth.

Although this is by no means the only fox legend involv-
ing royalty, the more frequent subjects are the peasants and
villagers of the rural regions. In this setting most tales are
told of men's amorous involvements with vixens and of the
seducing of women by foxes, which sometimes resulted in
pregnancy. An interesting example of the latter was brought
about by a fox imposter who posed as a Buddhist saint. The
story takes place during the T'ang dynasty (A.D. 618–906)
in the province of Shansi and has as its chief figure a young
girl who lived at home with her widowed mother while her
brother served in the army. One day mother and daughter
were visited by one such Bodhisatva, who appeared riding
on a cloud. He announced to the mother that he was pleased
with the virtue of her house and that he wished to abide in
it but that neither she nor her neighbors must ever speak of
it to anyone:

They accordingly admonished each other to hold their tongues,
and the Bodhisatwa had intercourse with the girl, so that she
became pregnant. A year passed by, and the brother came home;
but the Bodhisatwa declared that he did not desire to see any
male creatures, and prevailed upon the mother to drive her son
out. The latter thus being unable to approach the saint, used
his money for securing the help of a Taoist doctor, and finally
found one who applied his arts on his behalf. They thus discovered that the Bodhisatwa was an old fox; sword in hand,
he rushed into the house, and despatched the brute.[26]

[26] De Groot, *op. cit.*, pp. 592–93.

According to general belief, the offspring born from such unions tended to develop like other children and to merge with the human community. They were recognized as fox children only by others like them and by priests. Doubtless, the existence of such legends was frequently used as a convenient explanation for illegitimate birth. Yet they were invariably taken at face value and most certainly appeared entirely plausible when the mother was feeble-minded or deranged and thus presented conclusive evidence of supernatural mischief.

The fox lore quoted so far has largely been drawn from the early writings on the subject, since they provided the pattern for the numberless later tales. Before leaving the earlier period, reference must be made to a rather unusual story, some features of which are suggestive of the Oedipus legend. It was included by Yü Pao in chapter 18 of his collection of marvelous tales, the *Sou-Shên-Chi*, which was written in the early part of the fourth century and much quoted and altered in the T'ang dynasty.[27]

The story is laid during the Tsin dynasty (A.D. 265–419) in the Chehkiang province. It tells of a farmer and his two sons who were harvesting their field. The father's work had taken him away from his sons, and when he returned, and without apparent provocation, he began to berate and beat them. On reaching their home, the dismayed sons complained to their mother, who asked the father why he had hurt them. The astonished father, unaware that anything out of the ordinary had happened, declared that it must have been the work of a fox demon who had impersonated him and sent his sons out into the fields to destroy it. The demon did not appear, however, and when the father went to seek his sons, in the fear that something evil had befallen them, the young men attacked and killed him, believing him to be the demon. Meanwhile, the fox again assumed the shape of their father and had entered their dwelling. When the sons returned and told him of the slaying, the imposter and their mother expressed their joy.

For years the young men remained ignorant of their dreadful deed until one day a priest revealed to them that

[27] Wylie, *op. cit.*, p. 154.

their father was known to be an evil person. This conversation was carried back to the father, who exhibited such a fearful rage that the sons fled to warn the priest. But the latter, sustained by his righteousness, bravely entered the house. At first sight of him, the imposter turned back into an old fox and was slain by the sons. Only then did they realize that earlier they had killed their real father. They tried to atone for their fearful violation of filial piety by burying their father in a proper grave and by mourning him for a long period. Yet life had become altogether unbearable, and shortly afterwards one son killed himself and the other sank into profound melancholy and died of remorse.

The protagonists of this tragedy appear to be completely innocent targets of a vicious prank. Unlike the ancestral spirits which strike in retribution for insults or neglect, the fox generally prefers harmless and sometimes even virtuous victims for his malign play. There are a few exceptions, however, and among them the following story is of particular interest, since it appears to deal with a case of vicarious guilt. Its locale is Yedo (now Tokyo), its period the second decade of the nineteenth century, and it is told in the *Tōen Shōsetsu* (1825).[28] The victim, a young girl who lived with her mother, was found to be insane and exhibited unmistakable signs of fox possession. When she was subjected to searching questions, the answers were given by a voice recognized as that of a fox. In accounting for the reasons for the girl's abstraction, the fox revealed that "her mother, a widow, had illicit intercourse with a silk merchant who often passed the night in her house." After having made these revelations, the fox "went out" of the patient, the silk merchant fled, the widow was sent back to her native village, and the girl, now completely restored, went to the house of relatives. This case suggests that the weight of the guilty knowledge of her mother's improper conduct so preyed upon her as to cause this emotional disturbance. Unable because of consideration of filial piety or fear of loss of face to reveal this secret, she unconsciously took refuge in the fox disguise and so achieved her purpose.

During the millennia of recorded fox lore, frequently speculations were made about possible common traits among

28 De Visser, *op. cit.*, pp. 87–89.

those particularly predisposed to fox possession. A significant comment on this subject was that by Kojima Fukyu in the early eighteenth century.

> The fox is an animal of Darkness to the uttermost degree. Therefore the external evil [in the shape of the fox] enters people whose Light-spirit has diminished. In general, exaggeration of joy, anger, sorrow, pleasure, love, hatred and greed causes man to lose his original character and to become empty, and only possessed of the spirit of Darkness. How could it happen otherwise on such occasions but that bad demons should enter into him?[29]

The implication of this passage seems entirely clear. Did the author really believe in his supernatural imagery, or did he use it only because it was the idiom of his day? He points to the early subtle changes of personality, which are rarely noticed except in retrospect, and describes them as mere exaggerations of normal emotional behavior. They progress at so gradual a pace that the disturbance becomes evident only when the disease is full-blown. "It causes man to be empty and only possessed of the spirit of Darkness." What better characterization could one find of melancholia, of depression, and of all the other forms of alienation which were, according to Far Eastern thought, but stages of the same process?

Irrespective of whether Kojima Fukyu actually accepted fox possession or simply pondered the mysteries of the diseased mind, the folk belief of the Far East almost invariably ascribed preternatural causes to all forms of aberrant behavior, including sexual disturbances such as frigidity and impotence, nymphomania and satyriasis. Indeed, the association of sex and psychological aberrations in fox lore is frequent. It was equally prevalent in China and Japan and also existed in most other forms of animal and spirit possession. This emphasis seems particularly remarkable in that sexual inhibition was generally not a dominant feature in the mores of the Far East.[30] Much additional study will be required to

[29] *Kojima Fukyu, Heishoku waku-monchin* (1737), as quoted by De Visser, *op. cit.*, p. 101.

[30] This was particularly true prior to the Ming dynasty when most supernatural beliefs had crystallized. See R. H. Van Gulik, *Sexual Life in Ancient China: A Preliminary Survey of Chinese Sex and Society from* ca. *1500 B.C. until 1644 A.D.* (Leyden: E. J. Brill, 1961).

arrive at a full understanding of this phenomena. Future research might wish to examine the role played by the traditional Oriental desire for numerous male offspring. The fear of failure in fulfilling this desire may well have been a contributing factor to the extraordinary sexual preoccupation, which so easily assumed pathological dimensions.

Another conspicuous feature of most Oriental stories relating to mental disease is the apparently sudden onset of the derangement without noticeable premonitory symptoms, whether they were caused by haunting ancestors, Tengu, foxes, or other specters. Equally prominent are the reports of the abrupt cures either by exorcism or other violent measures to hasten the departure of the intruding demon. Although it is probable that the subtle prodromata, which generally preceded the obvious "madness," were not recognized as such, as has been indicated above, the narrators doubtless also made use of poetic license in telescoping the events so as to render their stories more dramatic.

The most important conclusion to be drawn from the study of Oriental folklore is that inherent in the belief of the spectral origin of mental disease there is a definite assumption of its reversible nature and curability. Each aberration had its specific cause, and a curative magic was directed towards the expulsion of the offending agent. Since many of the ceremonies were associated with violence that may have acted somewhat in the nature of shock treatment and all of them involved an intensive preoccupation with the patient, it is likely that the treatment was often effective. Above all, the belief in demonic powers made the patient an innocent victim and placed the correction of his derangement beyond the influence of rational treatment and into the hands of priests. As a result no stigma was attached to mental disease, and society was ready to receive the patient on pre-illness terms as soon as his behavior became normal.

Although the learned medical literature in China and Japan was concerned only with theoretical and philosophical aspects of mental disease and was particularly emphatic in its prophylactic recommendations, these writings were of little practical influence among the general population, few among whom were even able to read. The prevailing ideas, as has been shown from the examples in folklore and popular literature, were those of the supernatural. Hence, there was the development of two psychiatric attitudes which existed side by side with little interplay, but apparently also without hostility or professional jealousies. Herein lies the greatest difference between the history of Far Eastern and Occidental thought.

In the Western world, on the other hand, where this dichotomy did not exist, once the supernatural had been ex-

FIG. 6. Treatment of hysterical woman. (From Sokei Dojin, *Byo ka su chi* ["Health Handbook for the Patient"], 1834.)

cluded from all causative connections with health and disease, hysterical manifestations became once more the sole responsibility of the physician, and the question arises what, if anything, had medicine to offer as treatment for hysteria? The few medical publications of the early Middle Ages, as mentioned earlier, adhere firmly to the Hippocratic tradition of uterine causation. Included among these are the writings of the Byzantine physicians, of whom Oribasius of Pergamon (A.D. 325–400) and Aëtius of Amida (A.D. 502–75) are the most familiar. Since the latter's description of "uterine spasm"[31] clearly describes a hysterical attack and introduces some independent ideas as to its causation, it will be summarized here.

According to Aëtius, the uterus remains in its normal position during a hysterical attack, but is seized with violent contractions which then similarly affect the other organs. These spasms reach the heart by way of the arteries, the brain by way of the spinal marrow, and the liver through the veins. Thus the supposed ascent of the uterus to produce the manifestations in the upper regions of the body does not actually occur and the remote sensations, including the "globus hystericus," are in no way occasioned by a displacement of the organ. The prodromata of the attack are sadness, pains, anxiety, and weakness and a dulling of the eyes. At the end of the attack a fluid is discharged from the uterus. Aëtius observed that the disease manifests itself most frequently in winter and spring and generally in young women. It is caused, he believed, by a cooling of the uterus during menstruation.

ARABIAN AND SALERNITAN CONTRIBUTIONS

Arabian physicians preserved the heritage of the medicine of antiquity during the Middle Ages.

Occidental scientists and physicians are generally wont to regard the spread of science and medicine as flowing from West to East, rarely realizing that in the very beginning of Western civilization the flow took the opposite direction and that it was the East, i.e., the Near East, Egypt, and

[31] *Tetrabiblion* XVI, 67.

Mesopotamia, that produced the earliest scientific thoughts which gradually found their way into Greece and formed the foundation of Greek learning so proudly hailed as the beginning of Western science.

Similarly, in the Middle Ages, when the well of scholarship was drying up in the Western world, it was the Near East that took over the heritage so casually abandoned. Thus began the so-called Arabic period of medicine which was actually not altogether as Arabic as it was Muslim. The Muslim Empire, founded by its spiritual father, Mohammed, swiftly and irresistibly became the most powerful of its day, welding together within its own borders Europe and the Near East and preserving in its march of conquest the learning of classical antiquity. In addition to the traditional war booty extracted from their conquered enemies, the Muslim warriors confiscated whatever manuscripts or other evidence of learning they could find. They also brought back with them anybody who they assumed might translate these treasures into their own tongue.

Rarely were these translations into Arabic undertaken directly from the original Greek but generally by several different persons, first into Syriac and finally into Arabic. Much later they were retranslated in tortuous stages, often by way of Hebrew, into Greek and Latin; and it was through the inevitable misinterpretations that mistakes and completely new meanings were introduced into the classical writings of Hippocrates and Galen. In this process words like azimuth, zenith, nadir, and many others were washed back into our current scientific vocabulary. At the same time a number of substances were introduced by Arabian pharmacists into our materia medica of which they are important parts to this very day, among them colchicum, camphor, senna, nutmeg, cloves, and alcohol.

The period of the so-called Arabic medicine falls into three sections. The first is the one just discussed in which Syrians and Jews performed their invaluable services as translators from the Greek. The second period was of considerably greater originality. Muslim physicians now produced writings based upon their own medical experience and made original contributions to the development of medicine. The best known among them was the Persian Muham-

med ibn Zakaria, called Rhazes (A.D. 865–925), who had
studied medicine in Baghdad and became that city's leading
physician. He was a voluminous writer who wrote more
than two hundred books. Of these the most important is
known to the West under the name *Liber Continens* and, as
its title indicates, is a compilation of all the knowledge of his
day. Rhazes also was the author of one of the first disease
monographs in medical history dealing with smallpox and
measles and their differentiation from each other.

Worthy of note is another Persian physician whose name
in the Western world was Haly Abbas (A.D. ?–994). He became famous as the author of the *Royal Book* of the art of
medicine which was translated in the late twelfth century
from the original Arabic into Latin. Haly Abbas had much
clinical experience and observed well. Thus he noted that
temporary states of depression tend to afflict both boys and
girls at the beginning of puberty. He considered love a form
of melancholia. Because of the direct influence of Greek
tradition on Muslim thought, it is not surprising to find Haly
Abbas writing about the cause of hysteria in ancient terms
of the womb being a wild animal longing to satisfy its hunger
for semen.

The greatest of all Muslim physicians was beyond doubt
Ibn Sina, the "Prince of Physicians," known to posterity as
Avicenna (A.D. 980–1037). Like Rhazes and Haly Abbas before him, Avicenna was also a Persian. Innumerable exciting
legends surround his life. His experiences and writings concerned themselves with all aspects of healing and human
thought, including philosophy and psychology which he
described in the *Canon* in such a profound and complex
fashion that only the most learned of his day were able to
comprehend him.

While the three leading Muslim physicians did not write
much about hysteria, other important writers recorded their
observations on that disease. Among these, Serapion the
Elder (ninth century) denied that hysterical disturbances
are related to irregularities of the menses, and he reiterated
the Galenic theme that they result solely from sexual abstinence, since also according to his observations only widows
and spinsters are subject to the disease. Avicenna, "the
Prince" of the Arabic physicians, added, as an alternative

etiology, amenorrhea to seminal retention as the result of sexual abstinence, but he considered the former as offering a more favorable prognosis than the latter.

The revival of medicine in Europe began in Salerno in southern Italy. From this center emanated the one remaining publication bearing on hysteria, which should be mentioned in this brief review of medieval literature on the subject. This book, the *Passionibus mulierum curandorum* ("On the Cure of Women's Diseases"), was thought to have been the work of Trotula, certainly the most famous of the very few women authors in the history of medicine. It is neither certain nor very probable that such a person, and one with that name, ever existed. According to popular belief, however, Trotula was a prominent woman physician in the southern Italian city of Salerno, where an important lay medical school flourished from the ninth to the thirteenth century. Her personality and the dates remain subjects of unresolved historical controversy. It has even been stated that as the wife of a leading Salernitan physician, Platearius, she was the foremost of the learned "Women of Salerno" (*Mulieres Salernitanae*) who practiced gynecology and obstetrics during the eleventh and twelfth centuries. Actually, the only historical evidence is the small gynecological treatise mentioned, which is based upon older sources as well as on what appears to be first-hand observation. This book is unique in that it deals with subject matter forbidden to clerical physicians; it could emanate only from Salerno because that was the center of the lay physicians. By the time it was first printed in the sixteenth century it had been copied by hand so often that the extant versions differed somewhat from one another. All bore the same lengthy title however, and to a degree covered the various subjects mentioned: *On Curing the Sicknesses of Women Before, during, and after parturition never before published in which is set forth the accidents, diseases, and passions of the female sex; the care of infants and children from birth; the choice of a nurse and other matters related to this; ailments touching upon both sexes; finally the experiences of various illnesses together with certain medicines contributing to the beautification of the body.*

Discussion of hysteria, under the time-worn heading, "On Suffocation of the Womb," appears in the fourth chapter of the treatise. It begins with a brief exposition of the basis of the symptoms and the most characteristic manifestations: "Sometimes the womb is choked; sometimes it is lifted upwards and there results a subversion of the stomach and a loss of appetite due to a weakening of the circulation. Sometimes women faint and the pulse seems to vanish if it is not felt for deeply. Sometimes the woman is convulsed, her head is brought to her knees, she lacks sight and cannot speak; her nose is twisted, her lips are compressed, she grits her teeth, and her breathing is shallower than normal."[32]

Graphic as this description is, it differs little, if at all, from most of those of the early Greek writers. That the theories of Galen were also accepted is evident from one of his cases which she cites. This patient had lost her voice and her pulse and had ceased to show any signs of life—which may occur, Trotula asserts, in women if too much spoiled seed is retained and turns into poison.

Especially does this happen to those who have no husbands, widows in particular and those who previously have been accustomed to make use of carnal intercourse. It also happens in virgins who have come to marriageable years and have not yet husbands for in them abounds the seed which nature wished to draw out by means of the male. From this superabundant and spoiled seed a certain cold substance is formed which ascends to certain parts which by common use are called "collaterals" because they are neighbors to the heart, the lungs, and vocal organs, whence an impediment to the voice is wont to happen. Illness of this sort is accustomed principally to begin with a failure of the menses and when they cease and there is too much seed the illness is much more troublesome and prolonged especially when it takes possession of the higher parts.[33]

All the old methods are recommended as treatment for such states, including massaging hands and feet, applying fetid substances to the nostrils and cupping glasses to the groins, and anointing the womb with aromatic ointments. A new therapeutic element of extraordinary interest is

[32] *The Diseases of Women by Trotula of Salerno*, a translation of *Passionibus mulierum curandorum* by Elizabeth Mason-Hohl (Los Angeles: Ward Ritchie Press, 1940), p. 10.

[33] *Ibid.*, p. 11.

added, credited to an unidentified physician, Justinian, who prescribed "that a powder be made of the testicles of a fox or a kid and that this be injected [into the vagina] by means of a tampon."[34] Whether this is mere suggestion or an adumbration of hormonal treatment cannot be stated, but of unquestionably symbolic value was another recommendation by Justinian: that a carrot-shaped root of lovage,[35] which had been cooked and smeared with axle grease, be tied over the navel.

[34] *Ibid.*, p. 12.

[35] A member of the carrot family and part of the medieval pharmacopoeia.

CHAPTER VI

The Non-conformists

T HIS BRIEF CONSIDERATION of hysteria in the late Middle
Ages would be incomplete without mention of Arnald of
Villanova (*ca.* 1235–*ca.* 1314), whose extraordinary personality reflected and contributed to the pre-Renaissance stir-
rings of the thirteenth century. He was born and educated
in Spain and, although primarily a physician, he was also
trained in law and philosophy. In addition to these activities,
he served as a diplomat and was also known as an alchemist
and astrologer. In the last-named role he is said to have fore-
cast the early demise of King Peter III of Aragon, whom he
served as counsellor and physician, whereupon the clergy
accused him of practicing prophecy and had him banished
from Spain. Fleeing to France, he eventually settled at Montpellier where he was appointed to the medical faculty of the
university, in which position he attained considerable prominence. But further involvement with magic and alchemy
made him *persona non grata* in France also, and he was again
forced to flee, this time to Italy. He died in Genoa, reported-
ly while on a journey to give medical aid to ailing Pope
Clemens V. Despite the exalted status of his patient, Arnald's
name came under a cloud of heresy after his death.

THE SEARCH FOR NATURAL CAUSES

Arnald of Villanova was the most prominent of a group of
physicians who groped for a natural explanation for those
diseases that hitherto had been considered of demonic origin

by both laymen and clerics.[1] However, he believed in the magical origin of certain diseases and recommended prayers for their alleviation. The philosophical tenets of the group to which he adhered held that each man's personality is determined by a certain fragment of the "world-spirit" with which he is endowed and that the emanations of these qualities could affect others in his presence. Thus, healthy and serene persons impart pleasure to others, whereas those of the opposite constitution can even bring disease. Such transfer did not require physical contact; it was rather a spiritual reaction. In this manner a physician could affect a patient favorably or adversely, depending on whether the spiritual constitutions of the two were compatible. If they were reciprocally antagonistic, Arnald suggested a change of physicians.[2] The world-spirit, which was often equated with the medieval concept of the soul, was generally believed to be capable of bringing about somatic changes. The potency of the soul to affect the body was quaintly illustrated by Avicenna's assertion that a hen, after having fought with and conquered a rooster, will be so proudly convinced of her equality to the vanquished male that she herself will grow spurs.[3] In this vein also ran the explanations offered by medieval physicians for those somatic disturbances which lacked apparent causes. Faults of memory, speech, locomotion, and sexual function became explicable in the hazy context of uncongenial spirits.

It is strange that Arnald did not associate such symptoms with hysteria. Like most of his predecessors, he identified this disease only with paroxysmal disorders peculiar to females and, particularly, to sexually deprived women. The originality that characterized most of his voluminous medical writings was not apparent in his discussion of hysteria.[4] His one contribution to therapy, which is actually of greater social than medical interest, was a recommendation that

---

[1] Paul Diepgen, *Geschichte der Medizin* (Berlin: Walter de Gruyter, 1949), Book I, 215–18. See also Diepgen, in *Archiv für Geschichte der Medizin* (Leipzig), III, No. 2 (1909–10).

[2] Diepgen: *Geschichte der Medizin*, p. 217.

[3] Quoted by Diepgen, *ibid.*

[4] *Breviarum* III, chap. ix, 1344 ff., in Arnaldi Villanovi *Philosophi et Medici Opera Omnium* (Basel: Conrad Waldkirch, 1585).

widows and nuns attain sexual release by friction via irritating suppositories inserted in the vagina.

From this brief summary it is apparent that Arnald's writings reflect the traditional medical views of the ancients and the Arabs in addition to the beginnings of a new trend that sought for natural causes of disease, to which he contributed his own observations. However, this was tentative groping for new truths rather than an attempt to overthrow established beliefs, and it did not constitute a challenge to the authority of the Church in medical matters that occurred during the Renaissance, which heralded a liberation from established controls.

Arnald of Villanova, a man of the Middle Ages, spanned the transition from theocratic to rational medicine, from healing by priests to healing by doctors. Yet he could not free himself entirely from belief in magic as a cause and cure of disease, or from ecclesiastic authority in medical matters. But this apparent progress in the evolution of human rights coincided with the beginnings of the witch mania, when the persecutions were relatively few and mild. Two centuries later, Paracelsus exemplified the spirit of the Renaissance, with its vaunted liberation of thought and respect for the dignity of man; and he challenged and even defied the authority of both church and state. And this occurred during the apogee of the witchcraft delusion and the most malevolent intolerances of the Inquisition. These paradoxes substantiate the suggestion made earlier: that epochs, like men, are eccentric, and that it is impossible to categorize them neatly or to fit them into labeled pigeonholes.

There is a temporal relationship which may in some degree explain these paradoxes. Arnald and his scientifically minded peers displayed but a modicum of scholarly skepticism which constituted a relatively minor threat to the social and religious status quo. Although the lay and Church authorities reacted to the danger of intellectual independence and scientific innovation by attacking the first deviationists and those who came under their influence, these were too few to constitute a real menace to the old order, and the repressions were consequently mild. In Paracelsus' day, however, the threat represented by the Protestant Reformation had become overwhelming and evoked the frantic persecution of the possessed, the bewitched, and the bedeviled, all of whom were damned as heretics.

PARACELSUS' "CHOREA LASCIVA"

Philippus Theophrastus Bombastus von Hohenheim, better known as Paracelsus (1493–1541), was a physician whose interests were as multiple as those of Arnald of Villanova. He too possessed a roving soul and could not be chained to one place or position. He gathered information and ideas from all types of people, wherever they were encountered. Considered a genius and a charlatan, hailed as a reformer of medicine and denounced as an ignorant quack, idolized by few but despised and persecuted by many, Paracelsus and his influence are difficult to assess. The judgments of time are rather in his favor. Garrison characterized him as "the most original medical thinker of the sixteenth century," and Sigerist spoke of him as "one of the most forceful personalities of the Renaissance." His short, tempestuous life was filled with strife and wandering, despite which he wrote voluminously on chemistry, natural philosophy, theology, medicine, and, very importantly, surgery.

Paracelsus spent most of his life in the cultural sphere of Germany. He was born at Einsiedeln, in Switzerland, and in his early youth moved with his family to Villach, one of the mining centers of Carinthia. His father was a physician from whom, presumably, he received his early education and his introduction into medicine. As a young man he worked in the mines of Villach and in the Tyrolean metallurgical laboratories, where his lasting interest in chemistry was born. Then he embarked on a long course of travel, during which he visited many countries, and traveled among all classes of people. He listened avidly to all and retained a vast fund of medical fact and folklore. Whether he had formal university training is not definitely known. He claimed the title of Doctor of Medicine, although his right to it was questioned by his detractors. If a degree was conferred on him, its source has not come to light.

His practice of medicine began in 1526, at the age of thirty, and from the start his unconventional methods aroused the suspicion and hostility of the other physicians. In that same year he purchased citizenship in Strasbourg and became a member of the guild to which surgeons belonged, as did also millers and grain dealers. But before he could settle in Strasbourg, he received the appointment of City Physician (*Stadtarzt*) of Basel (1527), which carried with it the professorship in medicine in the university of that city.

Paracelsus was deeply concerned with the stagnation of medical thought and education. He was filled with the spirit of the Renaissance, and he flung himself into a war against sterile dogma and opposition to change which was to continue throughout his life. He denounced the current medical and surgical practices, burned the book of Avicenna in a public bonfire, and, worst of all, lectured in German instead of Latin. The ire of the profession, as well as of the rest of the faculty, was quickly aroused, and, after a stormy eighteen months, he was driven from the city.

He spent the remainder of his life wandering from place to place preaching "heretical" doctrines and pursuing his medical practice with varying success. At times he was reduced to abject poverty. Throughout these years he wrote frenetically, on many subjects, winning a small number of ardent adherents but making many more enemies. These adversaries often prevented the publication of his books, many of which remained in manuscript until after his death.

Paracelsus violently attacked the Galenic-Arabic concepts and the natural philosophy upon which they were based. The system he offered as a substitute was largely rooted in chemistry with a liberal admixture of cosmology and astrology. Although no less irrational and incomprehensible than its predecessors, it did serve to loosen the iron grasp of medieval dogma and so helped to liberate thinking in medicine.

Paracelsus was in many respects a destructive iconoclast, offering little to replace that which he attempted to overthrow. The effectiveness of his diatribes was weakened by their acerbity and extravagance. And yet, his contributions cannot be disparaged; some of his passages show an extraordinary degree of wisdom and insight. In the preface to his treatise *On the Diseases that Deprive Man of his Reason*,[5] where he assigns natural causes for all illnesses, whether of body or mind, he wrote:

In nature there are not only diseases which afflict our body and our health, but many others which deprive us of sound reason, and these are the most serious. While speaking about the natural diseases and observing to what extent and how seriously they afflict various parts of our body, we must not forget to explain the origin of the diseases which deprive man of reason, as we know from experience that they develop out of man's disposition. The present-day clergy of Europe attribute such diseases to ghostly beings and threefold spirits; we are not inclined to believe them. For nature proves that such statements by earthly gods are quite incorrect and, as we shall explain in these chapters, that nature is the sole origin of diseases.[6]

Thus Paracelsus rejected the supernatural and returned to ideas similar to those of Hippocrates. Paracelsus' deviation from established medical authority is clearly revealed in his discussion of hysteria. Astutely, he listed it among the mental diseases "that deprive man of his reason." Had he stopped at this point, he might have carried his audience with him, but his rebellious disposition took him much further. Rather than accept the Hippocratic or the Galenic etiologies, he developed his own, but they lacked the clarity and logic of the older ones:

We have also to speak about the womb. It produces, though in another way, the same signs and symptoms as those appearing when the womb's natural condition is changed into an unfavorable one, which change results in a contraction of the uterus and takes away all reason and sensibility. The cause is that the matter on which the womb is internally nourished and kept alive destroys itself, like wine returning into vinegar. If the womb neither feels nor has the proper substance, then the substance has lost its right nature and is cold. This coldness causes a tension of the skin and of the lining of the womb, contracting

[5] According to Sudhoff, Paracelsus wrote this book in 1525 or 1526 when he was thirty-one years old and held a professorship at Basel. It was first published in Basel in 1567 under the title *Medici Aureoli Theophrasti Paracelsi Schreiben von den Krankheiten so die Vernunft berauben.*

[6] Henry E. Sigerist (ed.), *Four Treatises by Paracelsus*, trans. with introductory essays by C. Lilian Temkin, George Rosen, Gregory Zilboorg, and Henry E. Sigerist (Baltimore: Johns Hopkins Press, 1941), p. 142.

it into a kind of spasm, for it is an inherent quality and innate nature that all acid and cold of that kind give a sort of spasm or stinging to the whole body, with the exception of the flesh and bone. This causes coldness and sharp acid in the uterus, resulting in cramps and contraction, making the uterus like a log. The contraction, the tetanus and the spasm also force the other limbs into spasms and tetanus, for they become contaminated by the womb also. If such contraction takes place in the veins of the whole body, vapor and smoke come out of the womb to the organs around it, and if it touches the heart the convulsion is similar to epilepsy with all its symptoms, and no other organ but the heart is afflicted with it.[7]

This confused quasi-scientific analysis makes little sense to the modern reader. As in many of his writings, Paracelsus overthrows outworn concepts, but what he offers instead is of doubtful superiority. It is difficult to tell from his obscure writings whether he was always thoroughly conversant with the theories of the ancients whom he so violently rejected. The above-quoted "observations" on hysteria may simply be the result of his lack of understanding of the older sources. Strikingly new, however, are other thoughts on hysteria in a chapter "On St. Vitus Dance." He suggested, according to Zilboorg, in addition to the long-cherished sexual components, the importance of the unconscious in the development of hysteria. Paracelsus did this "not by way of inference or philosophic speculation, but by direct observational assertion."[8] To convey this idea, Paracelsus called the disease *chorea lasciva* and described the susceptibility of children to influences of which they are unaware:

> Thus the cause of the disease, *chorea lasciva,* is a mere opinion and idea assumed by the imagination, affecting those who believe in such a thing. This opinion and idea are the origin of the disease both in children and adults. In children the cause is also an imagined idea, based not on thinking but on perceiving, because they have heard or seen something. The reason is this: their sight and hearing are so strong that unconsciously they have fantasies about what they have seen or heard. And in such fantasies their reason is taken and perverted into the shape imagined.[9]

This idea was totally ignored by his contemporaries and did not re-emerge until the late nineteenth century.

[7] *Ibid.,* pp. 163–64.

[8] *Ibid.,* p. 132.   [9] *Ibid.,* p. 158.

A SATIRICAL VIEW OF THE NATURE OF WOMAN

Although Paracelsus was the most violent and arrogant opponent of the petrified authority exerted by academic medicine, others shared his revolt. Among these was his French contemporary François Rabelais (1483–1553), mainly remembered today as a cleric and author of the immortal satires *Gargantua* and *Pantagruel*. The diffuseness of Rabelais' activities, with a predilection for literature and social satire, naturally precluded strikingly important or effective contributions to medicine. He is quoted here primarily because of the delicious literary flavor of his comments which pertain to hysteria. Perhaps his only original addition is to be found in a statement, in which he implies that the manifestations of hysteria are susceptible to voluntary intellectual control on the part of the affected individual.

Actually, Rabelais divided his time between belles-lettres and medicine. He had studied at Montpellier, then a very famous seat of medical education, and subsequently lectured there on the works of Hippocrates and Galen, upon which he wrote important commentaries. His first literary production, *Pantagruel*, reflects his great medical erudition, as his satire is directed against both the medical profession and mankind in general. His ironic discussion of the womb is particularly pertinent to our subject because it refers to hysteria. The physician Rondibilis discourses as his spokesman, partly in jest and partly seriously:

Plato, you will recall, was at a loss as to where to class them, whether among the reasoning animals or the brute beasts. For Nature has placed in their bodies, in a secret and intestinal place, a certain animal or member which is not in man, in which are engendered, frequently, certain humors, brackish, nitrous, boracious, acrid, mordant, shooting, and bitterly tickling, by the painful prickling and wriggling of which—for this member is extremely nervous and sensitive—the entire feminine body is shaken, all the senses ravished, all the passions carried to a point of repletion, and all thought thrown into confusion. To such a degree that, if Nature had not rouged their foreheads with a tint of shame, you would see them running the streets like mad women, in a more frightful manner than the Proetides, the Mimallonides, or the Bacchic Thyades on the day of their Bacchanalia ever did; and this, for the reason that this terrible animal

I am telling you about is so very intimately associated with all the principal parts of the body, as anatomy teaches us.

I call it an "animal," in accordance with the doctrine of the Academics, as well as of the Peripatetics. For if movement, as Aristotle says, is a sure sign of something animate, and if all that moves of itself is to be called an animal, then, Plato was right, when he called this thing an animal, having noted in it those movements commonly accompanying suffocation, precipitation, corrugation, and indignation, movements sometimes so violent that the woman is thereby deprived of all other senses and power of motion, as though she had suffered heart-failure, syncope, epilepsy, apoplexy, or something very like death.[10]

It was Rabelais' opinion, apparently, that women could control this internal "animal" and suppress its desires by exercise of the will or by becoming absorbed in other activities, which today might be called "sublimation." As an example of the latter he cites ". . . Diana, who is constantly occupied in hunting, is called the chaste." To exemplify the former, he stated:

> I shall not go any further into this dispute. I merely would say to you that those virtuous women who have lived modestly and blamelessly, and who have had the courage to rein in that unbridled animal and to make it obedient to reason, are deserving of no small praise indeed. And I may, in conclusion, add that once this same animal is glutted, if glutted it can be, through that alimentation which Nature has prepared for it in man, then all these specialized motions come to an end, all appetite is satiated, and all fury appeased.[11]

THE POWERFUL MAGICIAN

Rabelais' ironic pen used but feeble disguise in portraying actual people. Thus the magician Herr Trippa in *Pantagruel*, who advises Panurge on how to avoid being cuckolded, is an easily recognizable caricature of the famous Cornelius Heinrich Agrippa de Nettesheim. This original, restless, revolutionary personality, who combined an interest in science with the occult, resembled both Paracelsus and Arnald of Villanova. His specific importance is that he was the teacher

---

[10] François Rabelais, *Pantagruel* in *The Portable Rabelais,* trans. and ed. Samuel Putnam (New York: Viking Press, 1946), pp. 477–78.

[11] *Ibid.*, pp. 478–79.

of Johann Weyer[12] (1515–88), the Dutch physician for whom Zilboorg has suggested the title "founder of modern psychiatry."[13] Agrippa's influence is apparent in the writings of his pupil, although he died when the latter was but twenty years old.

Upon his teacher's death, Weyer, desolate and liberated at the same time, went to Paris to study medicine. Having acquired his doctorate, he visited Africa, where Tunisian sorceresses (called *Les Théraphim*) excited his interest, then toured the Orient, and eventually returned to his native land where he became physician to Duke William of Cleves, one of the most enlightened princes of his day. In this tranquil environment, protected by his powerful friendship from the persecution and annoyance which his writings might have aroused, Weyer published two valuable books of medical observations covering a wide range of diseases. But the work which supports his fame and exhibits his unusual intelligence and erudition is on the trickery of demons, *De praestigiis daemonun et incantationibus ac veneficiis* (1563). Arranged in six parts, it deals successively with the devil's origin, fall, and power; malevolent magicians; witches; diseases ascribed to witches (*De iis qui lamiarum maleficio affecti putantur*); methods used to treat the possessed; and punishments recommended against sorcery and witchcraft.

In a long prefatory dedication, Weyer explains that his work is simultaneously theological, legal, philosophical, and medical.[14] Passages from the scriptures, exegeses from Hebrew texts, discussions concerning the law, commentaries on the soul—notably on the power of the imagination—and clinical observations are all inextricably intertwined. This conglomeration reveals the rather confused state of Weyer's views in relation to the supernatural: he believed in the devil and in magic; he believed in God, sincerely, and with solid faith. He was not a free thinker. His was a gentle spirit and

[12] Also known as Ioannes Wierus, Wier, Weiher, or Weier.

[13] Gregory Zilboorg, *The Medical Man and the Witch during the Renaissance* (Baltimore: Johns Hopkins Press, 1935), p. 109.

[14] The complete works of Johann Weyer are collected in a volume of more than 1,000 pages under the title: *Joannis Wieri illustrissimi Ducis Julioe Clevioe etc., quondam archiatri, OPERA OMNIA*. Amsterdam: apud Petrum vanden Berge, sub signo Montis Parnassi, 1660.

his ideas, presented with logic and persuasion, were quite devoid of violence or controversy.

When Weyer wrote about the stratagems of Satan in his conflict with the clerical views, he did not mention them as a sop to the opposition, but because he actually believed them. One could not expect even a liberal mind of the sixteenth century to reject totally and abruptly universal superstitions. But despite Weyer's conformity to the basic sixteenth-century superstitions, he was nevertheless astute enough to recognize genuine mental illness, and he differentiated it from fraudulent pretense or malingering. In the case of a woman who claimed to vomit ribbons which were daily introduced into her stomach by the devil, he noted that none of the gastric contents was mixed with the material ejected from the mouth. He found that she hid foreign bodies in her mouth, which she then brought forth with simulated effort. Similarly, he discovered the ruses of a little beggar girl who claimed to have lived for years without taking any nourishment or performing any natural functions. This child became such a celebrity that the senate of the city of Unna certified her as supernatural. Weyer went to live in the house which she shared with her older sister and proved that the miraculous abstinence was a farce. The young girl either stole food or had it brought by her sister, whom she called Habakkuk after the prophet who brought food to Daniel in the lions' den. Weyer was a superb observer, and though a skeptic, he was credulous. He could reconcile his adherence to prevailing superstitions with his scientific rationalism, his intelligence with his emotions, devilry with humanism. This ambivalence furnishes the clue to his conduct and writings and is clearly detected in all his works.

Weyer's beliefs can be summarized somewhat as follows: There are magicians who have made a pact with Satan which endows them with power to do evil, and they deserve the most severe punishment. But there are also persons, especially women, who, far from being accomplices of the devil, are his victims: sick, unfortunate, lonely women, they easily fall prey to the Great Prestidigitator, who fills their weak minds with hallucinations and dreams and makes them believe that they have committed crimes of which they are entirely innocent. These people are to be pitied rather than punished;

PLATE IV. Assembly of foxes, each preceded by his soul in form of a flame, known as *Kitsunebi,* or fox-fire. (Wood block print by Hiroshige [1797–1858].)

PLATE V. Young medical exorcist carrying sword and prickball with iron spikes and dagger in mouth for self-mutilation. (From De Groot, "The priesthood of animism," Vol. VI: *The Religious System of China* [Leyden: E. J. Brill, 1910].)

PLATE VI. William Harvey (1587–1657).

PLATE VII. Thomas Sydenham (1624–89).

they suffer from "passive witchery," or "repression," which is not a crime but an illness.

Being both medical and juridical, this theory had a dual merit. In cases of the latter kind, he urged acquittal of the accused, or at least milder forms of punishment, such as public reprimand or exile. He earnestly implored the courts to stop torturing and killing these innocents, and he added: "Don't you know that these poor women have suffered enough? Can you think of a misery anywhere in the world that is worse than theirs? If they do seem to merit punishment, I assure you, their illness alone is enough."

For these humane views, Weyer was violently attacked by many of his contemporary writers. One was Jean Bodin, the erudite economist who was attached to the court of Henry III in Anjou and author of *Démonomanie des Sorciers*. His reasoning was quaint: "Madwomen are never burned," he told Weyer, "and Hippocrates whom you should know better, teaches you on his part that those women who have their menses, are not subject to melancholy, madness, epilepsy." Bodin's arrogance in calling the words of Hippocrates to Weyer's attention is almost amusing in that Weyer, an excellent physician, was known to be widely read in the medical sources.

Weyer's ability to detect sickness in women where others only saw the perpetration of witchcraft derives from his medical skill, through which, he was enterprising enough, according to Garrison, "to treat amenorrhea from imperforate hymen by incision of the membrane." Diseases of women were of special interest to him, and he was therefore particularly sensitive to the behavioral changes of women in health and disease. By interesting himself in the practice of obstetrics and gynecology, which had long been the almost exclusive domain of midwives, Weyer was in step with his time. Encyclopedic compilations of gynecology appeared in the sixteenth century in a variety of editions and were widely read. Moreover, some of the most prominent medical men, both physicians and surgeons, included in their writings at least a brief discussion on the diseases of women. Although a good many of these chapters seem derivative and unoriginal, and betray little personal experience of the author, a few constituted important contributions to this long neglected field.

A SURGEON TREATS HYSTERIA

Predominant among such authors was the French surgeon Ambroise Paré (1517?–90), a contemporary of Weyer, whom he resembled in forthrightness and single-minded devotion to the healing profession. But unlike Weyer, whom posterity has identified almost exclusively with his book on witchcraft, forgetting his many other contributions, Paré has been remembered for his surgical achievements—which, admittedly, reflect his foremost, although not only, preoccupation. Obstetrics[15] and gynecology also figured importantly in Paré's long and fruitful career. He introduced podalic version among several other innovations, and he described and treated a great many different "diseases of the womb" and, hence, concerned himself with hysteria.

Paré, Paracelsus, and Vesalius are often mentioned as the trio that personified Renaissance medicine. As might be expected, their reforms and innovations aroused the resentment and hostility of the medical faculties, which was only intensified by the revival of interest in early classical medicine. The manifested resentment bordered on persecution. None of the three creative minds entirely escaped these conflicts with established medical authority.

Paracelsus' struggles have already been mentioned. Andreas Vesalius (1514–64), the great Belgian anatomist of the Renaissance, convinced himself rather slowly that some of Galen's anatomical descriptions were wrong. When, however, he openly asserted Galen's fallibility, vicious and slanderous attacks so disheartened him that he discontinued his scientific endeavors. He died a broken man at the early age of fifty.

Ambroise Paré was the only one of the three who was sufficiently successful in weaving the new into the old to breach the wall of resistance. Despite his humble origins and his meager training as an apprentice to a provincial barber surgeon, he rose to perhaps the most exalted position in the profession of surgery. When he reminisced, at the age of seventy-five about his training, he recalled: "I was resident

15 In addition to Paré's own writings on the subject, see Alan F. Guttmacher's amusing study, "Ambroise Paré Does a Delivery," *Bulletin of the History of Medicine*, IV, No. 9 (1936), 703–17.

in the space of three yeares in the Hospitall of Paris, where I had the meanes to see and learne divers workes of Chirurgery, upon divers diseases together with the Anatomy, upon a great number of dead bodies."[16] Shortly after completing this period of service he entered the army as a surgeon.

Throughout the rest of his long and productive life, Paré alternated between military campaigns and relatively quiet civilian practice in Paris, where he studied anatomy and wrote his many books. With each call to the service, his stature, confidence, and reputation grew. He served as body surgeon to four successive kings of France, beginning with Henry II, eventually attaining the position of *Premier Chirurgien* and *Conseiller du Roi*.

Paré's collected works reflect the vast range of his interests. Originally written in French, the only language he knew, they were translated into Latin to make them acceptable to the learned medical circle. Except for a Dutch edition, all the subsequent translations into many languages —including Japanese—were based on the Latin version rather than on Paré's original. They had a powerful influence upon his contemporaries and upon many subsequent generations of advanced surgeons all over the world. Although most of his writings had more than a spark of spontaneity and originality, his discussion of the etiology of hysteria was a largely derivative though peculiar amalgamation of Hippocratic and Galenic reasoning. His description of the manifestations of the disease were, however, quite original and were based upon his own personal observations of many and varied hysterical patients. Significantly, also, he spoke of hysteria as madness:

The strangulation of the womb, or that which commeth from the womb, is an interception or stopping of the libertie in breathing or takeing winde, becaus that the womb, swoln or puffed up by reason of the access of gross vapors and humors that are contained therein, and also snatched as it were by a convulsive motion, by reason that the vessels and ligaments distended with fulness, are so carried upwards against the midriff and parts of the breast, that it maketh the breath to bee short, and often as if a thing lay upon the breast and pressed it.

. . . .

[16] *The Workes of the famous Chirurgion Ambrose Parey, translated out of the Latine and compared with the French by Tho. Johnson* (London: R. Cotes & W. Du-gard, 1649).

For som accidents com by suppression of the terms [menses], others com by corruption of the seed, but if the matter bee cold, it bringeth a drousiness, beeing lifted up unto the brain, whereby the woman sinketh down as if shee were astonished, and lieth without motion, and sens or feeling, and the beating of the arteries, and the breathing are so small, that somtimes it is thought they are not at all, but that the woman is altogether dead. If it be more gross, it inferreth a convulsion; if it participate of the nature of a gross melancholick humor, it bringeth such heaviness, fear, and sorrowfulness, that the party that is vexed therewith shall think that hee shall die presently, and cannot bee brought out of his minde by anie means or reason: if of a cholerick humor, it causseth the madness called *furor uterinus,* and such a pratling, that they speak all things that are to bee concealed; and a giddiness of the head, by reason that the animal spirit is suddenly shaken by the admixture of a putrefied vapour and hot spirit: but nothing is more admirable, then that this diseas taketh the patient somtimes with laughing, and somtimes with weeping, for som at the first will weep and then laugh in the same diseas and state thereof.[17]

Although Paré adhered to the ancient etiologies of hysteria, which must have been well known in his day, he found it necessary to review them for his readers, particularly since he thought it possible to differentiate the causes according to the symptoms and the circumstances of life of the patient. He devoted a chapter to the question "How to know whether the strangulation of the womb com's of the suppression of the flowers [menses], or of the corruption of the seed."[18] He was convinced that the latter brought forth severer manifestations, which included difficulties in breathing that often reached the point of actual suffocation while the patient's body turned very cold. If these symptoms occurred, it seemed evident to Paré that "the woman is a widow; or els hath great store or abundance of seed, and hath been used to the companie of a man, by the absence whereof shee was before wont to be pained with heaviness of the head, to loath her meat, and to bee troubled with sadness and fear, but chiefly with melancholie."[19]

Paré further believed that enforced abstinence suppressed menstruation:

[17] *Ibid.,* Book 24, chap. 44, pp. 632–33.

[18] *Ibid.,* chap. 47, p. 634.

[19] *Ibid.,* p. 634.

When shee hath satisfied, and everie waie fulfilled her lust, and then presently on a sudden begin's to contain her self, it is verie likely that shee is suffocated by the suppression of the flowers, which formerly had them well and sufficiently, which formerly had been fed with hot, moist and manie meats, and therefore engendring much bloud, which sitteth much, which is grieved with som weight and swelling in the region of the bellie, with pain in the stomach, and a desire to vomit, and with such other accidents as com by the suppression of the flowers.

But all these symptoms were transitory:

Those who are free'd from the fit of the suffocation of the womb, either by nature or by art, in a short time their color commeth into their faces by little and little, and the whole bodie beginneth to wax strong, and the teeth, that were set and closed fast together, begin (the jaws beeing loosed) to open and unclose again, and lastly som moisture floweth from the secret parts with a certain tickling pleasure; but in som women, as in those especially in whom the neck of the womb is tickled with the Midwives finger, in stead of that moisture com's thick and gross seed, which moisture or seed when it is fallen, the womb beeing before as it were rageing, is restored unto it's own proper nature and place, and by little and little all symptoms vanish away.[20]

Paré diverged from the Galenic view respecting the retention of semen in men; he contended that the symptoms produced thereby were different from those of women but did not describe them. He further believed that the accumulated male sperm could always be "dissipated by great and violent exercise."

An above quotation from Paré, briefly mentions the means of bringing about recovery from the hysterical paroxysm. In another chapter he dealt more extensively with "The cure of the strangulation of the womb."[21] His methods were very similar to those widely used in antiquity, although they were rejected by Soranus and Galen as illogical according to their concepts and crudely violent in application. After loosening the patient's garments, Paré placed her on her back, called her loudly by name, and pulled her by the hair, especially the pubic hair, partly to cause enough pain to return the patient to her senses, but also "that the sharp and malign vapor ascending upwards, may bee drawn downwards." To

[20] *Ibid.*, p. 634.
[21] *Ibid.*, chap. 48, pp. 634–36.

hasten this return of the vapors, a medicated pessary was inserted into the patient's vagina, a cupping glass applied to the lower abdomen, and fumigation applied to the uterus. Paré met the challenging technical problem of conveying the fumes through the vagina with the same inventiveness that had earlier led him to design artificial hands and legs with joints that were actually movable. He designed an instrument to be made of gold or silver "into the form of a pessarie; at the one end thereof, that is to say, that end which goeth up into the neck of the womb, let there bee made manie holes on each side, but at the lower end let it bee made with a spring, that it may open and shut as you will have it. Also it must have two laces or bands by which it must bee made fast unto a swathe or girdle tied about the patient's bellie."[22]

Paré's complete return to the ancient views on hysteria, though seemingly a regression, was actually a scientific advance, because he bypassed the medieval superstitions and subsequent demonomania of the Renaissance. To be sure, Paré, like Weyer, was still deeply enmeshed in the superstitious beliefs of his day—they come to light in his discussion of monsters and freaks—about all subjects for which his intelligence and the sciences of his day offered no answers. Hysteria, however, was a disturbance he often encountered among his female patients, and he had found that many of the ancient etiological concepts seemed entirely reasonable to explain the bizarre behavior of the afflicted women.

Although Paré's origins were simple and he retained his close ties to the common people even when he reached the peak of his eminence, his interests encompassed all strata of society. His discussion of the factors predisposing towards hysteria offered a simple explanation for the differences in etiology among the various social classes and between the city and country population. Of the young ladies of the city he said:

Those maids that are marriageable, although they have the menstrual flux verie well, yet they are troubled with headach, nauseousness, and often vomiting, want of appetite, longing, an ill habite of bodie, difficultie of breathing, trembling of the heart, swouning, melancholie, fearful dreams, watching, with sadness

22 *Ibid.*, pp. 634–36.

and heaviness, becaus that the genital parts burning and itching, they imagine the act of generation, whereby it commeth to pass that the seminal matter, either remaining in the testicles in great abundance, or els powred into the hollowness of the womb, by the tickling of the genitals, is corrupted, and acquireth a venemous qualitie, and causseth such like accidents as happen's in the suffocation of the womb.[23]

In contrast, however, "Maids that live in the countrie are not so troubled with those diseases, becaus there is no such lying in wait for their maiden-heads, and also they live sparingly and hardily, and spend their time in continual labor."[24]

[23] *Ibid.*, chap. 54, p. 640.   [24] *Ibid.*

The defcription of a veffel made with a funnel or pipe for to fumigate the womb.

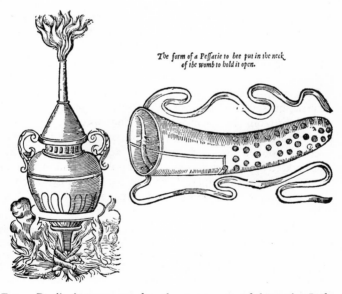

The form of a Peffarie to bee put in the neck of the womb to hold it open.

FIG. 7. Paré's instruments for the treatment of hysteria. Left: apparatus for uterine fumigation. Right: medicated pessary to be inserted in the patient's vagina; the holes made possible the conveying of the fumes into the uterus. (From *Works of Ambroise Paré*, Book 24, "On the Generation of Man" [London: Richard Cotes, 1649].)

The causal relationship between cessation of the menses and hysteria has been frequently mentioned. A reciprocal relationship in which amenorrhea may be caused by hysteria will be mentioned later. In either event, treatment of amenorrhea per se would be prophylactic as well as adjunctive in the management of hysteria. Paré's advice "on provoking the flowers or courses" was necessarily similar to the treatment of hysteria itself. But he distinguished between the treatment of young maids and women, recommending fumigation for the former "because they are bashful and shamefaced," whereas women who are or have been married should have pessaries inserted or, better even, horse-leeches placed within the neck of the womb.[25] Married women suffering from the suppression of the menses were also encouraged to engage in frequent and "wanton copulation with their husbands," whereas virgins had to content themselves with walking, dancing, and riding. The last, because it was perhaps the most acceptable exercise for gentlewomen (and they were the ones suffering most frequently from amenorrhea and hysteria), became a favorite therapeutic measure, and for centuries afterward hysterical patients were sent into the woods on horseback.

Paré was not only uncommonly experienced and observant; his scientific curiosity demanded explanation for all deviations from the norm which he encountered. Not completely satisfied with the most obvious and simplest explanation, he looked for additional and accessory causes. He enumerated all the conditions which could bring about cessation of the menses (apart from the natural causes such as "age, greatness with childe, and nursing of children") as follows:

The courses are suppressed or stopped by manie causses, as by sharp, vehement, and long diseases, by fear, sorrow, hunger, immoderate labors, watchings [wakefulness], fluxes of the bellie, great bleeding, haemorrhoids, fluxes of blood at the mouth, and evacuations in anie other part of the bodie whatsoever, often opening of a vein, great sweats, ulcers flowing much and long, scabbiness of the whole skin, immoderate grossness and clamminess of the blood, and by eating of raw fruits, and drinking of cold water, by sluggishness and thickness of the vessels, and also the obstruction of them by the defaults and diseases of the womb,

25 *Ibid.*, chap. 53, p. 639.

by distemperature, an abscess, an ulcer, by the obstruction of the inner orifice thereof, by the growing of a Callus, carbuncle, cicatrize of a wound or ulcer, or membrane growing there, by injecting of astringent things into the neck of the womb, which place manie women endeavor foolishly to make narrow. . . .[26]

That some of the physical causes have no bearing whatsoever on amenorrhea, and others appear to be the result rather than the cause of it, does not detract from the general astuteness of his observations. It is particularly noteworthy that he was aware of psychogenically produced amenorrhea. His interest in psychosomatic relationships is also evident in his discussion of masculinization, which he describes as follows: "Manie women, when their flowers or terms be stopped, degenerate after a manner into a certain manly nature, whence they are called *Viragines*, that is to say, stout, or manly women; therefore their voice is more loud and big, like unto a mans, and they become bearded."[27]

Whether masculinization has a psychogenic origin remains unresolved, although these endocrinological changes are generally believed to be the cause for emotional disturbance rather than the result. Paré, however, was convinced of the reverse sequence, and he cited two case histories which he took from the literature of Greek antiquity: "In the citie *Abdera* (saith *Hippocrates*) *Phaethusa* the wife of *Pytheas* at the first did bear children and was fruitful, but when her husband was exiled, her flowers were stopped for a long time: but when these things happened, her bodie became manlike and rough, and had a beard, and her voice was great and shrill. The verie same thing happened to *Namysia* the wife of *Georgippus* in *Thasus*."[28]

[26] *Ibid.*, chap. 51, p. 638.
[27] *Ibid.*   [28] *Ibid.*

CHAPTER VII

Hysteria in England

WE HAVE spoken of these Renaissance physicians of widely disparate origins who took the position that all disease forms, whether physical or mental, are based on natural changes and therefore should be totally within the province of medicine rather than religion. Thus Paracelsus from Switzerland, Weyer from the Netherlands, and Paré from France, together with many others not quoted here, have contributed towards returning medicine to the Hippocratic denial of supernatural influence. England's representative of this movement was a relatively little-known physician, Edward Jorden (1578–1632), who is perhaps best known for his study of the English mineral waters (1631). But his volume on a more distinct medical subject, *A Briefe Discourse of a Disease Called the Suffocation of the Mother,* is of special interest to this study.[1] The book, designed for both lay and medical readers, grew out of the author's involvement in a London trial in 1602 in which one Elizabeth Jackson was indicted before Lord Chief Justice Anderson for having bewitched fourteen-year-old Mary Glover. This bewitchment had thrown the girl into fits, had rendered her speechless and blind from time to time, had caused her throat and neck to swell, and had deprived her entire left side of

[1] The full title of this treatise is *A Briefe Discourse of a Disease called the Suffocation of the Mother. Written uppon occasion which hath beene of late taken thereby, to suspect possession of an evill spirit, or some such like supernaturall power. Wherein is declared that divers strange actions and passions of the body of man, which in the common opinion, are imputed to the Divell, have their true naturall causes, and do accompany this disease* (London: John Windet, 1603).

feeling and movement. Dr. Jorden, a fellow of the Royal College of Physicians, was one of four doctors asked to examine the afflicted girl and to express their views on whether sorcery or disease was involved. Jorden made a diagnosis of hysteria and, with one of his colleagues, gave testimony attributing the afflictions to natural causes. Nevertheless, the court ruled in favor of witchcraft and sentenced Elizabeth Jackson to the pillory and imprisonment.

THE SUFFOCATION OF THE MOTHER

Jorden wrote *A Briefe Discourse* to acquaint the public as well as the medical profession with diseases of this nature so that they would never again be mistaken for bewitchment, although they appear to have some features in common. His introductory arguments were largely concerned with establishing that only a physician was qualified to deal with maladies such as Mary Glover's. Thus, though it was presumably a certain sign of sorcery, if the affected woman failed to feel the pricking of a pin and the burning by fire, Jorden maintained that this "is so ordinary in the fits of the Mother," as he "never read any author writing of this disease who does not make mention thereof."[2] Equally firmly he refuted the following as signs of devilry: insensibility, convulsions, periodicity of the fits, the choking sensation when eating, and the commencement of fits at the sight of specific persons. All of these, he contended, were signs of disease, and, if cure was ever achieved through fasting and prayers, it was only due to the "confident perswasion of the patient to find release by that means." He devoted the rest of his treatise to a description of the origin and nature of hysteria. His initial remarks on the subject, restating the uterine theory, show little promise of new revelations:

This disease is called by diverse names amongst our Authors, *Passio Hysterica, Suffocatio, Praefocatio,* and *Strangulatus uteri, Caducus matricis, &c.* In English the Mother, or the Suffocation of the Mother, because most commonly it takes them with choking in the throat: and it is *an affect of the Mother or wombe wherein the principal parts of the bodie by consent do*

2 *Ibid.*, "The Epistle Dedicatorie," p. [iv].

suffer diversely according to the diversitie of the causes and diseases wherewith the matrix is offended.[3]

But out of this traditional exposition Jorden developed new ideas which involved other organs beyond the uterus as the primary site of hysteria. To be sure, he persisted in terming it a uterine disorder, but he remarked that other parts of the body suffer "by consent." This may occur, he said, in two ways: either some noxious substance, such as "vapors,"[4] may reach the secondary organ from the afflicted womb; or there may be a sympathetic interaction between the two organs which makes the second one a "partaker of grief."

Jorden, like most of his contemporaries, adhered to the Platonic idea that the soul was tripartite and seated in separate organs; the brain the animal faculty; the heart the vital faculty; and the liver the natural faculty. In hysteria each of the three faculties could be involved by emanations from the uterus or by sympathy with it. Involvement of the brain disturbed the animal faculty governing imagination, reason, and memory, and with possible impairment of intelligence or complete mental alienation. A further function of the animal faculty was to govern the five senses, locating their seats, correctly, in the brain, any one of which might become disordered or dulled by such emanations. It was thus that he explained the sudden losses of hearing or sight, or how "all parts are benummed or do not feele at all, or when they feele pain and offence, or when they feele things falsely and otherwise than they are." The third function of the animal faculty, control of motion, explained spasms, paroxysms, palsies, convulsive dancing, stretching, yawning, and all the other disorders of movement which accompany hysterical attacks. Thus, the cardinal symptoms of hysteria were all affections of the animal faculty, and since it was mediated by the brain, it is this organ which was the source of hysterical manifestations.

[3] *Ibid.*, chap. 2, p. 5.

[4] The term "vapors" originated about this time and referred to emanations from a disordered uterus which might ascend and produce symptoms in other parts of the body. This belief gained such credence that subsequently, particularly in the English literature, the term not only became synonymous with hysteria but was also descriptive of many lesser and insubstantial female behavioral peculiarities.

Jorden did not link hysteria and the heart, the seat of the vital faculty; he did, however, relate it to some disorders of the natural faculty located in the liver. These were digestive errors, but to Jorden they were insignificant compared to those of the animal faculty. A hundred years later these manifestations and symptoms excited much professional comment.

Jorden's transfer of the seat of all hysterical manifestations from the uterus to the brain constituted a major turning point in the history of hysteria. His conversion, however, was not entire. He added to the traditional factors of inter-rupted menstruation and sexual abstinence the idea that "the perturbations of the minde are oftentimes to blame for this and many other diseases. For seeing we are not maisters of our own affections, wee are like battered citties without walles, or shipps tossed in the sea, exposed to all manner of assaults and dangers, even to the overthrow of our own bodies." The phrasing of this passage, particularly the image of our frailty at the mercy of our emotions, like storm-tossed ships or vulnerable cities, is indeed felicitous. Similar pathetic inability to cope with "our own affections" has been expressed much more recently by modern masters of psy-chology.

This extraordinary perceptiveness is revealed again in Jorden's prescriptions for hysteria. He mentioned the tradi-tional physical approaches, but his real concern was to alle-viate the perturbations of the mind which, he felt, were actually responsible for the disease. He was the first to ad-vise anything resembling psychotherapy for hysteria. In the implementation of this advice, he suggested that not only the physician but also the patient's friends and attendants be involved.

Treatment was directed towards release of the particular emotional tensions suspected of being the causative agents. The doctor, with the aid of friends and relatives of the patient, was to attempt to appease jealousy and anger by good counsel and persuasion, to counteract hatred and malice by religious instruction, and to rout fears by encouragement, unfortunate loves by inciting hatred, and desires by arrang-ing their fulfilment. If gentle opposition failed to reach the patients, pretended agreement with their whims and fancies

might return them to normalcy. Occasionally, another per-
turbance superimposed upon the original one might help to
end the hysterical paroxysm. He recorded the following
story as an example of such treatment inadvertently effect-
ing a cure:

A yong Maiden also upon some passion of the minde, as it was
credibly reported, fell into these fits of the Mother, and being in
one of them, a Physition then present modestly put his hand
under her cloathes to feele a windie tumor which shee then had
in her backe. But a Surgeon there also present not contented
with that manner of examination, offered to take up her cloathes,
and to see it bare: whereupon the Maid being greatly offended,
tooke such indignation at it, as it did put her presently out of
her fit.[5]

His directions for psychotherapy resembled those recommended by Soranus a millennium and a half earlier; Jorden
was, however, the first to use them for the "cure of hysteria."

In the final statement of his *Briefe Discourse*, Jorden sums
up his rationale concerning the complementary nature of the
treatment of the body and the mind in hysteria, for "we doe
observe that most commonly besides the indisposition of the
bodie: here is also some melancholike or capricious conceit
. . . which being . . . removed the disease is easily overcome."

THE ANATOMY OF MELANCHOLY

Jorden's view of hysteria as an affliction of the mind *and* the
body were also shared by Robert Burton, the author of *The
Anatomy of Melancholy*. Burton, born at Lindley, Leister-
shire, in 1577, was apparently moved by trends and thoughts
similar to Jorden's, although Jorden's life was devoted to
the practice of medicine and Burton's to solitary meditation.
Burton lived the greater part of his life at Christ Church
College, Oxford, reading mathematics, divinity, astrology,
magic, medicine, and the classics. His literary monument,
The Anatomy of Melancholy, was first published in 1621
(seven years before William Harvey's discovery of the circulation of the blood); and it was revised continuously by
Burton up to his death in 1640. Suffering from melancholy,

[5] Jorden, *op. cit.*, chap. 7, p. 25.

Burton thought he might find surcease by the lifelong study of the subject. He justified his competence to write about melancholy by saying: "It is a disease of the soul on which I am to treat, and as much appertaining to a Divine as to a Physician." Burton considered himself a Divine by profession and a Physician by inclination and explained that in the theory of medicine, "I have taken some pains, not with the intent to practice, but to satisfy myselfe."[6] He wanted the book published in scholarly Latin and sadly related that "it was not mine intent to prostitute my muse in English," but the "mercenary Stationers [publishers]" who "print all, and pound out pamphlets on the leaves of which even a poverty-stricken monkey would not wipe,"[7] expected better sales from a book in the vernacular. The only passages left in Latin were those few concerning the sexual aspects of melancholia which the author, in his marginal notes, specified by "Good Master Schoolmaster, do not English this!"[8]

Burton was a man of vast erudition and of gentle mirth, which he often directed against himself; his prejudices were limited to "Papists." He spoke of himself as a melancholy bachelor, "a mere spectator of other men's fortunes and adventures, and how they act their parts." His concept of melancholy included a broad emotional range from the sadness of natural grief at separation and death through all aberrations from the norm to madness, under which heading could be grouped not only depressions but also most other illnesses now described as neuroses or psychoses. Burton deplored those who are "mad like Seneca's blind woman and will not acknowledge or seek any cure of it, for few see their malady, all love it." For bodily diseases a physician is sent for, "but for the diseases of the mind we take no notice of them: lust burrows us on the one side, envy, anger, ambition on the other. We are torn in pieces by our passions,

[6] Robert Burton, *The Anatomy of Melancholy* (now for the first time with the Latin completely given in translation and embodied in an *all-English* text), ed. Floyd Dell and Paul Jordan-Smith (New York: Tudor Publishing Co., 1948).

[7] *Ibid.*, p. 23.

[8] Floyd Dell and Paul Jordan-Smith in the edition quoted here violated this injunction since they felt that "these matters are not nowadays so frightful." *Ibid.*, p. viii.

as [by] so many wild horses, one in disposition, one in habit; one is melancholy, another mad; and which of us all seeks for help, does acknowledge his error, or knows he is sick?"[9]

Among his many varieties of melancholy, Burton included hysteria, which he colorfully called "Maids', Nuns' and Widows' Melancholy."[10] His speculations on the etiology are interesting only inasmuch as they combined the most ancient views with those that were introduced in his day. He included therein the implication of the brain "by consent" only and the belief that "a fallen uterus and spoilt menstrual blood are general causes, for, in a word, the whole malady proceeds from that inflammation, putridity, black smoky vapours, &c., from thence comes care, and anxiety, obfuscation of spirits, agony, desperation, and the like." Widows with much care and sorrow, nuns, and elderly spinsters were the primary victims, but others were not altogether excluded. It is difficult to tell, however, whether he believed emotional distress to be a part of the uterine involvement, as either the cause or the result of it.

With his admitted empathy for the melancholic, it is not surprising that Burton displayed more concern for the emotional sufferings of the patients than for the physical phenomena of the attack. He described these victims as being in despair, the elderly often weary of their lives and prone to suicide. "Some of the younger women see visions, confer with spirits and devils, they shall surely be damned, are afraid of some treachery, imminent danger, and the like."[11] Others of all ages "will not speak, make answer to any question, but are almost distracted, mad or stupid for the time." These extraordinarily sensitive observations bespeak close scrutiny of many female sufferers; one can only wonder whether they were made before he entered his monastic retreat at Oxford.

So far as treatment was concerned, Burton simply summarized the older methods. Like his many predecessors, he thought the surest remedy was to see them married to good husbands. In suggesting this, Burton assured his readers that "I write not this to patronize any wanton, idle flirt, lascivious or light housewives, which are too forward many times, unruly, and apt to cast away themselves on him that comes next."

[9] *Ibid.*, p. 57.   [10] *Ibid.*, p. 353.   [11] *Ibid.*, p. 355.

Those unable to find husbands, or whose station or employment precluded marriage, should lead a simple and disciplined life, for he shared the general belief that hardworking women were rarely troubled by hysteria. The usual victims were "Noble Virgins, nice Gentlewomen, such as are solitary and idle," who live an easy life yet are strong and healthy and beset by general discontent. Burton did not pity them, for they were in a position to find easy outlets that would fill their empty lives. He did, however, feel great compassion for such women "that out of a strong temperament . . . are violently carried away with this torrent of inward humors, and though very modest of themselves, sober, religious, virtuous . . . yet cannot make resistance."[12] Once such women have recognized the nature of their longings and passions, or have even given in to them, their particular melancholy will set in and may become entirely incurable.

Here Burton stopped, apparently amazed at the path along which his reflections had taken him, and exclaimed, "But where am I? Into what subject have I rushed? What have I to do with Nuns, Maids, Virgins, Widows? I am a Bachelor myself, and lead a Monastick life in a College. I am truly a very unfit person to talk about these subjects." However, after extensive further apologies concerning his transgression into such an unsuitable discussion, he decided to add a few words on behalf of these distressed women. Rather than holding them guilty, he found the fault for their misery with "those tyrannizing pseudo-politicians," parents, guardians, and friends who, in their selfish concern for their own ends, ignored the sufferings of the women in their charge and did nothing to prevent their sorry plight.

But most reprehensible did he, who himself had chosen a life of celibacy and chastity, hold the "Popish Monasteries" that bound men and women to vows of chastity "to lead a single life against the laws of nature, opposite to religion . . . and humanity, so to starve, to offer violence to, to suppress the vigour of youth." This blunt assertion of the evils of enforced sexual abstinence has surprisingly contemporary overtones. Indeed, so violent was his opposition to the waste of the physical and mental health of the victims of these

12 *Ibid.*, p. 365.

religious injunctions that his diatribes became impassioned. Comparing the torments of the flesh with roaring flames, he wrote: "They will by all means quench their neighbour's house, if it be on fire, but that fire of lust, which breaks out into such lamentable flames, they will not take notice of." Later on, he abruptly terminated this subject with a brief verse:

> Lest you should think that I do plead
> Some certain maid's or widow's need,
> I'll say no more.[13]

Although Burton and Edward Jorden were contemporaries and expressed very similar views on hysteria, there is no evidence that they knew each other, or each other's work. Jorden's *Briefe Discourse,* as already noted, was written largely to disabuse the laity of its preoccupation with witchcraft. Burton wrote of the "Maids', Nuns' and Widows' Melancholy" with the chief purpose of giving comfort to those who were afflicted and to prove that these symptoms were not caused by "Devils, as they suppose, or that they are bewitched or forsaken of God, but from natural and inward causes; that so knowing them, they may better avoid the effects or at least endure them with patience." While still convinced of the uterine origins, both authors associated emotions with hysteria and spoke of the brain in connection with the disease. According to Burton, the brain was involved "by consent." Jorden had gone even further in identifying the brain as the seat of the clinical manifestations. This new emphasis on the brain presaged a *neurological phase* in the history of that disease. Characteristically, such major transitions in medical thought were not total and abrupt; they tended to evolve gradually. Thus it was that many writers subsequent to Jorden, only slowly relinquished the older concepts of the uterine etiology, although they placed increasing emphasis on the role of the nervous system.

The first clear expression of conviction that the seat of hysteria was in the brain was made by the French physician Charles Lepois (1563–1633), more commonly known by the Latinized version of his name, Carolus Piso. He was consulting physician of Duke Charles III of Lorraine and later dean of the medical faculty of Pont-à-Mousson, at the time when

13 *Ibid.,* p. 357.

that university was at its height. There he published an important treatise on hysteria that was based on extensive clinical experience: "We believe we are correct in concluding that all the hysterical symptoms . . . have been attributed to the uterus, the stomach and other internal organs for the wrong reason. All [these symptoms] come from the head. It is this part which is affected not by sympathy but *idiopathically* and produces motions which make themselves felt throughout the entire body."[14] In support of this theory he recorded many of his observations; in one concerning a hysterical young girl suffering from fits, he spoke of "a collection of liquid accumulated in the hind part of the head and here collected with the effect that it swells and distends the beginnings of all the nerves."[15]

As a corollary to his disbelief in the uterine theory of hysteria, Piso came to the conclusion that hysteria was not restricted to women. This idea, as will be recalled, was first tentatively voiced by Aretaeus and Galen. Piso was bolder when he stated, "The hysterical symptoms are almost all common to both men and women."[16]

Beyond his theoretical conclusions, Piso contributed important clinical observations on hysteria gathered in his practice. He had seen hysterical patients suffering from cutaneous anesthesia, from deafness, blindness, and aphonia, and he had watched the development of hysterical tremors and paralyses of the extremities. With reference to the latter he wrote about a young girl, a neighbor as well as a patient, whom he had occasion to observe through several hysterical attacks. He noted that after the second paroxysm her arm retained a tremor which turned into paralysis after the third attack.

Headache, which he had come to recognize as an important hysterical manifestation in both men and women, served as an irrefutable argument in favor of his etiological theories. He reasoned that headache must have the same cause in both sexes and thus ruled out any involvement with the womb.

[14] C. Piso, *Selectiorum observationum et conciliorum de praeteretis* (Pont-à-Mousson, 1618). (Italics mine.)

[15] Translated from Piso as quoted by Cesbron, *Histoire critique de l'hystérie*, p. 98.

[16] *Hysterica symptomata omnia fere viris cum mulieribus sunt communia.* Piso, *op. cit.*, p. 181.

WILLIAM HARVEY AS GYNECOLOGIST

Neither Piso nor his successors succeeded in completely abolishing the uterine etiology. Among those who continued to espouse a mixture of all the old versions of the uterine etiology was the great William Harvey. His writings on hysteria are of special interest, since at times he merely repeated the ancient statements without giving them any personal shading, while at others his remarks revealed his perspicacity and the acuity of his observations. Thus while describing the uterus in a totally logical fashion, he went on to repeat uncritically the ancient views on the cause of a hysterical attack: "No one of the least experience can be ignorant what grievous symptoms arise when the uterus either rises up or falls down, or is in any way put out of place, or is seized with spasm!"[17] But in an actual attack, Harvey was again the superb observer who saw concurrent "mental aberrations, the delirium, the melancholy, the paroxysms of frenzy, as if the affected person were under the dominion of spells."[18] Thus far, Harvey the observer! He continued, however, to blame the uterus as the source of a wide variety of physical and emotional states. Quoting Galen, and perhaps adding his own clinical conjecture, he said: "How many incurable diseases also are brought about by unhealthy menstrual discharges or from over-abstinence from sexual intercourse when the passions are strong!"[19]

Harvey seems to have had a great many patients who suffered from "*furor uterinus* and melancholy." He detailed the histories of two, one "a noble lady who for more than 10 years laboured under" this illness, the other also suffering for a long period. Strangely enough, but quite in keeping with Harvey's own prediction, both women were cured after they suffered uterine prolapse, in the course of which the over-heated wombs were cooled by external air. The

[17] William Harvey, *On Parturition* in *The Works of William Harvey, M.D.*, trans. and with "A Life of the Author" by Robert Willis (London: Sydenham Society, 1847), p. 542.

[18] *Ibid.*, p. 543.   [19] *Ibid.*, p. 545.

cure persisted even after the uterus was returned to its proper place.

Obviously, Harvey's practice which included many female patients, gave him a great deal of gynecological experience that he frequently related, in some fashion or other, to hysteria. Another case recorded in his study *On Parturition* concerned the wife of a clergyman whom he treated for "a hidden ulcer in the uterine cavity." Harvey's therapy consisted of intrauterine injections which caused the uterus to "contract suddenly and become as hard as a stone." When this occurred, Harvey relates, "various hysterical symptoms showed themselves, such, I mean as are generally supposed by physicians to arise from constriction of the uterus, and the rising of 'foul vapours' therefrom." This condition persisted until Harvey had applied soothing remedies which relaxed the opening of the uterus and permitted the expulsion of the injected fluid together with the pus of the ulcer "and in a short time the patient recovered."[20]

Harvey's *Anatomical Exercises on the Generation of Man* was almost as familiar to his contemporaries as was his treatise on the circulation, and it is not surprising that his remarks on hysteria were known to those who were interested in the study of that disease. Among these was Thomas Willis (1622–75), the famous physiologist and neuroanatomist (after whom the Circle of Willis is named). Although he was a peasant's son, Willis completed his medical studies at Christ Church College, Oxford, and later became professor of natural philosophy at that university. He moved to London in 1666, where he developed a highly successful and fashionable medical practice. His most important studies, begun at Oxford but continued in London, were those on the central nervous system. In the preparation of his publication on the anatomy of the brain, he had the collaboration of two other prominent scientists of his day, the physiologist-physician Richard Lower and the great architect and mathematician Christopher Wren.[21]

[20] *Ibid.*, p. 546.

[21] Thomas Willis, *Cerebri anatome, cui accessit nervorum descriptio et usus* (London, 1664).

NEUROLOGISTS BEGIN TO STUDY HYSTERIA

The fortunate concatenation of an unsurpassed familiarity with brain structure and function and a clinical practice which necessarily included many patients with hysterical complaints led Willis to formulate the theory of the cerebral origin and seat of hysteria. This new concept was initially promulgated in a series of polemical monographs in a controversy with the equally well-known London anatomist and physician Nathaniel Highmore (after whom the maxillary antrum is named).

In a book that gained wide popularity, Highmore expressed his belief that hysterical attacks arose "from the blood, most impetuously rushing on the Lungs." Although Willis thought it "almost unlawful to dissent from this famous man,"[22] he nonetheless rejected Highmore's theory and instead proposed "that the Distemper named from the Womb is chiefly and primarily Convulsive, and chiefly depends on the Brain and the nervous stock [system] being affected."[23] The irregularities of the movement of the blood, which appeared of such importance to Highmore, Willis considered but secondary manifestations arising from visceral spasms. According to Willis, hysterical fits were caused, like all other convulsive movements, by the "Spirits inhabiting the Brain, being now prepared for Explosions." Their point of origin, he maintained, was generally in the head; occasionally it was in the womb, but the latter organ did not cause them any more frequently than did any other organ.[24] He did admit, after all, an occasional uterine starting point of the disease.

[22] The publications arising from this polemic are the following: N. Highmore, *Exercitationes duae quorum prior de passione hysterica; altera de affectione hypochondriaca* (Oxford, 1660); Thomas Willis, *Pathologiae cerebri et nervosi generis in quo agitur de morbis convulsivis* (1667); N. Highmore, *De passione hysterica et affectione hypochondriaca* (1670); Thomas Willis, *Affectionum quae dicuntur hystericae et hypochondriacae, vindicata contra responsionem epistolarum Nathanaelis Highmore* (London, 1670).

[23] Thomas Willis, *An Essay of the Pathology of the Brain and Nervous Stock in which Convulsive Diseases are Treated of*, trans. S. Pordage (London: Dring, Leigh, and Harper, 1684), p. 71.

[24] *Ibid.*

In general, however, most of Willis' arguments were designed to disprove the role of the uterus in hysteria. His
practice furnished him the necessary support for his arguments, since his patients included women of every age and
condition—"rich and poor, Virgins, Wives and Widows"—
who were susceptible to hysterical diseases. He observed
symptoms "in Maids before ripe age, also in old women after
their flowers have left them; yea, sometimes the *same kind
of Passions infest Men*."[25] Thus Willis was the next after
Carolus Piso, with whose writings he was familiar, to be convinced by his own clinical experiences that hysteria was not
limited to the female sex and hence could not truly arise
from the uterus. Nevertheless, he maintained that women,
because of their weaker animal constitution, were by far
more susceptible to hysteria than men, for "Women, from
any sudden terror and great sadness, fall into mighty disorder of spirits, where men from the same occasion are
scarcely disturb'd at all."[26]

Willis was too much the scientist to base his views solely
on impressions derived from his medical practice, and he
used cogent anatomical arguments when refuting the uterine
theory. "The Womb," he said, "is of so small bulk in Virgins
and Widows, and is so strictly tied by neighbouring parts
round about, that it cannot of itself be moved, or ascend
from its place."[27]

In another passage Willis even showed by post-mortem
dissections that beyond any doubt the origin of hysteria is
"within the bounds of the head." His autopsies of patients
who had suffered from hysteria but died of other afflictions
disclosed in each instance that the uterus was untouched by
disease. He went on the describe "in the hinder part of the
head, the beginning of the nerves [were] moistened and
wholly drowned with a sharp serum." Of course, this latter
observation was false, but from it he developed a theory
which is even more confusing, if possible, than any of the
preceding ones: "Having weighed these and other reasons,
we doubt not to assert the Passions, commonly called Hysterical, to arise most often, for that the animal spirits possessing the beginning of the Nerves within the head are in-

[25] *Ibid.*, p. 69. (Italics mine.)

[26] *Ibid.*, p. 74.   [27] *Ibid.*, p. 69.

fected with some taint." We thus find under the guise of the new science of neuroanatomy a resurrection of the ancient concept of "animal spirits" that is hazier than any uterine theory.[28]

More worthy of quotation is Willis' description of the place of hysteria in the medical practice of his time. His charges could be applied to medicine in all the succeeding centuries, not excepting our own.

The hysterical passion is of so ill fame among the Diseases belonging to Women, that like one half damn'd, it bears the faults of many other Distempers: for when at any time a sickness happens in a Woman's Body, of an unusual manner, or more occult original, so that its causes lie hid, and a Curatory indication is altogether uncertain, presently we accuse the evil influence of the Womb (which for the most part is innocent) and in every unusual symptom, we declare it to be something hysterical, and so to this scope, which oftentimes is only the subterfuge of ignorance, the medical intentions and use of Remedies are directed.[29]

Lord Russell Brain has described Willis as "the Harvey of the nervous system," because he developed his neurological findings not from speculative theories but from his anatomical observations and pathological studies and because he attempted to correlate what he observed post-mortem with the patient's symptoms during life. Willis derived his hypothesis of exploding animal spirits in the brain from this scientific approach.

The following quotation from Lord Brain's recent article notes that Willis

opposed the current view that the origin of what we call focal seizures lay in the part in which the spasm or sensation appeared, and declared his opinion that the primary cause was always in the brain, "to wit that the spirits inhabiting it being disposed to explosions, and there being exploded, bring on or cause every Falling Evil."

But Willis was not content with this generalization. Where in the brain, he asked himself, does the explosion originate? He rejected the view that it was cortical in origin, because he had seen severe cortical damage occur without producing

28 *Ibid.*

29 For a brilliant discussion of the origin and evolution of the term animal spirits see Walther Riese, *A History of Neurology* (New York: MD Publications, Inc., 1959), pp. 50–52.

convulsions. He came to the conclusion that "the spirits inhabiting the middle of the brain are the primary Subject of the disease. . . . Since the assault of the Epilepsie urging the insensibility, and great disorder, is for the most part the first Symptom, and all the pathognomick, it may be concluded that the Animal Spirits lying within the middle of the Brain itself are affected before others; and that therefore that part is the principal seat of the disease.[30]

Lord Brain points out that the above explanation for the convulsive manifestations of epilepsy could also be used to explain the hysterical symptoms formerly attributed to suffocation of the womb, with the one difference that the discharge of animal spirits provoking epilepsy took place in the middle parts of the brain, whereas those causing hysterical convulsions arose at "the beginning of the nerves within the head." Further exegesis of the Willis concept hints at the transmission of the convulsive disposition through the vagi and intercostal nerves to the viscera of the chest and the abdomen.

Lord Brain's sympathetic interpretation of Willis' theories gave him reason to believe that they contained modern neurological scientific discoveries. To his contemporaries, however, Willis' etiological hypotheses must have remained obscure and, at best, offered no practical aid in the selection of therapeutic measures. To the physician of that era, as indeed to doctors of all periods, the cure was the most important aspect in medicine. The particular preoccupation with treatment in the seventeenth century, to judge by the volume of current literature, was due to large numbers of patients in their practice who were considered to be hysterical and who clamored for help.

Willis, too, despite his scientific interests had so many "Noble Virgins" and "very Noble Ladies" among his patients who suffered from various forms of hysteria that he felt bound to devote attention to therapy. He could not, however, offer a single innovation; and, instead, he attempted to endow the old treatments with new rationales to make them fit his neurological theories. Thus, he applauded the old custom of putting tight bandages or plasters upon the

[30] Russell Brain, "The Concept of Hysteria in the Time of William Harvey," *Proceedings of the Royal Society of Medicine*, LVI (April, 1963), 321-23.

region of the navel not because they restrained the uterus, but because they "repress and compel into order . . . the spirits from leaping forth . . . wherefor when the explosions there about to be made are restrained, the convulsive fit is wholly prevented."[31] He further believed that by binding the patient's abdomen and epigastrium the ascent of the globus and "the progress of the symptoms towards the upper parts" could be stopped.

He discussed further the age-old practice of treating hysterical attacks by applying odoriferous substances, which he also reconciled with his theory of the animal spirits.

As to the various effects of odors, to wit, that sweet things bring on the fit, but stinking things drive the same away, it may be said, that the former do loosen the animal spirits, by pleasing them, and too much release them from their wonted tasks of influence, and so provoke them ready to be exploded, in such disorders, yea and as a flame put to them, do somewhat inkindle them: but on the contrary, stinking things repress the spirits, drive them back from excursions and exorbitances, and compel from them their explosive force.[32]

Among such remedies Willis recommended asafoetida, castor, galbanum—in short, the old array of evil-smelling substances, all of which he considered anti-spasmodic and anti-convulsive and effective in both sexes. But, he said, since "these Distempers most often happen to the Female Sex, in whom the menstrual flux and other accidents of the womb, do challenge a part in the morbific cause; therefore medicines respecting the various dispositions of the womb, are to be added to the former, and many ways to be compounded with them."[33] Obviously, there is little point in any further discussion of Willis' remedies and manipulations, since they lack novelty and only by specious and tortuous argument can they be at all related to his etiological theories. In this respect he was joined by the other leading physicians of his time, including William Harvey, who dropped their laboratory theories when confronting their patients; they did, in fact, lead double lives as scientists and physicians with little reciprocal influence of one phase of their activities on the other. This duality of science and tradition-bound em-

---

[31] *An Essay of the Pathology of the Brain . . .*, p. 75.
[32] *Ibid.*   [33] *Ibid.*, p. 78.

piricism in therapy was characteristic of the period when rational investigation began to displace unsupported speculation.

The England of the seventeenth century, the century of the Royal Society's foundation, as well as of the Great Plague and the London Fire, was richly blessed with poets and philosophers and with scientists and physicians of all persuasions. Shakespeare and Bacon, Locke and More, Boyle and Wren, Newton and Halley were but a few of the most prominent of the many superb thinkers of their period. In the field of internal medicine, this century of genius, which put the stamp of premium on individualism, produced one of the greatest clinicians of all time—Thomas Sydenham (1624–89). His contemporaries honored him with the designation "English Hippocrates." This title is particularly apt, because Sydenham not only revitalized the long-stagnant field of internal medicine, he also reintroduced essential features of Hippocratic medicine, bedside observation, expectancy in treatment, and reliance upon the powers of nature abetted by the physician.

In the light of the great fame of Sydenham, the known facts about his life are rather scanty. That he was born in Winford Eagle, Dorset, in 1624 is firmly established. Nothing, however, is known about his youth until he entered Magdalen Hall, Oxford, at the age of eighteen. His stay there was very brief and the causes for his leaving are uncertain. There is good reason to believe, however, that he withdrew in order to bear arms in the Parliamentary revolution, in which cause his family was deeply involved. Whatever the explanation, he returned after an absence of nearly four years, during which time education at the university had also undergone something of a revolution. Old doctrines, hallowed simply because of their antiquity and unchallenged authority, had been rooted out by the general ferment of the political upheaval.

The consequent improvement of scholarship and learning was of great benefit to Sydenham, who soon after his re-

turn decided to pursue the study of medicine. He received
the Bachelor of Medicine degree in 1648 at Oxford and then,
presumably, spent a further period of study at Montpellier,
although definite evidence of the latter is lacking as is even
the exact date of the opening of his medical practice in
London. It is certain that he did not become a licentiate of
the College of Physicians until 1663, at the age of thirty-
nine. Evidently Sydenham did not consider his medical
education complete, for he took his Doctor's degree in medicine in 1676, when he was fifty-three years old and curiously not from Oxford but from Cambridge.

In the interim between the two degrees, in 1666, he published his first book, *On the Method of Treating Fevers*.
That it was reviewed in the *Transactions* of the recently
founded Royal Society indicates that Sydenham had attained
considerable prominence as a physician by that time. In 1678
Sydenham suffered a particularly severe attack of the gout,
a disease that had plagued him since the age of twenty-five.
Pains and persistent hematuria so weakened him that he was
required to spend several months convalescing in the country to recover his strength. The years that followed, although never free from pain, were active and successful
ones. Further publications appeared, some in repeated editions in many countries and eventually in the form of collected works (*Opera universa*). Sydenham died in 1689 after
intensified suffering from gout aggravated by renal calculus
and massive hematuria.

Sydenham was not an outgoing person and he had few
close friends among his colleagues. Towards his patients,
however, he displayed a warm concern which won him the
gratitude and esteem that he needed. One of the few human
touches in the scanty available data about him was supplied
by Dr. Johnson, who related that when a young physician[34]
who later attained great fame first engaged in the practice
of medicine, he consulted Dr. Sydenham on what authors he
should read. Sydenham directed him to *Don Quixote*, saying,
"It is a very good book, I read it still." Although this anec-
dote may be apocryphal, it is certain that Sydenham was
not a great reader of medical works either of the past or of

[34] Sir Richard Blackmore (1650?–1729).

his own day. Apart from Cervantes, his favorite authors were Hippocrates, Cicero, and Bacon.

Sydenham believed the role of medicine to be a simple one. He felt that because of the limitations and fallibility of the human mind, causes must remain unknown and, therefore, scientific theories were of little value to the practitioner of medicine. Instead, when at a patient's bedside, he must rely on his powers of observation and on his fund of experience. According to an admiring reviewer of his first published book, Sydenham's advice was "to permit Nature to do her own work, requiring nothing of the physician, but to regulate her when she is exorbitant, and to fortify her when she is too weak."[35] The reviewer was particularly impressed by the fact that Sydenham used methods which he would choose to have applied for the treatment of his only son, were he to fall ill.

Sydenham based his concept of disease on Hippocrates' but he went far beyond his venerated professional ancestor. He spoke not of disease but of *diseases,* each of which was a recognizable entity with a natural history of its own. He emphasized that each belonged to a separate and distinct species which could be described in the same manner as a botanist described plant species. This is, in essence, the basis of modern medical thinking; and, indeed, to find the first clear clinical picture of various illnesses one frequently refers to Sydenham.

Sydenham was not a prolific writer, but his words were charged with meaning. In an informal and unpretentious style he presented his observations for the guidance of his contemporaries, sometimes written specifically in response to inquiries. Most familiar among his writings are those on epidemics and epidemic constitution and treatises on dropsy, fevers, venereal disease, and St. Vitus' dance, also known as Sydenham's chorea. His most highly esteemed work is undoubtedly the *Treatise on Gout,* which he wrote in 1683 after having suffered from this affliction for more than thirty years.[36]

[35] An Account of Dr. Sydenham's Book, entitled, *Methodus curandi Febres, Propriis observationibus superstructa,*" *Transactions of the Royal Society,* London, May 7, 1666.

[36] This was also reviewed in *Transactions of the Royal Society,* London, 1683.

Hysteria was the subject of one of Sydenham's most valuable but relatively less well known works. Perhaps because
the subject is concealed in the non-descriptive title *Epistolary Dissertation*, this treatise has received not so much notice as many others. In truth, it is a landmark in the history
of hysteria. Written without dependence upon any other
writer and only vaguely related to preceding or contemporary thought, it introduced a fresh approach to the disease
and an unequaled understanding of the psyche of its victims.

Sydenham might never have written on hysteria without
special invitation. In the last quarter of the seventeenth century it became known among some English physicians that
he had developed a new insight into the definition and treatment of hysteria. These findings had not been published and
his colleagues were concerned that because of his frail health
he might never have the opportunity to put his thoughts on
paper. Finally, on November 17, 1681, Dr. William Cole
(1635–1716) of Worcester, a medical author of considerable
repute, addressed a letter to the great physician urging him
to communicate his observations "concerning the so-called
hysterical diseases," which had long exercised the wits of
physicians and eluded the recognized methods of treatment.

Sydenham's reply to this request shows that he was highly
pleased with the deferential inquiries of his noted colleague
and was quite willing to reveal his thoughts on this disease,
which were indeed novel to the medical profession of his
day. Early in *Epistolary Dissertation*, his answer to the
"most illustrious and learned" Dr. Cole, Sydenham stated
that he had been led to the treatment of hysteria because he
had observed that next to fever it was the most common of
diseases.[37] This statement may have astounded even the
seventeenth-century physicians who wrote so much about
hysteria, but had not learned to recognize it except in its
convulsive or paroxysmal forms. Astonishing also must have
been his assertion that not only women but men, too, could
be counted among its victims, for it was much more emphatic than any such previous statement. The following
sentences are quoted verbatim, for no paraphrase could do

[37] *The Works of Thomas Sydenham, M.D.*, trans. and with a "Life
of the Author" by R. G. Latham (London: 1848), II, 54.

justice to their clarity of definition and their sagacity of observation:

Of all chronic diseases hysteria—unless I err—is the commonest; since just as fevers—taken with their accompaniments—equal two thirds of the number of all chronic diseases taken together, so do hysterical complaints (or complaints so called) make one half of the remaining third. As to females, if we except those who lead a hard and hardy life, there is rarely one who is wholly free from them—and females, be it remembered, form one half of the adults of the world. Then, again, such male subjects as lead a sedentary or studious life, and grow pale over their books and papers, are similarly afflicted; since, however much, antiquity may have laid the blame of hysteria upon the uterus, hypochondriasis (which we impute to some obstruction of the spleen or viscera) is as like it, as one egg is to another. True, indeed, it is that women are more subject than males. This, however, is not on account of the uterus, but for reasons which will be seen in the sequel.[38]

Proceeding from this introduction, Sydenham first of all warned:

The frequency of hysteria is no less remarkable than the multiformity of the shapes which it puts on. Few of the maladies of miserable mortality are not imitated by it. Whatever part of the body it attacks, it will create the proper symptom of that part. Hence, without skill and sagacity the physician will be deceived; so as to refer the symptoms to some essential disease of the part in question, and not to the effects of hysteria.

He then described the various manifestations which he recognized to be of hysterical origin, listing among them recurring violent headaches, occasionally followed by vomiting, violent coughing, and spasms of the colon. Sydenham cautioned that differential diagnosis of pains of apparently visceral origin may be difficult: "It may be hysteria or it may be a calculus; and unless there have been some antecedent mental emotion . . . the former may be mistaken for the latter." Cases where pain in the bladder and retention of urine occurred he found even more difficult to diagnose. In connection with "hysteria on the stomach," Sydenham observed continuous vomiting and diarrhea.

He turned from hysterical afflictions of the internal organs to those of the external parts, "the muscular flesh of

---

[38] *Ibid.*, p. 85. All of Sydenham's subsequent quotations are taken from the *Epistolary Dissertation, loc. cit.*

the jaws, shoulders, hands, legs and ankles, sometimes causing pain and sometimes swelling." Even some forms of
toothache were not exempted from his list of hysterical
complaints, and "of all pains . . . the most certain [to be of
hysterical nature] is the pain in the back." Polyuria he considered an almost unfailing symptom of hysteria in females
and of hypochondriasis in males.

Sydenham's recognition of the emotional concomitants of
these physical disturbances was equally perspicacious. He
wrote of the incurable despair of patients, their belief that
they must suffer all the evil that befalls mankind, their pre-
sentiment of further unhappiness. He described their pro-
pensity to anger, jealousy, and suspicion and pointed to their
very occasional intervals of joy, hope, and cheerfulness; their
daytime moods, mirrored by their dreams, were haunted by
sad forebodings. "All is caprice," he said; "they love without
measure those whom they will soon hate without reason."

With deep compassion for these patients, Sydenham compared their physical and mental sufferings to life in a pur-
gatory wherein they expiate crimes committed in a previous
state. Yet he emphasized that these men and women were
not insane. He even went so far as to say that "those who
thus suffer are persons of prudent judgment, persons who
in their profundity of meditations and the wisdom of their
speech far surpass those whose minds have never been exerted by such stimuli." Despite Sydenham's insistence on the
sanity of the hysterical patient, he nevertheless recognized
the manifestations to be of mental origin. Jorden had believed them to have their origin in the head, and Willis, in
the brain; and both the authors were aware of the frequent
association of emotional disturbances with hysterical phenomena. *Yet the definite inclusion of hysteria itself among
afflictions of the mind was the contribution of Thomas
Sydenham.*

Among the mental symptoms described above is depression. Some of the patients showing evidence of this today
would be considered to be suffering from the cyclic form
of this emotional imbalance. It is, of course, not to be expected that a physician of Sydenham's day could differentiate between the two in view of the dearth of information
on mental disease in the seventeenth century.

Sydenham's explanation of the pathogenesis of hysterical disorders included remote or external as well as proximate and direct causes. He explained the former as follows:

The remote or external causes of hysteria are over-ordinate actions of the body; and still oftener over-ordinate commotions of the mind, arising from sudden bursts of anger, pain, fear of other similar emotions. Hence, as often as females consult me concerning such, or such bodily ailments as are difficult to be determined by the usual rules for diagnosis, I never fail to carefully inquire whether they are not worse sufferers when trouble, low-spirits, or any mental perturbation takes hold of them. If so, I put down the symptoms for hysterical; a diagnosis which becomes all the more certain whenever a large quantity of limpid crystalline urine has been voided. To such, and such like mental emotions bodily derangements may be added, e.g., long fasting and over-free evacuations (whether from bleeding, purging, or emetics) which have been too much for the system to bear up against.

His ideas of direct cause, like those of Willis, involved "animal spirit."[39] But whereas Willis fancied "explosion" of such spirits, with localization of their effect dependent upon their source, Sydenham advanced a simpler, more logical, and more credible hypothesis. He believed an imbalance of the mind-body relationship gave rise to disturbances in that corporeal part that happened to be weakest at the moment.[40] The framework of the mind he held to be far more delicate than that of the body, "a structure consisting in the harmony of eminently excellent and almost divine faculties; so, whenever the constitution of the same shall, by any means, have become interrupted and broken down, the ruin will be great." Sydenham emphatically stated:

[39] It is extremely difficult to find a satisfactory explanation of the meaning of the term "animal spirits" (*spiritus animales*). Although the term originated in antiquity, its meaning shifted constantly, and Sydenham himself seems to have been somewhat uncertain about the nature of these spirits to whom he attributed such far-reaching influence. He conceived of them as dominating both mind and body, for "it is from the irregularity of the spirits that the inconsistency both of mind and body . . . so prevalent with both the hysterical and hypochondriacal take birth. The strength and constancy of the mind . . . depends most especially upon the . . . spirits which are at the top of the scale of matter, and on the very verge of the immaterial entity."

[40] Centuries later this was described by Freud as "das organische Entgegenkommen in der Neurose."

It is clear then, to me, that it is not any corruption of either the semen or the menstrual blood . . . to which this disease is to be referred. It is rather the faulty disposition of the animal spirits. There is no malignant halitus to the parts affected, no perverse deprivation of the juices, no congestion of acrid humours. There is the cause I have assigned, and no other.[41]

Is his concept any less rational or believable than our modern imputations to the mind?

Although not the first, as has been stated, Sydenham's expression of the belief that hysteria could extend to both sexes was by far the most explicit. The medical profession, bound by the literal meaning of the term hysteria, had paid little attention to the earlier statements. Indeed, more than two centuries later, and even after Charcot had demonstrated hysteria in males at the Salpêtrière, some physicians insisted that since *hystera* was Greek for uterus, it was impossible for men to be hysterics. Sydenham escaped such criticism from his literal-minded colleagues by calling the masculine version of hysteria "hypochondriasis." His alliance of hypochondriasis and hysteria was perfectly logical. After it was introduced by Smollius in 1610,[42] hypochondriasis became the subject of many treatises, in which the hypochondrium was accorded a role similar to that of the uterus in hysteria.[43] Just as "uterine suffocation" gave rise to many physical and mental disorders in women, so *suffocatio hypochondriaca* caused numerous derangements of the abdominal viscera and, specifically, of the spleen.[44] The latter was supposed to be the cause of the melancholy which frequently accompanied the physical complaints.[45]

Although hypochondriasis was not explicitly restricted to the male, similar complaints in females were classed as hys-

41 *The Works of Thomas Sydenham*, p. 95.

42 G. Smollius, *Trias maritima, proponens per introductionem trium aegrotantium, sororum morbosarum, domesticarum, hypochondriacae spleneticae; hypochondriacae meseraicae; hypochondriacae phantasticae; ortum et interitum.*

43 For example, C. Van Diik, *De suffocatione hypochondriaca* (Leyden, 1665); R. Westhoff, *De affectu hypochondriae* (Argentorati, 1668); H. G. Herfelt, *De affectione hypochondriaca* (Duisburg on Rhine, 1678).

44 Nathanael Highmore, *Excertitationes duae quarum . . .*

45 The eleventh edition of the *Encyclopaedia Britannica* (1911) still lists "the spleen" as synonymous with hypochondriasis.

teria. In Sydenham's day the word "hypochondriasis" did not connote morbid preoccupation with one's physical health. This narrower definition was introduced in 1822 by Jean Pierre Falret,[46] who described false beliefs about an impaired state of health as characteristic of hypochondria. Sydenham's views on etiology and pathogenesis evoked little interest on the part of the English physicians of his time. And later, when authors quoted him, they did so partially out of context and with reservations. The eventual permanent abandonment of the belief that hysteria had a uterine origin and that it occurred only in females came about quite independently and with no direct reference to the writings of Sydenham. This transition will be traced in subsequent chapters.

But Sydenham's therapy of hysteria, quite in contrast to his etiology, was eagerly adopted by his fellow physicians. As already mentioned, his approach to treatment in general was pragmatic and reasonable in the Hippocratic spirit. As such, therefore, his management of the hysterical patient was directed towards the cause of the disturbance. This, at once, demanded complete rejection of the old and traditional measures which were directed towards tempting or repelling the wandering womb to its normal site.

It cannot be expected, however, that the avenues of general therapy could be changed altogether, even though specific treatment had been altered by Sydenham. And so we find him treating patients with hysteria by the conventional measures which were designed to purify and fortify the blood. It was his belief that hysteria and hypochondriasis gave rise to an accumulation of "putrid humors" which impaired the organs whose function it was to purify the blood and thus caused the physical affliction. Bleeding and purging were the universal remedies for such putrid humors and these he employed. Having bled and purged his patients, he administered medicines that "fortified the blood," such as iron filings. Riding on horseback was recommended, not with the idea of jolting a dislodged uterus back into place as earlier physicians had suggested, but merely because of the beneficial effects of exercise.

Irrespective of the actual therapeutic efficacy of Syden-

[46] Jean Pierre Falret, *De l'hypochondrie et du suicide* (Paris, 1822).

ham's measures, there can be do doubt that, taken together with his deep personal interest in the patient's welfare and the powerful suggestion thus generated, he was eminently successful in his treatment. Moreover, while his remedies per se lacked novelty, his modes of dispensing them differed greatly from traditional practices.

Sydenham was uncommonly flexible, adjusting his treatment to the special requirements of each case. He was extremely cautious in the amount of bleeding and purging and avoided these methods completely in cases with physical debilitation. He administered his blood-building remedies with the same caution, aware of individual reactions to different medicines and cognizant of the fact that to some patients his "hysterical pills" were absolutely repugnant. In such cases he omitted medication altogether, relying entirely on time, "the prince and pattern of physicians."

Shortly after Sydenham's death, a book on the "Practice of Physick" was published by an Italian physician, Giorgio Baglivi (1668–1706), which importantly advanced the understanding of the emotional basis of "nervous diseases." Baglivi referred to Sydenham's work with the highest praise and, in turn, was himself widely quoted by subsequent writers in other countries. Literature in the centuries preceding our own, whether scientific or belletristic, was international in a way that does not exist today. This was partly because Latin was the language common to all the learned of the entire Western world; it was probably also because the total literary output of the time was minute compared to the unremitting deluge of printed matter today. Individual books in the past had an importance that commanded immediate and general attention. Although some translation into various vernaculars was done, this was not essential for international participation.

Baglivi, whom Pope Clement XI appointed to the chair of medical theory in the Collegio della Sapienza in Rome, was noted both for his prominence as a physician and for his contributions to muscular physiology, including the first differentiation between smooth and striped muscle fibers. He is chiefly remembered for his mechanical interpretation of bodily function, but he also made sensitive appraisals of the impact of emotions on health. Baglivi belonged to the iatromechanist school which likened the body to a machine composed of many smaller mechanical units; he compared the teeth to scissors, the chest to bellows, the stomach to a bottle, the viscera and glands to sieves, etc. At the bedside, however, he disregarded these theories and devoted himself entirely to the patients and their specific diseases. He was a physician in the best tradition of Hippocrates and Sydenham.

HYSTERIA: A PASSION OF THE MIND

Of surpassing interest in this context are his ideas concerning hysteria in *De praxi medica*, which Baglivi published in 1696. This book reveals the clinical acuity of its author in all aspects of medical practice. It also contains a chapter entitled "The Cure of the Diseases of the Mind; and the Method for giving their History." This is an impressive contribution in that it introduces the concept of psychosomatic medicine. By its inclusion of hysteria among the disturbances of the mind it added invaluably to the history of hysteria, and its influence is evident in the works of many subsequent writers.

Baglivi was actually one of the first physicians to write at length on mental disease in its modern connotation and as an integral part of medicine. Furthermore, he expressed the belief that certain physical diseases are of psychogenic origin:

> All Men have their own Cares, and every one lies under a bitter Necessity of spending almost all the Periods of his Life, in attending the doubtful Events of his Labour. Now this being true, 'tis equally a Truth obvious to all Men, that a great Part of Diseases either take their Rise from, or are fed by that Weight of Care that hangs upon every one's Shoulders; . . .[47]

Hysteria, in his opinion, one form of mental disease, was also caused by passions of the mind. Sydenham had considered the emotions as concomitants of hysteria, but Baglivi believed them to be its cause.

[47] George Baglivi, *The Practice of Physick, reduc'd to the ancient Way of Observations, containing a just Parallel between the Wisdom of the Ancients and the Hypothesis's of Modern Physicians* . . . (2d ed.; London: Midwinter, Linton, Strahan, etc., 1723), chap. 14, pp. 160–72.

Because of his preoccupation with the emotional background of physical suffering, he urged all physicians to
question their patients carefully about the "occasional cause"
of their illnesses and particularly about the "passions of the
mind." Baglivi considered this train of inquiry much more
pertinent than that of "running on without any further En-
quiry, and promiscuously imputing all diseases to a fabulous
Fancy of Repletion." The assumption that overindulgence
was a cause for hysteria and other "nervous diseases" had
become so deeply ingrained in Baglivi's contemporaries that
even he admitted that repletion could give rise to certain disorders; but he stated with considerable heat that passions of
the mind give rise to many more diseases, especially among
persons of consequence, "most of whom have other things to
think of than overcharging their Stomach with Gluttony or
Drunkenness."

Baglivi felt it necessary to examine three specific questions: (1) whether the passions of the mind have an influence
upon the body; (2) how that influence is conveyed; and
(3) by what means are diseases arising from these passions to
be cured. His answer to the first question was unreservedly
affirmative and was supported by examples from his own
observations. The first of these, dated "*Anno* 1690" reads as
follows: "In *Dalmatia*, I saw a young Man seiz'd with violent
Convulsions, only for looking upon another Person that lay
groveling upon the Ground in a Fit of an Epilepsy."[48] He
also referred to the writings of other unspecified authors
among which he discovered many accounts of the power of
imagination upon the organs of the body. From all this he
gathered that those of genteel breeding and more delicate
emotional sensitivity are more susceptible to disease than are
the "meaner sort of person." These are often of rustic origin,
less sensitive and better able to cope with grief and worry.

Baglivi shared the opinion of his day that affliction with
diseases of the mind would sooner or later manifest itself by
gastrointestinal symptoms, largely brought about by de-
creasing appetites and disinterest in food. For this reason he
warned that no cure should ever be begun with the common
practice of purging, bleeding, or any other medicines that

[48] *Ibid.*, p. 161.

further aggravated the patient's debility. He urged, on the contrary, measures to overcome debility and promote vigor.

Baglivi, despite his clinical astuteness, was so carried away by his conviction of the power of the mind over the body that he fell into the same error encountered today: occasional failure to note the existence of physical disease when it coincides with emotional disturbance. The following is a particularly interesting example of an obvious cancer being overlooked.[49] The fact that the symptoms were uterine in origin probably evoked the suggestion of hysteria and led him to believe they were the physical response to hysterical emotional imbalance.

If a Patient is seiz'd with an Illness during a Passion of his Mind, it uses sometimes to last as long as the Passion; and will rather shift to a Disease of another Form, than quit him altogether. I observed this particularly of late in a Woman of forty Years of Age, that was thrown by the deepest Passions of Mind into a great Flux of Blood from the Womb, of which she was cur'd, after using several Remedies for the space of three Months. But the same Concern, and Passions even of greater Violence, continuing for almost a Year, she was no sooner cur'd of that Flux of Blood, than she was seiz'd with a running from the Womb, that was sometimes white, and sometimes particoloured. After this Running was stopt, she was seiz'd with Anguish at Heart, Anxiety of the Breast, extream Weakness, Leanness, Inappetency, Thirst, a lingring slow Fever, a falling off of the Hair, and the like; which continued, and held out for six Months against all the Power of Remedies. To compleat her Misery, she was taken first with the Swelling of her Legs, then with an Ascites, and at last with an Universal Dropsy all over her Body. After all, being worn out with Care, and miserably tortur'd for five Months with a Legion of Illnesses, she remov'd to the other World.[50]

Baglivi's answer to the second specific question, how mental influences are conveyed through the body, leaves much to be desired. In fact, he made no serious attempt to account for the "Mechanick Way" in which the passions of the mind produce disease. But, his silence on the subject is quite understandable in the light of how subtle and complicated the relationship seems to us. Apparently he felt such challenge to be beyond human comprehension, "considering that the

[49] I am grateful to Dr. Lester S. King for calling this passage to my attention.

[50] *The Practice of the Physick,* p. 164.

most tow'ring Genius's of all Ages, have fatigu'd themselves
in vain upon this Solution; and that scarce any, besides
Cartes [Descartes], have advanc'd any thing upon the Head,
that bears a Colour of Reason." He therefore thought that
"it will be allowable in us to skip these knotty Difficulties,
that relate but little to the Cure of Diseases."[51] He considered it much more important to do what had never before
been done: to obtain good and clear histories of every passion and care of the mind. He wanted histories of all the
physical diseases that were thought to arise from emotional
suffering; he wished to know their symptoms, their incidence, their duration, their transformation into other illnesses, their method of treatment, and all the factors that
might aggravate them.

Baglivi stressed the fact that emotionally unstable persons
are much more prone to frequent and intractable illness than
are those of more rugged mental makeup, that the psychogenic ailments may give rise to serious and even fatal illness
in such individuals. "Some thro' Indignation and Impatience,
turn the slightest Disorders into long and mortal Diseases:
Thus a Cough, contracted by Indignation and a customary
Trick of Coughing, degenerates very easily into a Phthis-
ick."[52]

The final section of Baglivi's *Practice of Physick* is devoted to his third question, namely, the treatment of these
diseases. He stated first

that almost the whole of the Cure lies in the Patient's own Breast;
that is, in a Mind well fortify'd with Patience, Fortitude, Pru-
dence, Tranquility, and the other moral Vertues, without which
all Manner of Remedies, and all the Efforts of Physicians, will be
e'en a'most vain and useless. For the Remedies in the Apothe-
caries Shops, that go by the Name of Exhilarating, Antimelan-
cholick, Comforters of the Heart and Memory, Whets for the
Genius, etc. are rather invented to favour the Pomp of the Art,
than to dispel the bitter Cares of the Mind, or to rouze a drooping
Spirit.[53]

He did not mean to imply a therapeutic nihilism, but rather
that treatment should consist of general measures that act
upon the blood and penetrate into the innermost recesses of
the body. He was certain that persons who are unable to

[51] *Ibid.*, p. 165.   [52] *Ibid.*, p. 169.   [53] *Ibid.*, p. 167.

control their passions and are plagued by hypochondria or melancholia could be helped even though they appear hopelessly incurable. Among the measures he recommended were bathing, proper diet, physical exercise, travel to foreign countries, hunting and riding in the country air, music, and dancing. All these, he assumed, gradually repair the body by virtue of the soft and gentle delight they give to the mind and thus "reduce the disorderly Motions of the Imagination to their Primitive Regularity."

Baglivi exhorted the physician to employ his greatest wisdom and to assume a fearless self-assurance to help the patient regain his tranquillity. He urged humoring the patient, promising recovery, and suggesting ways and means to alter the patient's profession, domicile, or way of life.

I can scarce express what Influence the Physician's Words have upon the Patient's Life, and how much they sway the Fancy; for a Physician that has his Tongue well hung, and is Master of the Art of persuading, fastens, by the mere Force of Words, such a Vertue upon his Remedies, and raises the Faith and Hopes of the Patient to that Pitch, that sometimes he masters difficult Diseases with the silliest Remedies; which Physicians of greater Learning could not do with nobler Remedies, merely because they talk'd faintly, and with a soft dead Air.[54]

No modern physician, whether he is a psychiatrist or an internist, would take issue with Baglivi on the therapeutic value of such measures.

THE PURITAN ON HYSTERIA

The American Colonies, remote and with sparse opportunities for communication with the mother countries, were necessarily slow to apprehend and adopt changing ideas. There were, of course, exceptions. Sydenham's work, for instance, was first seriously mentioned in American literature by Cotton Mather. This is not particularly surprising, since Mather was a fellow of the Royal Society and undoubtedly had access to the reviews of the Sydenham publications. In any event, he first referred to them in a medical treatise, typically entitled *The Angel of Bethesda*, which he

[54] *Ibid.*, p. 171.

completed in 1724 when he was sixty-four years old.[55] The
design of his book and its title reveal Mather's dual concern
with religion and medicine, but his primary role was that of
a clergyman. As such, his purpose in the book was to lead
the reader unto God and thereby to achieve "The Cure of a
Sin-sick Soul" which was "what all Invalids ought to reckon
their Grand Concern."[56]

Although the book was never published[57] and hence failed
to exert significant influence upon Mather's contemporaries
and his century, it is nevertheless interesting to note the reactions of this intensely religious person to hysteria. Mather
obviously never realized the essential identity of the persons
he condemned as witches and those whom he later described
as hysterics. In all persons, he suggested, there was a substance to which he gave the Hebraic name *Nishmath-Chajim*,
a "Spirit in Man" or "The Breath of Life." He considered
this soul or spirit "the most successful physician in the
world," somewhat contradictorily, since it was apparently
both healer and sufferer. Thus the *Nishmath-Chajim* required strengthening and invigorating when the melancholy
of hysteria took hold of the patient, and this could be
achieved by means of tranquillity. In support of this theory
Mather quoted Baglivi's earlier mention of diseases being
caused by the "Weight of Cares lying on the Minds of
Men." He quoted another physician, Giovanni Bonifacio, as
saying, "Tranquillity of Mind will do strange things towards
the Relief of Bodily Maladies," and he cited Friedrich Hoffmann's treatise on the achievement of longevity by means of
mental tranquillity. To Mather the clergyman tranquillity
meant piety, and his recommendations read as follows:

By practising, the Art of Curing by Consolation, you may carry
on the Experiment. I propound then: Lett the Physician with
all possible Ingenuity of Conversation, find out, what Matter of
Anxiety there may have been upon the Mind of the Patient;

[55] I am indebted to the Massachusetts Historical Society for their
kindness in making available to me the transcript of Mather's manuscript. See also Otho Beall, Jr., and Richard H. Shryock, *Cotton
Mather, First Significant Figure in American Medicine* (Baltimore:
Johns Hopkins Press, 1954), pp. 53 ff.

[56] *Ibid.*, p. 136.

[57] In 1954 excerpts were published by Beall and Shryock, *ibid.*

what there is that has made his Life uneasy to him. Having discovered the Burden, lett him use all the Ways he can devise, to take it off. Offer him such thoughts as may be the best Anodynes for his distressed Mind; especially the right Thoughts of the Righteous, and the Ways to a Composure upon religious Principles. Give him a Prospect, if you can, of sound Deliverance from his Distresses, or some Abatement of them. Raise in him as bright Thoughts as may be; and scatter the Clouds, remove the Loads, which his Mind is perplexed withal; especially, by representing and magnifying the Mercy of God in Christ unto him.[58]

Mather's beliefs concerning hysteria are thus a composite of his own spiritual theories and the practical observations of Sydenham. His treatment combined both elements and emphasized a holy and easy mind together with vigorous physical exercise. An incidental observation gleaned from Mather's book is that he used only the masculine pronoun when referring to hysterical patients.

A brief digression to another early eighteenth-century publication offers a somewhat different flavor. Bernard de Mandeville in *A Treatise of the Hypochondriack and Hysteric Passions,* published in England in 1711, spoke of hysteria allegorically in the form of a dialogue between Misombedon, the father of the patient, and Philopirio, the physician. The wife was suffering from melancholia and the daughter from hysteria. In response Philopirio prescribed a vigorous regimen of horseback riding, passive exercise, and massage for the daughter which required at least three hours in both the morning and the afternoon. The father, taken aback by the excessive severity of the regimen, respectfully inquired whether this therapy, which seemed rather modern to him, could not be replaced by a much older one, that is, whether marriage might not be as effective as all those exercises. The doctor's answer was decidedly negative for a variety of reasons which he developed with great clarity.

I never prescribe an uncertain Remedy, that may prove worse than the Disease; for not to speak of the many inconveniences, the advising it often puts People to. In the first place it may fail, and then there are two People made unhappy instead of one; Secondly, it may but half Cure the Woman, who lingering under the remainder of her Disease, may have half a dozen Chil-

[58] *Ibid.,* pp. 145–46.

dren, that shall all inherit it. A Physician has a publick Trust reposed in him: His Prescriptions by assisting some ought never to prejudice others; besides that a Young Lady has no reason with the same Fortune to expect such an agreeable Match, whilst she labours under so deplorable an Infirmity, as if she was in perfect Health; therefore let her either be first Cured, and then Marry without being injurious to her self, her Husband, or her Posterity; or else remain single, with this Comfort at least in her Affliction, that she is not liable of entailing it upon others.[59]

This brief answer is replete with new thought. Countless physicians had recommended such marriages, but none before had expressed an interest in the result of a marriage of a hysterical patient or in the fate of her spouse. The fact that marriage might fail to be a cure, that the children might be affected, and that unhappiness might be multiplied had never before been the concern of physicians. Needless to say, de Mandeville's exceptional therapy in no way weakened the tendency of later physicians to advise marriage.

[59] Denis Leigh, *The Historical Development of British Psychiatry* (New York: Pergamon Press, 1961), I, 23–27.

CHAPTER VIII

The Controversial
Century

THE TIME-HONORED CONVENTION of historians to divide the continuum of history into periods of one hundred years creates the impression that a century is a firm historical unit rather than a by-product of the decimal system. Certainly such divisions are often arbitrary. If any century deserves to be treated as a cohesive unit, however, particularly from the medico-historical point of view, it is the eighteenth. In its course were laid the foundations for what we call modern or scientific medicine.

Although most medical historians have felt strongly about the contributions of this century, their evaluations of its characteristics differ greatly. Baas considered it "the most important century in the history of culture and particularly the sciences," a century of enlightenment that demonstrated its humanitarian idealism in medicine and the allied sciences as well as in politics and philosophy. Pagel shares this enthusiasm and adds that this period was one of emancipation from religious and political domination, when science could flourish unhampered by any external pressure. Fielding H. Garrison, the eminent American medical historian, summarized the era in terms which are somewhat less rapturous than those of his German colleagues. To him the eighteenth century produced much "tedious and platitudinous philosophizing," formalism dominated literature and music, and medicine abounded in "theorists and system-makers." Each of these characterizations has merit. Taken together they evoke a more accurate concept of the century.

Because of the great accretion of scientific knowledge in the period immediately preceding it, eighteenth-century medicine had achieved a complexity unknown earlier. The wisdom of antiquity was still part of the physician's intellectual background, and to it had been added the innovations generated during the seventeenth century. In fact, the full impact of many of the important discoveries of the earlier period was not felt for many decades. This was true also of the practical application of Harvey's discovery of the circulation of the blood in 1628 and of the revelations of the early microscopists. Sydenham's clinical wisdom, as has been stated, was adopted by few of his contemporaries immediately. In the course of the eighteenth century, however, all these achievements became part of medical thinking and furnished the basis for clinical practice and further scientific experimentation.

These developments were, of course, also reflected in the history of hysteria in which several streams of thought were amalgamated. Of these, the neurological phase became dominant. The literature on hysteria increased in bulk as well as in quaintness, and it will therefore be possible to discuss only a limited number of the most important writings on the subject.

Among these works is one that created a great deal of fame for its author and that was more important because of its widespread popularity than for its intellectual or scientific content. Its title, too, is interesting; *The English Malady or a Treatise of Nervous Diseases of All Kinds as Spleen, Vapours, Lowness of Spirits, Hypochondriacal, and Hysterical Distempers.*[1] Its author, George Cheyne, a Fellow of the Royal Society, had also published books on gout and scurvy, as well as *The Natural Method of Cureing the Diseases of the Body and the Disorders of the Mind, depending on the Body.*

The familiarity of Cheyne's *English Malady* demands its inclusion in a history of hysteria, even though its affectation and absurdities are such that it scarcely merits elaborate dis-

[1] George Cheyne, *The Natural Method* . . . (London: Strahan & Leake, 1773).

cussion. By the term "English Malady" Cheyne refers to hysteria, hypochondriasis, melancholy, and all similar states which lead to a morbid heaviness of the spirit. He considers this a specific trait of the English, for reasons which will be mentioned later.

Cheyne, like Burton, professed to suffer from the disease of which he wrote. In his preface he stated that the work had lain finished for several years, having been "intended as a Legacy and Dying-Speech, only to my Fellow-Sufferers." Its ante-mortem publication was due only to the urging of his "warmest Friends" who were perturbed by the late frequency and daily increase of wanton and uncommon suicides, which they attributed to the English Malady. In order to impress his readers all the more with the authenticity of his own malaise, he appended "the Author's own Case at large." But in contrast to those of Burton, Cheyne's references to his own distress seem inconsequential. His symptoms were almost entirely of a gastrointestinal nature, which in his opinion were indeed the predominant manifestations of hysteria and, actually, of most nervous diseases. His preoccupation with regimen as the key to physical and mental health, which brought forth his *Natural Method of Cureing Body and Mind*, also shapes his prophylaxis and therapy of the malady. A great part of his book is, therefore, devoted to the description of a proper regimen of life. The details of these rules and regulations need not be described here. What is of interest, however, are his notions of the remote causes of the malady; they have a striking modern ring. Cheyne was among the earliest of the medical writers to ascribe an increase of mental disease to the increased complexity of modern civilization. He mentioned political and economic factors and especially the deleterious effects of affluence and luxury. "The frequency of these nervous Distempers of late, especially among the Fair Sex," he attributed to those substances which were the result of the encroachment of foreign and esoteric customs and products upon English life, such as coffee, tea, chocolate, and snuff.

He also blamed lack of exercise and the preference for spectator rather than participatory sports because people wished to be entertained and forgot how to entertain themselves. And, "to convey them with the least Pain and Uneasi-

ness possible from Motion or slavish Labor . . . Coaches are
improv'd with Springs [and] Horses are taught to pace and
amble.[2]

Since our Wealth has increas'd, and our Navigation has been
extended, we have ransack'd all the Parts of the Globe to bring
together its whole Stock of Materials for *Riot, Luxury,* and to
provoke *Excess.* The Tables of the Rich and Great (and indeed of
all Ranks who can afford it) are furnish'd with Provisions of
Delicacy, Number, and Plenty, sufficient to provoke, and even
gorge, the most large and voluptuous Appetite. The whole *Controversy* among us, seems to lie in out-doing one another in such
Kinds of Profusion. *Invention* is rack'd, to furnish the Materials
of our Food the most Delicate and Savoury possible: Instead of
the plain *Simplicity* of leaving the Animals to range and feed in
their proper *Element,* with their natural Nourishment, they are
physick'd almost out of their Lives, and made as great *Epicures,*
as those that feed on them; and by *Stalling, Cramming, Bleeding,
Lameing, Sweating, Purging,* and *Thrusting* down such unnatural and high-season'd Foods into them, these Nervous Diseases
are produced in the *Animals* themselves, even before they are
admitted as Food to those who complain of such Disorders. Add
to all this, the *torturing* and *lingering* Way of taking away the
Lives of some of them, to make them more delicious: and the
Dressing of them, by culinary Torments while alive, for their
Purchaser's Table: All which must necessarily sharpen, impoison,
corrupt, and putrify their natural Juices and Substances.[3]

Cheyne argued that the practice of overeating and under-
exercise were compounded by "the present Custom of Living so much in great, populous, and over-grown Cities."[4] He
found that in London—"the greatest, most capacious, close
and populous city of the globe"[5]—nervous disorders were
most frequent and symptoms most bizarre. To make his explanation more topical, he blamed the climate and lack of sun-
shine as the specific reason for the English Malady. Cheyne's
further deliberations add little to the history of hysteria,
since most of his arguments and scientific facts are obviously
borrowed from other writers, including Sydenham and
Willis but without the clinical insight of the former or the
scientific spark of the latter.

[2] Cheyne, *op. cit.,* p. 52.   [4] *Ibid.,* p. 52.
[3] *Ibid.,* pp. 49–50.   [5] *Ibid.,* p. 54.

THE ADVENT OF NERVOUS DISORDERS

The qualities that Cheyne lacked were possessed to a super-
lative degree by Robert Whytt (1714–66). This Scottish
physician and physiologist was a product of the Edinburgh
School at the time when medical education and practice at
the university in that city were pre-eminent in Great Britain.
Whytt's education began under Alexander Monro I, founder
of the medical faculty of Edinburgh. He then went to London to study under Cheselden and Winslow and, finally, to
Leyden to become a pupil of Boerhaave, who had been
Monro's mentor and who was at the time the greatest clinician in all Europe. Whytt's keen intelligence and scientific
turn of mind, sharpened by this superb medical education,
assured him a brilliant career in medicine. He returned to
Edinburgh, where, at an early age, he became Professor of
Medicine. Later he was appointed Physician to the King and
elected President of the Royal College of Physicians. Whytt
manifested an interest in neurology very early and was soon
considered the leader in this newly founded and rapidly expanding science. He pioneered in experimental physiology
of the nervous system and reported numerous significant
observations, pertaining particularly to the mechanisms involved in reflex action.

Whytt, whose neurological investigations reached from
the laboratory to the bedside, published his clinical observations in a treatise *Nervous, Hypochondriac or Hysteric Disorders* in 1764.[6] Since the publication of Willis' book on
nervous diseases[7] almost one hundred years earlier, the term
"nervous" had become widely used, but apparently with
very hazy specifications of its meaning. Whytt's initial endeavor was to clarify this expression, particularly as it related to hysteria. In his preface he stated that the disorders
which were the subject of his book had variously been called
flatulent, spasmodic, hypochondriac, or hysteric and, most

[6] Robert Whytt, *Observations on the Nature, Causes, and Cure of
those Disorders which have been commonly called Nervous, Hypochondriac, or Hysteric: to which are prefixed some Remarks on the
Sympathy of the Nerves* (3d ed.; Edinburgh: J. Balfour, 1767).

[7] *Pathologiae cerebri et nervosi generis specimen* (Oxford, 1667).

recently, "nervous." Since this designation had usually been applied to many apparently varied and obscure symptoms, it had often been said, and is still being said today, "that physicians have bestowed the character of *nervous* on all those disorders whose nature and causes they were ignorant of."[8] Whytt conceived his task as that of erasing this inference and narrowing the use of the term to conditions actually resulting from disorders of the nervous system. He included in this category hypochondriasis and hysteria. He explained that "since, in almost every disease, the nerves suffer more or less, and there are very few disorders which may not, in a large sense, be called nervous, it might be thought that a treatise on nervous diseases should comprehend almost all the complaints to which the human body is liable."[9] But the disorders he spoke of were those which "in a peculiar sense deserve the name of nervous" because they were largely "owing to an uncommon delicacy or unnatural sensibility of the nerves, and are therefore observed chiefly to affect persons of such a constitution."

Whytt asserted that his reasoning on the nature and causes of nervous disorders avoided all uncertain hypotheses and therefore had no recourse to any "imaginary" flight, repercussion, dispersion, confusion, or explosion of the animal spirits; in fact, he clearly doubted the existence of these spirits. Although admittedly uncertain about the minute structure of the nerves, he nonetheless asserted that they were endowed with sensibility and that it was through nervous connections between all parts of the body that sensation, motion, and other functions were brought about.[10] Beyond these speculations Whytt did not dare go. He admitted that he was dealing with a *facultas incognita* because the interactions of the nerves could only be deduced and not confirmed. Yet he was sure that observation of natural phenomena would yield information. One such observation was "that the increased secretion of tears, occasioned by the passions of the mind proceed from them [the sensibility or sympathy of the nerves] and not from any compression of

---

[8] Whytt, *Observations on the Nature, Causes, and Cure . . .* , p. iii.

[9] *Ibid.*, p. iv.

[10] *Ibid.*, p. v.

the lachrymal glands by the neighbouring muscles as had been commonly imagined."[11]

In order to elaborate this idea further he spoke "Of the Structure, Use, and Sympathy of the Nerves":

> Nothing makes more sudden or more surprising changes in the body, than the several passions of the mind. These however, act solely by the mediation of the brain, and, in a strong light, shew its sympathy with every part of the system.
>
> Such is the constitution of the animal frame, that certain ideas or affections excited in the mind are always accompanied with corresponding motions or feelings in the body; and these are owing to some change made in the brain and nerves, by the mind or sentient principle (By the sentient principle, I understand the mind or soul in man, and that principle in brutes which resembles it.): but what that change is, or how it produces those effects, we know not: as little can we tell, why shame should raise a heat and redness in the face, while fear is attended with a paleness.
>
> But although, in these matters, we must confess our ignorance; yet, from what we certainly know of the action of the nerves, we can easily see, that a change in them may occasion many of those effects which are produced by the passions.[12]

These and many other effects of the emotions Whytt attributed to "the laws of union between the soul and the body." Subject to these laws are a great many bodily changes, such as increased heart beat from anger or rage, palpitation from terror, turning pale from anger or fear and diminution or increase of perspiration, unrelated to temperature, in response to emotional changes. To the last-mentioned he also related diarrhea due to fear, which "may be a consequence of obstructed perspiration, or of that debility and relaxation which grief is observed to bring on the alimentary canal."[13]

Whytt made a special study of all these involuntary changes and came to the astute conclusion that they were obviously designed to "free the body of something hurtful," thus to serve the "principle of preservation, without which we should often cherish, within our bodies such causes as would sooner or later end in our ruin." Frequently, the principle of self-preservation involved motions which increased rather than lessened the existing physical distress. But vomiting excited by inflammation of the liver, by pain and swell-

---

[11] *Ibid.*, p. vii.   [12] *Ibid.*, pp. 60–61.   [13] *Ibid.*, p. 65.

ing from a bad tooth, or by similar discomfort showed that
the mind acted neither perversely nor ignorantly but triggered these reactions in the best interest of the patient.

In some cases Whytt encountered "anomalous sympa-
thies" which he could not explain by the principle of self-
preservation and which he suggested might be "in consequence of the uncommon weakness or delicacy of a particular organ . . . although the other parts of the body are not
affected."[14] They might also stem from a weak or unnatural
constitution of the nerves. Thus he explained the phenomena
observed in his hysterical and hypochondriacal patients.

Whytt introduced this subject by quoting the observations of the "sagacious Sydenham" to the effect "that the
shapes of *proteus,* or the colours of the *chameleon,* are not
more numerous and inconstant, than the varieties of the hypochondriac and hysteric disease."[15] He also defended
Sydenham's thesis of the identity of both ailments, although
he hastened to add that in women hysterical symptoms occur
more frequently and are more sudden and violent than are
the hypochondriacal in men.[16] He repeated an earlier argument of Willis, as though it were his own, that women who
are regular in their menses and have no uterine ailment do
not always escape hysteria, while others who suffer from
tumors and prolapse are often not affected. Whytt decided
to describe only the most "common and remarkable" of the
endless number of symptoms, but their listing alone occupies
four pages of his book.

When he came to the causes of hysteria, Whytt introduced factors decidedly at variance with his lucid, perceptive statements regarding the influence of the mind. He
listed successively, wind, a tough phlegm, worms in the
stomach or bowels, improper quantity or quality of food,
and scirrhous obstructions of the viscera or the lower abdomen.

Only the final point relates directly to his earlier reasoning: "Thus doleful or moving stories, horrible or unexpected
sights, great grief, anger, terror, and other passions, fre-

[14] *Ibid.,* pp. 78–79.   [15] *Ibid.,* p. 95.

[16] *Ibid.,* p. 102. Among his many contemporaries who persisted in
considering them separate diseases was the famous Friedrich Hoffmann,
System. med., III, chap. 5, 4.

quently occasion the most sudden and violent nervous symptoms. The strong impressions made in such cases on the brain and nerves often throw the person into hysteric fits, either of the convulsive or fainting kind."[17] As illustrations, Whytt wrote that Francis Bacon was said to have fainted whenever he saw an eclipse of the sun and that an unnamed lady who looked through a telescope at the comet of 1681 was "struck with such terror that she died soon afterwards."[18] Here he also quoted Baglivi's story about the young man of Dalmatia who saw a person in an epileptic fit and was then affected in the same manner.

Unlike Baglivi, who considered himself unqualified to investigate these matters, Whytt had definite ideas about the reaction of emotions upon the body. As examples he cited blushing in shame, increased salivation at the sight of food, discharge of tears in sadness, and many other physical reactions to emotions, as proof of the existence of an interaction between various parts of the body by way of the nerves. He believed other examples demonstrated an even more amazing interaction, which he called "sympathy," between the nervous systems of different persons, that various motions and even symptoms of diseases were often transferred from one to another. The organ receptive to these impressions and responsible for the transmission of this imitative urge to the nerves was the mind or *sensorium commune*. Having reached this point of deduction, however, Whytt, like Baglivi before him, was forced to admit that it was entirely unknown "in what manner the passions, or the morbid matter of the nervous diseases change the state of the brain or *common sensorium*, and occasion such disorders."[19]

As mentioned above, Whytt's list of hysterical symptoms was an extraordinarily long one.[20] It included those manifestations which had been considered typical throughout the ages, such as paroxysms, sudden sensation of cold, trembling and shivering, and feelings of oppression and suffocation. He included physical pains which resembled those of rheumatism and which suddenly migrated from one location to

[17] Whytt, *op. cit.*, pp. 206–7.   [18] *Ibid.*, p. 214.   [19] *Ibid.*, p. 307.

[20] *Ibid.*, chap. vi, entitled "Observations on Some of the most remarkable Symptoms of the Nervous, hypochondriac, and Hysteric Kind," pp. 218–320.

another; he also mentioned fleeting pains in the head arising from the "nerves of the *pericranium*," as well as protracted headaches. As many of his predecessors, he spoke of hysterical fainting, catalepsy, and wind in the stomach. Whytt further listed "nervous or spasmodic asthma," "nervous cough," "giddiness," "dimness of sight," and "low spirits" as frequent hysterical manifestations. Among the symptoms that he seems to have gathered from his own practice, as well as from contemporary literature, he described a great craving for food, which he called *fames canina* (canine voraciousness).[21] He had observed that during this state the patients were quite free from other complaints; but as soon as their voraciousness abated and their appetites became normal, their usual ailments reappeared.

Of particular interest to Whytt was the periodicity of some forms of hysterical afflictions. Like most of the physicians since his day, Whytt wondered why certain patients should suffer from migraines which returned at regular intervals. He knew that intermittent fevers recurred at regular periods, and he had also seen epileptic patients have fits once or twice ever day or once in two days at almost precisely the same hour. What was it that accounted for such regularity in hysterical headaches? Was it a mechanical process that recurred at a given time? Whytt had come to realize that the answer to this question was beyond his power, and he took comfort in the "obscurity of nature" which was so frequently encountered and never yielded satisfactory explanations. Rather than worry about the unanswerable, he was resigned to his limitations and admitted that "in both natural philosophy and medicine, it is often sufficient, at least for the purposes of life, to know the certainty of some particular phenomena, altho' we cannot account for them."[22]

Whytt believed that as a rule hysterical disorders were less dangerous than they were troublesome and lasting. Nevertheless, he made every attempt to find the right treatment for each patient, thus following the precepts of both Sydenham and Baglivi. He realized that, although certain aspects of the disease were common to all sufferers, there was a specific history in each separate case and treatment therefore

21 *Ibid.*, p. 234.   22 *Ibid.*, p. 301.

had to be highly individualized to meet specific needs. He sagely warned that patients should not expect their physicians to perform miracles and instructed his colleagues "that it is generally in the power of medicine to relieve, it is frequently beyond the power of art to eradicate the disorders we now treat of, and therefore it may often be of use to intimate this to our patients."[23] He further insisted that patients share with their physicians the responsibility for the success of treatment, but without their perseverance in taking medicines, in following a diet, and in taking their exercise, they simply could not expect significant or lasting benefit.

Many of Whytt's prescriptions were those listed by Sydenham, including vegetable bitters, mineral waters, quinine, steel filings, cool and dry air, light and sparing food, small amounts of wine, and active or passive exercise. The thoughts of both Sydenham and Baglivi are also apparent in some other aspects of Whytt's regimen, which included amusement: "The mind ought to be diverted and kept as easy as possible; since nothing hurts more the nervous system, and particularly the concoctive powers [digestion], than fear, grief and anxiety."[24]

He prescribed opium very frequently to palliate symptoms—for its tranquillizing effect on the emotional state rather than for its direct pain-relieving action—because such drugs "weaken, during the time of their operation the sentient power of the nerves."[25] Familiarity with the action of this drug is revealed by his warning that while occasionally it has an exhilarating effect, it often acts as a depressant and should not be given to "low-spirited people." He had encountered some patients who could not tolerate opium at first; but he was so firmly convinced of its beneficial effect that he started these patients with small doses, increasing them gradually in order to build up the patient's tolerance. Following the practice of his day, Whytt used opiates in large doses, carrying his therapy to the point of inducing chronic constipation, which, in turn, he attempted to overcome by a variety of medicines. Since they were such extraordinarily keen observers, it is strange that neither

[23] *Ibid.*, p. 324.   [24] *Ibid.*, p. 349.   [25] *Ibid.*, pp. 351-52.

Sydenham nor Whytt nor any of the later physicians who
followed their example ever revealed any awareness of the
dangers of addiction inherent in opium therapy.

THE NOSOLOGICAL CONFUSION

Whytt's recognition of hysteria as a disorder of the nervous
system was shared by his Continental colleagues, some of
whom had embarked on the endless and initially fruitless
task of nosology. François Boissier de Sauvages (1706–67),
one of the most influential among those who attempted to
classify diseases according to their clinical manifestations, included hysteria, perforce, in this orderly arrangement. His
Nosologia methodica[26] was the culmination of a lifelong
study that attempted to do for diseases what the Linné had
done for plants.[27]

Like many of his English colleagues, Sauvages classified
hysteria among the diseases of nervous origin and stated that
the hysterical passion, or the vapors, was characterized by
general or localized convulsions and by exaggerated fears of
death or chronic invalidism. Hysteria, or the vapors, he said,
constituted the majority of all chronic diseases among
women, and men too were subject to it. The immediate
cause of the disease could be an intense love affair, or a life
frantically devoted to pleasure, either of which carried with
it exaggerated sensitivity and irritability and an intolerance
of minor inconveniences. To this point, Sauvages' definition
closely resembled that of his British colleagues. He differed,
however, in one important aspect in saying that men were
subject to hysterical affliction: he did not equate hysteria
with hypochondria. Rather, he suggested, somewhat darkly,
that "the hypochondriacs are rarely subject to hysterical
affections." Consequently, he classified hysteria separately
from hypochondria, a tradition which became quite general
with subsequent nosologists. He introduced new confusion

26 François Boissier de Sauvages, *Nosologia methodica sistens morborum classes* (Amsterdam, 1763).

27 For an excellent discussion of this "Urge to Classify" see chap. ii,
pp. 9–34, and "Appendix," in Karl Menninger, *The Vital Balance* (New
York: Viking Press, 1963).

however, by describing seven different forms of hysteria, such as verminous, chlorotic, menorrhagic, febrile, certain visceral forms, and *hysteria libidinosa*. Since reference to voluntary or involuntary sexual abstinence as a cause of hysteria had almost completely disappeared from the scientific literature of the seventeenth and eighteenth centuries, this category of libidinous hysteria is an interesting revival of the Galenic concept.

In this connection mention must be made of the great Dutch physician, Gerhard Van Swieten (1700–1772), who, at the invitation of Empress Maria Theresa of Austria, left Holland for Vienna where he developed the famous "old" Vienna School of Medicine. He was a disciple and protégé of Hermann Boerhaave (1668–1738), undoubtedly the most distinguished physician of Europe in the eighteenth century. To Boerhaave belongs the credit of having introduced clinical teaching in medicine, and his efforts are responsible for the glory attained by the medical faculty of the University of Leyden. Among his pupils are most of the distinguished figures in medicine and surgery of his time, and his influence was thus extended to all of the Western world.

Boerhaave was mighty in achievement, but his literary output was scant. What he did write was so pithy that each word was charged with meaning. Van Swieten did for his master what Galen did for Hippocrates, expanding the epigrammatic aphorisms into the *Commentaries*, which filled eighteen volumes.[28] Hysteria was one of the many subjects commented upon.[29]

Van Swieten was apparently unwilling to relinquish either the uterine or the nervous cause of hysteria and arrived at the solution that, depending on the circumstances, perhaps both could cause it. He coined the term "spasmodic anxiety" to denote the nervous constitutions in which the slightest stimuli might give rise to major convulsions in those who were naturally predisposed to hysteria. As to the uterus as a

[28] Gerhard Van Swieten, *Commentarii in Aphorismos Boerhaavii* (Leyden, 1745).

[29] Boerhaave refers to hysteria only as a predisposing cause of epilepsy and related to it. See Gerhard Van Swieten, *The Commentaries upon the Aphorisms of Hermann Boerhaave* (2d Eng. ed.; London: Horsfield & Longman, 1765), X, Sec. 1075, 351.

proximate cause he wrote, "It cannot be denied, that corrupted humours, collected in the cavity of the uterus, or lodged in the vessels dispersed through its substance, by erroding or irritating this nervous part, may produce the worst complaints."[30] On the other hand, he also offered his own variation of the theory of nervous origin. He explained that there were no signs or symptoms of uterine disease, "that such extraordinary motions are excited in the nerves dispersed through the abdominal viscera, which afterwards disturb the whole brain, and produce the strongest convulsions."[31]

Clearly, Van Swieten's views on hysteria, unoriginal and vague as they were, would hardly merit inclusion in this history were it not for the prominence of the author and the attention given to his writings by his contemporaries and successors. More worthy of comment are those writings of a relatively obscure French physician, Joseph Raulin (1708–84), whose treatise on vaporous affections deals with hysteria in a highly original manner.[32]

THE VAPORS

The term "vapors," we must remember, originally denoted emanations from the disordered uterus which, floating upwards, produced the various somatic manifestations of hysteria. In later usage "the vapors" became equated with hysteria, and in Raulin's time this term was being used with increasing frequency as a euphemism. Raulin, too, employed the terms "vapors" or "vaporous affections" to designate hysterical disorders, but he made it clear that vapors in their original sense could not cause hysteria. Inasmuch as this exonerated the uterus as an essential cause of such affections, the malady could conceivably also occur in men. This is not to say that Raulin altogether discarded all the traditional beliefs in obstructions or suppressions of the menses. He considered them one of the causes of the hypothetical nerv-

[30] *Ibid.*, p. 374.   [31] *Ibid.*, p. 375.

[32] Joseph Raulin, *Traité des affections vaporeuses d'un sexe avec l'exposition de leurs symptômes, de leurs différentes causes et la méthode de les guérir* (Paris, 1758).

ous perturbation: "One understands by the term 'affliction of vapors' such states as general convulsive movements, or of local spasms or convulsions which involve one or more viscera, occurring either simultaneously or successively, displaying various symptoms, depending upon the sensibility and irritability (of the mechanical power) of the affected parts; and also upon the quantity and quality of their causes."[33]

As to manifestations, Raulin described ringing in the ears which is among the prodromata of the hysterical crises; he enumerated the syncopes, the cough, the globus, the urinary retention, the paralyses, and the oedemata. Like Baglivi and Whytt, he also noted the contagiousness of hysteria and said, "This illness in which the women invent, exaggerate, and repeat all the different absurdities of which a disordered imagination is capable, is sometimes epidemic and contagious."[34] In connection with a hysterical bout of hiccups, Raulin told of a curious epidemic. "A girl of twenty-three years . . . was attacked by a violent and continuous hiccup. She was admitted to the Hôtel Dieu and was placed in a room with four other women who suffered from various different diseases. Three days later, they were all attacked by hiccup and convulsions of such violence that it took four men in order to hold just one of them. The hiccup and the convulsions had come upon all four at the same time."[35]

He also studied hysteria of the male extensively. "Every day we see 'vaporous men' with the sensation of a globus. These are the men who are subject to all other symptoms of the vapors. Men are by no means exempt from the effects of the imagination. Bartolin reported the observation of one who suffered a colic at the same time that his wife began to suffer labor pains."[36] However, while Raulin considered vapors a disease of both sexes, like all previous observers he believed it to occur predominantly in women. He thought that it was an essentially feminine sensitivity that responded to the slightest stimulus, that gave rise to an infinite number

[33] *Ibid.*

[34] *Ibid.*, "Discours préliminaire," p. 20.

[35] *Ibid.*, p. 24.

[36] The Bartolin referred to here is Danish anatomist Thomas Bartholin (1616–80).

of vaporous symptoms, and that occurred in women who were ruled by violent passions and who dwelt upon fear, sadness, and surprise.

Despite Raulin's observation of the suggestibility of hysterics, Baglivi's realization of the impact of emotions on physical health, Sydenham's assumption of the role of animal spirits, and Willis' and Whytt's relation of hysteria to the nervous system, the basic concept of hysteria remained unchanged for two thousand years. The essence of this concept was that hysteria was a physical disorder. It is interesting that the man who introduced the word "neurosis," and first classified hysteria among the neuroses, Cullen, clung even more firmly to the somatic etiology.

William Cullen (1712–90) was one of the most important physicians of his time in Great Britain. Although a contemporary of Whytt, he survived him by twenty-five years; thus, his influence extended almost two generations beyond that of his compatriot. A product of the Edinburgh School, a pupil of Alexander Monro I and perhaps even a fellow student of Whytt, Cullen became the most outstanding of the British clinical teachers of the eighteenth century. He was instrumental in founding the medical school of Glasgow (1744) and held chairs of medicine and chemistry at both Glasgow and Edinburgh. He was the first to give clinical lectures in medicine in Great Britain and also among the first to address his audiences in the vernacular instead of in Latin.

Cullen's lectures were published in a book entitled *First Lines of the Practice of Physic* which appeared in numerous editions throughout his lifetime and was frequently republished after his death. This book presents the concept of medicine which he had evolved and which he considered new and revolutionary. He rejected the theories of Stahl, which imbued the "rational soul" with the powers to prevent disease or bring about cure. Cullen equated this soul with what had earlier been identified as nature and he violently denied the healing powers of nature. He thus attacked Hippocrates himself and the large body of medical thought which was seeking a return to Hippocratic medicine. Cullen decried expectant therapy and advocated aggressive treatment by bleeding, purging, and vomiting.

Although Cullen is identified with the term "neurology," there is a great disparity between his and the modern scientific interpretation of this word; his conception of the nervous system bore little relation to that of the present. In short, he saw all of life as a function of nervous energy and disease as a nervous disorder. What these terms actually signified was never made clear. As did other physicians of his time, he too attempted to establish a classification of diseases. By his definition all diseases had to be confined to disorders of the nervous system, and since only two deviations of this system could be envisaged—namely, excessive or diminished tonus—the limits for nosological arrangement of all the ailments of body and mind were extremely narrow. Within this tight complex he recognized only four principal categories of diseases: fevers, cachexias, local disorders, and "neuroses," which also comprised hysteria. As already mentioned, he held that all disease was manifested by deviations in tone, which represented malfunction of the nervous system. Yet, somehow a category of disorders characterized by spasm or atony was segregated from the rest and included under the term "neurosis." It was for this reason, and not because of its psychic concomitants, that hysteria, obviously a spastic or convulsive disorder, fell under the heading of "neurosis."

Cullen's neurological and neuropathological contributions stopped with his nosological arrangement, at least so far as hysteria was concerned. Indeed, this man who thought himself to be a ruthless innovator, and whom the world regarded as the creator of a totally new system of medicine, contributed not a single new idea to the etiology and therapy of hysterical disorders. Yet, out of a welter of earlier and rarely acknowledged sources, he created the impression of an entirely new concept, convincing enough to gain important adherents all over Europe and even in America.

Like most authors on the subject, Cullen introduced his discussion of hysteria with a description of the general character of the illness.[37] He drew the traditional picture of a paroxysmal attack preceded by the voiding of large quantities of limpid urine and accompanied by a globus, loss of consciousness, general muscular contraction, including the anal sphincter, and retention of urine. These paroxysms alternated with bouts of laughter and crying, "false imagination," and some degree of delirium. Ostensibly from his own observations, he found the disease to be more frequent in women than in men, especially from the age of puberty to thirty-five years. He saw it related to the menstrual period, to young widowhood, and to passions of the sensitive mind. "It occurs especially in those females who are liable to the Nymphomania; and the Nosologists have properly enough marked one of the varieties of the disease by the title of *Hysteria Libidinosa*."[38] Clearly, this refers to Sauvages whose *Nosologie* furnished the word and the concept for *hysteria libidinosa*. It is probably also from this source that Cullen found support for his notion that hysteria and hypochondria were totally different diseases. It is important to recognize that the meaning of Cullen's term "neurosis" bore little relation to its modern connotation.[39] Indeed, it is difficult to follow Cullen's thought about a definition of neurosis.

THE UTERINE THEORY RETURNS

As to the pathogenesis of hysteria, Cullen was lost in a maze of confusion. For instance, as to the etiology, he thought it would "be obvious that its paroxysm began in the alimentary canal, which is afterwards communicated to the brain, and to a great part of the nervous system," and then he went on to correlate it with menstrual difficulties "and with the diseases that depend on the state of the genitals." He concluded by agreeing with the time-worn deduction

[37] William Cullen, "Of the Hysteria or the Hysteric Disease" in *First Lines of the Practice of Physic*, with notes by John Rotheram (Edinburgh: Bell, Bradfute, etc., 1796), pp. 98–115.

[38] *Ibid.*, p. 104.

[39] See Walther Riese, "The History of the Term and Conception of Neurosis," in "Pre-Freudian Origins of Psychoanalysis" in *Science and Psychoanalysis* (New York: Grune & Stratton, 1958), pp. 66 ff.

"that the physicians have at all times judged rightly in considering this disease as an affection of the uterus and other parts of the genital system." The only innovation is that for the first time the ovaries were included in the picture of hysteria and were mentioned as being particularly affected in this disease. Cullen made no pretense of explaining by what means genital disturbances affected the brain and caused the hysterical convulsions. His study of epilepsy had convinced him that this disease was caused by a dilation of the blood vessels in the brain. This led him to suggest that hysteria might result from a turgescence of blood in the genital system. Having established this arbitrary analogy, he concluded that the indications of treatment were the same in both diseases.

It is clear that Cullen's work contributed nothing to the development of understanding or treatment of hysteria; rather, because of his great international influence, it had a retarding effect. Among those influenced by Cullen's teachings, despite the vacuity of their content, was his most ardent disciple, the great American physician, Benjamin Rush (1745–1813), who was the first in his country to write on the subject of psychiatry.[40] But it must be said for Rush that his views on hysteria were tempered by his own observations, which pointed strongly towards psychosomatic implications. Rush wrote a non-medical essay in 1788 on the influence of the Revolutionary War upon the minds of the people. He suggested that the impact of this struggle variously affected the human body through the medium of the mind. He found that "many persons of infirm and delicate habits, were restored to perfect health, by the change of place or occupation, to which the war exposed them. This was the case in a more especial manner with hysterical women, who were much interested in the successful issue of the contest." He cited similar observations made by his teacher, "the same effects of a civil war upon the hysteria, were observed by Doctor Cullen in Scotland, in the years 1745 and 1746." Rush went on to state: "It may perhaps help

[40] Benjamin Rush, *An Inquiry into the Influence of Physical Causes upon the Mental Faculty* (Philadelphia, 1786); *Medical Inquiries and Observations upon the Diseases of the Mind* (Philadelphia: John Grigg, 1812).

to extend our ideas of the influence of the passions upon diseases, to add, that when either love, jealousy, grief, or even devotion, wholly engross the female mind, they seldom fail, in like manner, to cure or to suspend hysterical complaints."[41]

Rush's reflections on hysteria also suggested that this disease had slowly become a token of social distinction. This observation may have grown out of the assumptions by such men as Rabelais, Robert Burton, and, later, Joseph Lieutaud (1703–80) that hysteria befalls only the well-born and the idle. Servants and laboring persons had neither the time nor the tolerant environment to indulge in hysterical complaints or paroxysms. Rush was a deepdyed democrat, a signer of the Declaration of Independence, and a persistent fighter for social equality. He was sensitive to a social change in the incidence of hysteria, at least in America, which he attributed to the extension of luxurious habits to the common people, stating, "The HYSTERIC and HYPOCHONDRIAC DISORDERS, once peculiar to the chambers of the great are now to be found in our kitchens and workshops. All these diseases have been produced by our having deserted the simple diet, and manners, of our ancestors."[42]

The static quality of British thinking and writing on hysteria was suddenly illuminated by a brilliant and imaginative Frenchman, who was as revolutionary as the period in which he appeared. Philippe Pinel who did for psychiatry what Harvey did for the science of physiology is, of course, a celebrated figure in the annals of psychiatry. Strangely, however, he has been overlooked by those who have concerned themselves with the history of hysteria.

The revolutionary spirit of the late eighteenth century, marked successively by the American and the French revolutions, extended far beyond those countries and the direct political consequences: it touched upon all classes of society and all walks of life; it affected even the inmates of the

41 Rush, "An Account of the Influence . . . of the American Revolution upon the Human Body," in *Medical Inquiries and Observations* (3d ed.; Philadelphia: Hopkins and Earle, 1809), I, 238.

42 Rush, "An Inquiry into the Natural History of Medicine among the Indians of North America and a Comparative View of their Diseases and Remedies with those of Civilized Nations" (1774) in *Medical Inquiries and Observations*, p. 157.

PLATE VIII. Physician examining lovesick girl. (After a painting by Gerard Dou [1613–75].)

PLATE X. Lithograph of J.-M. Charcot (1825–93) showing a hysterical patient in his famous clinic at the Salpêtrière.

insane asylums. Throughout western Europe, England, and the newly constituted United States individual physicians were motivated by the ambient concepts of equality and the brotherhood of man to alter their ideas about those "deprived of reason." But it was in Paris, as a direct consequence of the French Revolution, that the most dramatic steps were taken—namely, breaking the chains that had traditionally bound insane persons and restoring them to the status of human beings. The name of Philippe Pinel is indelibly associated with this event because, although he was neither the only one nor the first to seek humane treatment for mental patients, he was doubtless the most vocal and the most effective.

In a world that considered insanity incurable and lunatics devoid of sensibilities, Pinel's thoughts on mental disease and his therapeutic recommendations blazed a new trail in medical thinking. Out of his efforts and example psychiatry emerged as a new discipline in medicine. For this leadership Pinel's name is widely known; somewhat less familiar are the man and the contents of his writings, revolutionizing as they were, upon the contemporary scene.

Pinel was born in 1745, the son and grandson of physicians. His mother died at an early age, a misfortune that probably had a great deal to do with shaping his personality and his later professional interests and accomplishments. He was diffident and withdrawn and early developed an interest in the humanities, especially in philosophy. He never lost his love for Virgil and the thinkers of his own era, Locke, Condillac, Voltaire, and Rousseau. Although he was later strongly attracted by the sciences and chose medicine as his vocation, he found solace in scholarly literature. After he received his medical degree in 1773 at the age of twenty-eight, Pinel, not yet ready to embark on his definitive career, turned once more to a scholarly life in the humanities, first in Montpellier and later in Paris. After further educational experience, he entered into the practice of medicine in Paris and soon found his attention drawn to diseases of the mind. This interest was at first personal, aroused by compassion for a friend who had become insane. Pinel visited him daily and made detailed records of his illness. At the same time he read all available books on the subject of mental diseases, which thus became his principal interest for the rest of his life. In the course of this development he joined the medical staff of a Petite Maison, a private psychiatric institution where he continued his investigations and published his earliest observations on disorders of the mind.

These publications gained him considerable reputation and led eventually, in 1793, to an appointment to the staff of the Bicêtre, the large public mental hospital for men. A year later he was put in charge of the Salpêtrière, an equally large institution for female patients. The number of patients in each hospital was at least eight hundred. The Salpêtrière won renewed fame a century later under the leadership of Charcot. At about the same time Pinel also received a professional appointment at the University of Paris. Pinel held these eminent positions with distinction for many years; up to his death at the age of eight-one he was still actively at work at the Salpêtrière.

Pinel published his two major works, the *Nosographie Philosophique* (1798) and the *Traité médico-philosophique sur la manie* (1801), early in his tenure at the Salpêtrière. Both treatises were frequently revised and expanded; they afford the clearest insight into his psychiatric reforms and practices at the two major mental institutions in Paris. His prolonged and intensive involvement in the humanities fostered in Pinel a felicitous literary style which characterized all his writings.

The treatise on mania eventually appeared as an inclusive textbook of psychiatry under the title *Traité médico-philosophique sur l'aliénation mentale* (1809). This treatise opens with "a general plan of work," which acquaints the reader with the earliest problems confronting Pinel upon his accession to hospital duty at the Bicêtre.

On my entrance upon the duties of that hospital, every thing presented to me the appearance of chaos and confusion. Some of my unfortunate patients laboured under the horrors of a most gloomy and desponding melancholy. Others were furious, and subject to the influence of a perpetual delirium. Some appeared to possess a correct judgement upon most subjects, but were occasionally agitated by violent sallies of maniacal fury; while those of another class were sunk into a state of stupid ideotism [*sic*] and imbecility. Symptoms so different, and all comprehended under the general title of insanity, required, on my part,

much study and discrimination; and to secure order in the establishment and success to the practice, I determined upon adopt-
ing such a variety of measures, both as to discipline and treatment,
as my patients required, and my limited opportunity permitted.[43]

Pinel embarked upon his study of mental disease with the
same method of investigation that was then practiced in all
the other departments of natural science—namely, "to notice
successively every fact, without any other object than that
of collecting materials for future use; and to endeavor, as far
as possible, to divest myself of the influence, both of my
own prepossessions and the authority of others." He personally interviewed each of the patients to learn their presenting symptoms and to observe "their characteristic peculiarities." Detailed records were instituted for each of the
old patients and all successive admissions. His meticulous
case histories reveal that many patients, although they had
been institutionalized for prolonged periods, had hardly ever
been seen by a physician, and never before had been the
object of anyone's interest.

The therapeutic measures introduced by Pinel were, by
modern criteria, simple enough; by the standards of his day,
they were startlingly novel. No less startling were their
effects. The chronic inmates responded so well that they
could be released to their homes, albeit they had periodic
recurrences. These favorable results led him to entirely new
conclusions about the origin and curability of mental disease: "Few subjects in medicine are so intimately connected
with the history and philosophy of the human mind as insanity. There are still fewer, where there are so many errors
to rectify, and so many prejudices to remove. Derangement
of the understanding is generally considered as an effect of
an organic lesion of the brain, consequently as incurable; a
supposition that is, in a great number of instances, contrary
to anatomical fact."[44]

These ideas were revolutionary indeed, for at that time
mental disturbances were considered incurable because, as
Pinel truly said, they were uniformly accepted as the result
of organic brain disease. His fervent belief in the curability

[43] Philippe Pinel, *A Treatise on Insanity* (Sheffield, England, 1806),
p. 46.
[44] *Ibid.*, p. 49.

of most mental diseases had the most important practical consequences. It demanded complete revision of the institutional care of the insane, which had until then been predicated on the futility of therapy in this category of human diseases. Physical labor for convalescent patients was initiated in the hospitals under his directorship. He arranged for a variety of occupations by inducing Paris manufacturers to supply patients with work "which fixed their attention and allured them to exertion by the prospect of a trifling gain." He also obtained from the government a piece of land adjacent to the hospital which was converted into a farm where the patients could engage in healthy outdoor labor. This scheme was highly recommended for all similar institutions, because "the fatigues of the day prepare the labourers for sleep and repose during the night. Hence it happens, that those whose condition does not place them above the necessity of submission to toil and labour, are almost always cured; whilst the grandee, who would think himself degraded by any exercises of this description, is generally incurable."[45]

Pinel was convinced that his patients' chances for recovery would be greatly enhanced if they could be segregated according to the nature of their mental illness. In order to bring this about, he had to classify mental diseases, which, of course, he accomplished as mentioned in the *Nosographie*. Initially, his nosographical efforts encompassed all diseases of the body and the mind then known and divided them into five classes: fevers, inflammations, hemorrhagic diseases, neuroses, and organic lesions.

This classification bears a superficial resemblance to that of Cullen, to whose work Pinel referred on several occasions, particularly concerning the word "neurosis." But the resemblance ends with the use of a similar terminology. To Cullen, neuroses were distinctly physical afflictions; to Pinel, they were part of what he called mental alienation. As such they could be "moral" or "physical" in nature and occasionally a concatenation of both. If we translate "moral" and "physical" into their more modern counterparts, "functional" and "organic," we can appreciate the enormous advance

[45] *Ibid.*, p. 64.

of Pinel's thinking over Cullen's. Pinel's concept of moral causes of insanity fitted in with his frequent inability to find physical changes in patients' brains at autopsy. This concept also validated "moral treatment," similar to modern psychotherapy, which consisted of regular, lengthy conversations with the patient that probed into the nature and origin of his disturbance.

The neuroses, Pinel's fourth class of diseases, were vested with a connotation that is close to our present understanding of the word, since it included disorders of the nerves as well as psychoneurotic disturbances. Hysteria was naturally included among the neuroses and was discussed under the heading "Genital Neuroses of Women." This suggested that Pinel recognized hysterical conditions in women only, but he described similar conditions in men under different headings. Pinel himself indicated a parallelism when he said that "the genital neuroses of the woman are as many and varied as those of the man."[46] Here he refers to sterility and frigidity as well as to nymphomania or *furor uterinus,* which is "for the woman what satyriasis is for the man."[47]

NYMPHOMANIA OR FUROR UTERINUS

Pinel believed that nymphomania and other genital neuroses of women generally displayed their first symptoms at the time of puberty. "Nymphomania," he said, "is most frequently caused by lascivious reading, by severe restraint and secluded life, by the habit of masturbation, an extreme sensitivity of the uterus, and a skin eruption upon the genital organs."[48] The symptoms are described as follows:

In the beginning the imagination is constantly obsessed by lascivious or obscure matters. The patient is in a state of sadness and restlessness; she becomes taciturn, seeks solitude, loses sleep and appetite, conducts a private battle between sentiments of modesty and the impulse towards frantic desires. In the second

---

[46] Philippe Pinel, *Nosographie philosophique ou la méthode de l'analyse appliquée à la médecine* (5th ed.; Paris: J. A. Brosson, 1813), III, 285.

[47] *Ibid.,* p. 285.   [48] *Ibid.,* p. 287.

phase she abandons herself to her voluptuous leanings, she stops
fighting them, she forgets all rules of modesty and propriety; her
looks and actions are provocative, her gestures indecent; she
begins to solicit at the moment of the approach of the first man,
she makes efforts to throw herself in his arms. She threatens and
flares up if the man tries to resist her. In the third phase her
mental alienation is complete, her obscenity disgusting, her fury
blind with the only desire to wound and to revile. She is on fire
though without fever, and finally, she manifests all the different
symptoms of a violently maniacal condition.[49]

He further illuminated this graphic description by two
case histories. The first concerned a young woman whose
marriage to an impotent husband triggered the most violent
hysterical reactions. The second, described in even greater
detail, was a report of a young girl only just past the period
of puberty who had secretly become involved in an amorous
liaison with a young man of lowly origin. She was discovered and separated from her lover and reacted at first by
experiencing painful dreams. A few days later she began to
display obscene and lewd behavior. Eventually, it became
difficult to restrain her from walking about in the nude,
from assuming lascivious poses, and from inviting sexual in-
timacies from any man who came near her. She scarcely
slept and became increasingly deranged. Pinel considered
these two cases typical and stated that "many examples of
this affection can be found in the mental hospitals for
women."[50]

When he came to a discussion of hysteria, Pinel stated
that in spite of the mass of material written about it, it was
still "an example of obscurity and confusion" because it had
always been studied in its variety of complications and in
relation to analogous diseases without first examining its own
specific character. He criticized Cullen, Sauvages, and even
Whytt for this lack of definition. Because of the multiplicity
of opinions, Pinel considered it necessary to analyze the
characteristic symptoms of the illness in its pure form before
passing on to the various complications. This he found best
illustrated by one specific case history of a hysterical girl
who had been under his care for a long time. It runs as
follows:

[49] *Ibid.*, pp. 287–88.   [50] *Ibid.*, p. 287.

A young girl of dark complexion and a strong and healthy constitution fell at the age of 17 years without any known cause into a kind of mania, or rather into a succession of extravagant acts which consisted in her talking to herself, jumping about, taking off her clothes and throwing them into the fire. This state continued for five months and disappeared during the summer as a result of various distractions and frequent journeys into the country. Then came her first menstrual period. Shortly afterwards, however, a retention of the menses set in. After the third month she again manifested hysterical outbursts which recurred every month, and displayed the following symptoms: at first, disgust with her daily life, frequent tears without cause, somber and taciturn behaviour; shortly afterwards she lost the ability to speak, her face became discolored, there was periodic tightening of her throat, feelings of strangulation, congestion of the salivary glands; and afterwards, abundant salivation, as though mercury had been used, inability to open her mouth, because of muscle spasm; tetanus-like rigidity of the rest of the body, pulse scarcely perceptible, respiration slow but regular, bowels constipated and the urine limpid.

These symptoms persisted for three or four days during which there was complete abstinence from food; afterwards a voracious appetite set in and all the natural functions were reestablished. This calm continued for seven to eight days, even occasionally for ten-twelve days, but afterwards the attacks renewed themselves with the same violence.[51]

In a footnote Pinel added that during these attacks the patient's ability to hear, far from being abolished or suspended, appeared to gain a new degree of sharpness. An excellent violinist was called to play for the patient during several of her attacks and, although she seemed insensitive to the charms of the music, she was actually so much affected by it that after having regained the complete use of her senses she avowed the music had thrown her into a kind of voluptuous rapture.

Pinel continued to observe the patient. Relating her disturbance to her irregular menstruation, he instituted a number of treatments which succeeded in bringing about the lagging *"évacuation sexuelle."* All the physical symptoms then ceased but the apathy, depression, and anorexia persisted. Eventually he returned the patient to the country for fresh air and bodily exercise and her regular menstruation returned. Thus she regained her physical and mental health,

[51] *Ibid.*, pp. 290 ff.

but Pinel, "in order to forestall any relapse," emphatically "insisted upon the necessity of a marriage before the onset of winter."

This lengthy report is important as it represents Pinel's conception of hysteria. The somatic manifestations and their physical concomitants in no way minimized his belief in the moral or psychogenic basis of the disease. Involved here is a predisposition to emotional instability to which were added stimulation by voluptuous conversation and reading, abuse of sexual pleasures or deprivation after a long period of great sexual enjoyment. The physical malfunctions, such as the diminution or suppression of the menses which might trigger hysterical attacks, were in fact themselves brought about by the mental disturbances.

More significant in revealing Pinel's inclusive grasp of hysteria than the specific section he devotes to this disease in its most overt manifestations are his random remarks seeded throughout the entire discussion of neuroses.[52] These tangential observations indicate that he recognized hysterical disturbances when his contemporaries failed to suspect them; particularly in cases of disorders of the senses, he never failed to consider the possibility of their being symptoms of hysteria which had to be combatted as such. He described a young girl who was apparently totally deaf and had severe headaches whom he succeeded, by constant active attention, in curing of both complaints. He was less successful, however, with another "vaporous" woman, thirty years of age, who complained of total blindness. Nevertheless, he felt certain that there was no organic disease, for not only did her eyes appear healthy but the movements and reflexes were completely normal, which he tested by exposing her eyes to the sunlight. Although the patient insisted that she was unable to distinguish the brightest day from the darkest night, her iris was rotated away from the sun and her pupils contracted in the strong light and enlarged when the light grew weaker.

Further examples of Pinel's perspicacity emerged in his discussion of aphasia. He tells of a woman who after having given birth to a child suffered from a hemiplegia "of which

[52] *Ibid.*, pp. 4, 5, 15–16, 19, 52, 201, 204, etc.

she was cured when she made a trip to take the waters at Bourbonne." Two years later she suddenly lost the ability to speak, although she retained the faculty of understanding. She indicated by gestures and writing that she understood all that was said to her but that it was impossible for her to answer. Pinel refused to accept this aphasia as a permanent impairment and by attention and treatment gradually induced her to utter sounds which eventually were recognizable as words and even sentences. The treatment was completed when she went to a spa to take the waters, which was then believed to be the sovereign remedy for most ailments.

Pinel's most important contribution to the understanding of hysteria was his deviation from the increasingly sterile and repetitive neurological basis that had emanated from Great Britain for nearly two hundred years. To be sure, the early efforts of Jorden and Willis to supplant the belief in witchcraft by one in the affection of the brain and the nervous system were important and forward-looking steps. Equally valuable was the work of Willis and Whytt which showed at post-mortem examinations that there were no pathological changes in the uteri of hysterical patients and that, therefore, the cause of the disease must be sought elsewhere. By the time of Pinel, however, the vague neurological hypotheses for hysteria had been repeated so often without the addition of any new thought that they had become practically meaningless. Even Cullen concluded his own "neurological observations" on hysteria by a return to the uterine theory of the ancients.

Because of his specialized interest and major hospital appointments, Pinel had vastly greater experience with mentally disturbed patients than had any of his predecessors. He was able to establish clinical pictures of the various mental diseases. His concept of behavioral disorders without demonstrable organic changes in the nervous system was also confirmed by post-mortem examinations. Pinel thus freed the brain, as Willis and Whytt had the uterus, from any organic etiological connection with hysteria.

In a similar fashion, his identifying amenorrhea, nymphomania, and sexual abstinence as hysterical manifestations was not a simple restatement of older views but the direct out-

come of his own observations. This reintroduction of sex
as a major factor in hysteria pointed the way to later developments that culminated with the work of Freud.

THE BEGINNINGS OF MEDICAL PSYCHOLOGY

The bridge between Pinel and Freud spanned several streams
of thought, however, and involved so many personalities
that only a few of them can be discussed here. Outstanding among these is Baron Ernst von Feuchtersleben (1806–
49), in whose book on *The Principles of Medical Psychology*[53] the terms "psychosis" and "psychiatric" were introduced in their modern sense and psychosis was differentiated from neurosis.[54] His emphasis upon the psychic
elements grew out of his admiration and emulation of "the
philanthropic Pinel," whom he credited with "being the
first who positively recommended the psychical method of
cure."[55] The term "psychiatry" in the form of *Psychiaterie*
is, of course, derived from the Greek *psyche*, meaning
"mind," and *iatros*, meaning "physician," and made its
earliest appearance in 1808 in the writings of Johann
Christian Reil.[56]

[53] Ernst von Feuchtersleben, *The Principles of Medical Psychology,
being the outlines of a course of lectures,* trans. H. Evans Lloyd, rev.
ed. B. G. Babington (London: Sydenham Society, 1847); originally
published as *Lehrbuch der ärztlichen Seelenkunde* (Vienna: Gerold,
1845).

[54] The physicians practicing "psychiatrics" were referred to by
Feuchtersleben as "psychological physicians," "psychopathic physicians," and "psychiatric physicians." *Ibid.*, pp. 33, 64, 65, 70, 249, etc.

[55] *Ibid.*, p. 65.

[56] Johann Christian Reil (1759–1813), whom Feuchtersleben quotes
frequently and with much respect, was an extraordinary personality.
He was not only the founder and original editor of the first scientific
periodical, the *Archiv für die Physiologie* which later became the
epoch-making *Müller's Archiv,* but he was also a neurologist of considerable acumen and is known in this field for the "island of Reil" in
the brain. Of particular importance to this study is the fact that he was
the first to found a journal of psychiatry, the *Magazin für psychische
Heilkunde* (1805–6), which he subsequently changed into his *Beyträge*
(1808–12). His pupil C. F. Nasse continued the journal under the title
Zeitschrift für psychische Ärzte (1818–22).
Reil shared Pinel's devotion to the humane treatment of the insane
and published his *Rhapsodieen über die Anwendung der psychischen*

Feuchtersleben, a Viennese, was the first of a long series of prominent authorities on mental diseases to emanate from the German-speaking school. The initial Italian leadership in both general medicine and in psychiatry had been assumed successively by France and Britain. Austria and Germany lagged behind, until the nineteenth century, when they rapidly gained world dominance in all the medical sciences.

Feuchtersleben was a contemporary of the brilliant triumvirate Skoda,[57] Rokitansky,[58] and von Hebra,[59] who were responsible for reviving the medical fame of the University of Vienna. In this genial climate he developed into one of the most original, liberal, and progressive thinkers in the field of mental disease, although he has subsequently seldom been accorded the acclaim he deserves. Even in his own century, except for a brief initial spurt of enthusiasm, his work was largely ignored. But during his short life his *Principles of Medical Psychology* was so in demand in his native Vienna that the publisher, in order to supply his own customers, was forced to recall those copies that had been distributed to the trade.

In England *Principles of Medical Psychology* was translated and published by the Sydenham Society, a rare token of recognition. To appreciate this unusual distinction one must read a few passages from the editor's preface, which indicate that as a rule only works of deceased authors and

---

Kurmethode auf Geisteszerrüttungen (Halle, 1803), to this effect. Strangely enough, however, his "psychological method of healing" included the stimulation of violent reactions. Reil believed in arousing anger, hostility, and guilt feelings, the latter by means of a theater in mental hospitals where employees would take roles of judges, prosecutors, avenging angels, and reviving corpses who would judge patients' behavior and possible transgressions or sins.

[57] Josef Skoda (1805–81) was the leading clinician of the New Vienna School and the exponent of its therapeutic nihilism. He taught in the *Allgemeine Krankenhaus* and was the first member of the medical faculty to lecture in German. His treatise on percussion and auscultation (1839) led to the use of the term "Skoda's resonance."

[58] Carl Rokitansky (1804–78) was a brilliant and successful pathologist whose lasting fame was marred by an adherence to unsupported doctrines.

[59] Ferdinand von Hebra (1816–80) was the founder of the histological school of dermatology.

those which had much earlier received the stamp of public approbation were included in the series of the Sydenham Society publications. "Newly published books like newly discovered ores, may be rich or poor; but to test their value, they require that the stream of time should flow over them.[60] The Society departed from its usual practice in the case of Feuchtersleben's book because of "the great interest which medical psychology at this time excites." This is an extremely interesting statement which seems to link the past and the present. It also explains the sudden spurt of psychiatric publications on the Continent and in England. German readers were already familiar with his writings, especially his poetry and a small volume of psychological aphorisms, *Zur Diaetetik der Seele* ("On the Dietetics of the Mind," 1858).

Feuchtersleben was born in Vienna in 1806, the son of a prominent and aristocratic court official. The status of medicine as a career is obliquely delineated in the biographical introduction to the English edition of *Medical Psychology*.[61] The author states that the old Baron Feuchtersleben could easily have enabled his son to pursue "a more brilliant career than medicine offers to its votaries, had not a love of independence, and a thirst for natural science, led him to make choice of our profession." Ernst von Feuchtersleben took his Doctor's degree in medicine at the University of Vienna in 1833 and subsequently became a member of its faculty and ultimately its dean. In 1840 he was elected secretary to the newly founded Imperial and Royal Society of Physicians and shortly afterwards began to concern himself with the study of "psychiatric medicine." His lectures in this field attracted so much attention by their brilliance and their departure from traditional teachings that a new mental institution was built according to his views and specifications.

Feuchtersleben's awareness of mental activity and its derangements was a measurable advance in the evolution of medical psychology. His ideas, although built on his own

[60] *Principles of Medical Psychology*, p. v.

[61] For a succinct appreciation of the work of Feuchtersleben, see Erna Lesky, "Wiener Psychiatrie im Vormärz" in *Gesnerus*, XIX (1962), 119–29.

observations, were necessarily grounded upon the writings of his predecessors. He freely acknowledged this in the introduction to his book, stating that "the history of a science is the science itself." Recognizing his own development to be the result of the sum total of the prior efforts to understand mental disease, he felt particularly indebted to Georg Ernst Stahl, who brought psychology into medical science. However, as Feuchtersleben stated, "this union yet awaits completion by the blending of both sciences either at the present, or some future time." One cannot help wondering whether this union has yet been completed today.

Stahl (1660–1734) has been mentioned several times heretofore in connection with his endeavor to identify the soul with essential vitality. According to the "Animist" or "Vitalist School," which he founded, all of the basic phenomena of life were governed by the soul, and through this agency the reciprocal relationship between the passions, or mental reactions, and the accompanying organic changes could be explained. Stahl insisted that there were no physical changes in the "substance of the mind" in mental diseases; he attributed disturbances merely to an abnormal relationship between mind and body. The organism was thus to be comprehended as a whole, composed of body and soul, which were intimately interrelated. These ideas show a distinct resemblance to Adolf Meyer's more recent concept of psychobiological integration.

Stahl's school dealt entirely with intangibles. Feuchtersleben went beyond this and acknowledged further indebtedness to more anatomically oriented physicians. He referred, for instance, to the work of S. T. Sömmering, whose many neurophysiological contributions included the explanation that man's greater intelligence was due to the larger size of the human brain compared to those of animals. Feuchtersleben was conversant with Joseph Gall's studies, which attempted to determine a cerebral localization of the individual emotions. He quoted Charles Bell's endeavors "to prove the existence of a double class of nerves, the one for sensation and the other for motion," and he paid frequent homage to Reil for his theories on the function of the nervous system.

At this juncture a new and rather surprising trend became manifest in the thinking regarding mental disease, with which Feuchtersleben concurred. As in the evolution of medical thought, which some two millennia earlier moved from religious and magical concepts towards philosophical, psychiatry in the eighteenth century emerged from the realm of mysticism and turned to philosophy. The dominant figure was Immanuel Kant (1724–1804), who claimed the traditional hegemony of the philosopher over matters dealing with the soul and all other factors relating to mind and emotions. On the basis of his own studies on perception and the nature of the human senses and their aberrations, Kant adjudged himself an authority on mental disturbances superior to physicians, even to those who were psychiatrically oriented.[62]

Kant's immersion in psychiatry went so far that he proposed his own classification of mental diseases as his contemporaries in other countries were doing. He postulated that the various aberrations could be equated with stages of the civilization of man. Thus, primitive man was free from the danger of mental disease, whereas the growing complexities of civilization posed increasing threats to man's personal freedom and hence his psychological balance. Doubtless, the intellectual climate that fostered Rousseau's belief in the "noble savage" and in the superior virtues of a *retour à la nature* contributed to these views. Many others, such as Cheyne, had linked the loss of simplicity of life with a greater expectancy of neurotic disturbances. But this proposition, stemming from the pen of a man of Kant's stature, called for study of environmental and social factors that contributed to emotional disturbances.

Feuchtersleben's praise of Kant was extravagant. He described him as "the man who in profundity and acuteness,

---

[62] This authority was acknowledged even by a physician of the stature of C. W. Hufeland (1762–1836), who submitted one of his books to the criticism of Kant because it touched upon mental health. Kant, in turn, sent to Hufeland a very small book of his own, which carried the disproportionately lengthy title *Von der Macht des Gemüths durch den blossen Vorsatz Seiner krankhaften Gefühle Meister zu sein* ("On the Power of the Mind to master One's Pathological Feelings [Sensation] through Sheer Will Power") (Leipzig: Philipp Reklam jun., 1929).

far exceeded all of us, who have mounted upon his shoulders."[63] This admiration to the contrary notwithstanding, Feuchtersleben resented Kant's excluding the physician from the study of psychology and the practice of psychiatry. He vigorously held that both these fields were distinctly the medical man's business, asking: "The question in dispute is, properly speaking, not whether the mind can become diseased, but whether the task of treating independent states of the mind by education, instruction, etc., is to be considered as belonging to the province of the physician or not? The present state of the world seems to reply in the negative, because since these moral influences are confided to the parents, teachers, the clergy, etc., and by diseases, in a non-figurative sense, only the somatic are understood, the physician has to do with them alone."[64] In keeping with his convictions about the unity of body and mind, he believed that only the physician was competent to comprehend and treat disturbances of the mind.

Although Feuchtersleben discussed hysteria in a specific chapter, his above-mentioned views were obviously related to his ideas on hysteria, and much additional information is to be found scattered throughout the entire volume. He termed hysteria a "sister condition" to hypochondriasis, as did his predecessors—the former occurring primarily in the female and the latter in the male. The two were distinguished from one another by "the psycho-organic difference between the two sexes." "Hypochondriasis" by that time had come closer to its present meaning and represented primarily an exaggerated fear of physical disease. This apprehension was augmented by the ever present threat of syphilis or of mercury poisoning following a course of its treatment. So prevalent was this form of hypochondriasis that it was noted as a "species" by some nosologists and termed *syphilis imaginaria*. Hypochondriacs were believed to be relatively immune to epidemics and contagious diseases because "of the concentration of their attention on themselves, and their consequently diminished receptivity for the external world."[65] This withdrawal explains the early nineteenth-

---

[63] *Principles of Medical Psychology*, p. 17.

[64] *Ibid.*, p. 72.   [65] *Ibid.*, p. 226.

century synonyms of hypochondriasis, namely, "melancholy" and "spleen," as it was called in England.[66] It was a form of depression which "if it did attack women, which sometimes happens, they are generally masculine Amazonian women."[67] By the same token it was Feuchtersleben's belief that "when men are attacked by genuine hysterical fits (globus hyst. &tc.) which certainly does occur, they are for the most part effeminate men."

Because of the greater delicacy of their nervous systems, women manifested hysteria more by abnormal peripheral motor and sensory phenomena than by the changes in mood so often displayed by men. This nervous sensitivity was supposed to result in a hyperirritability of the spinal cord which became known as *neuralgia spinalis*. The consequent exaggeration of reflex actions which were initiated by sexual factors resulted in the hyperkinetic responses of hysterical convulsions.

Other symptoms analyzed by Feuchtersleben were localized pains in various parts of the body and "hyperaphia," a condition of such extreme and general sensitivity that even the slightest touch was intolerable. He also listed the *globus hystericus*, and further the *clavus hystericus*, i.e., the feeling as if a nail were being driven into a certain spot on the head. He spoke of transient swellings, "anathymiasis," which appear in various regions; and of tonic and clonic convulsions which terminate in sudden and unrestrained laughter.

The psychogenic predispositions to both hysteria and hypochondriasis were selfishness, over-privilege with satiety and boredom, excessive scholarliness, as well as the misfortunes of life. In women he blamed particularly "the female education," which he called the shame of our times: "It combines everything that can heighten sensibility, weaken spontaneity, give a preponderance to the sexual sphere, and sanction the feelings and impulse that relate to it." This artificially heightened persistence of sexual tension "unfortunately remained unrelieved because of rapidly successive pregnancies or impotence of husbands." Women in the middle of their childbearing period were found by Feuchters-

---

[66] Where there continued a belief in a national disposition.

[67] *Principles of Medical Psychology*, p. 225.

leben to be particularly disposed towards hysteria, although he also encountered it during puberty and the climacterium. But most frequently he saw it in those who remained unmarried "and in whom both the want of exercise in those sexual functions intended by nature for use and disappointed desire or hope, or at least the feeling of having failed in their earthly destination, are to be taken into account."[68] Freud's colleagues would have been considerably less shocked by his emphasis on sex had they been more conversant with the older literature on the subject of hysteria.

Although Feuchtersleben spoke of "hysteria" and "hypochondriasis," he did not consider them to be distinct entities. Rather, he believed that they represented symptomatically the effect of a multitude of noxious circumstances upon a sensitive organism. As such, they were a stage in the life history of the susceptible individual and their outcome varied. They might yield to treatment and entirely subside. Often, as the climacteric approached, they assumed a low-grade chronic form which he described as "its own milder yet substantial imitation." But also there were other possibilities, such as paralysis or insanity. This dynamic concept of mental disorders, of which hysteria was one aspect, is probably Feuchtersleben's most significant contribution. He based his treatment on this dynamic concept. Thus, active symptomatic therapy directed at any particular stage in a disorder which endures throughout the life of an individual is futile. Unless thoroughgoing changes could be induced in the patient and his environment, such symptomatic treatment could yield but temporary results at best. Inasmuch as both predisposing and immediate causes varied exceedingly, no single regimen could be laid down; management had to be planned to fit the particular individual.

Guided by this principle, Feuchtersleben geared his therapy to three aspects of the disease, i.e., its causes, its manifestations, and the prevention of recurrences. In the Hippocratic tradition, he asserted that *the prime art of the psychiatrist is to know when to do nothing*. Such therapeutic restraint applied particularly to administration of narcotics which were so prevalent in Feuchtersleben's day. He con-

[68] *Ibid.*, p. 228.

sidered them contraindicated because their blunting of the
sensorium impaired the efficacy of psychotherapy. He also
cautioned against their injurious side effects, notably a progressive mental deterioration. It is strange that with his wide
experience and perspicacity he failed, as did his predecessors,
to recognize or at least to mention the hazards of narcotic
addiction. In quite a modern-sounding manner he advised the
physician to establish rapport with the patient without, however, permitting too great a familiarity, which would inter-
fere with the doctor's influence. Insofar as possible, the
patient should be treated as if he were sound of mind, and he
must be permitted "himself to continue to spin the thread
which has been held out to him."[69]

As a further adjunct to treatment, Feuchtersleben felt
there should be continuous and intensified investigation of
the patient's dreams, "not because it is to be considered a
spiritual divination, but because as the *unconscious language*
[of the mind], it often very clearly shows, to those who can
comprehend its meaning, the state of the patient though he
himself is not aware of this."[70] He urged that "the interpretation of dreams deserves the attention and study of the
physician." Half a century later Freud answered this call.
Feuchtersleben was at times perplexed by the meaning of the
"dormant ideas" often relating to the distant past which are
prevalent in dreams. On one occasion he raised the question
whether ideas that one dreams properly belong to dreamers.
He questioned the justice of a certain Roman emperor who
had condemned a man to death because he had dreamed that
this person had tried to kill him.

Kant had suggested that "perhaps, without the wearying
but salutary pain of dreams, sleep would be death."[71] Feuchtersleben fully agreed, believing, as do many modern investigators, that one never sleeps without dreaming. He was certain that dreams were frequently psychologically significant
because they shed light on powerful but "obscured ideas."[72]
"Dreams may give a man historical information respecting
himself, . . . and the forgotten images of bygone days rise up

[69] *Ibid.*, p. 357.

[70] *Ibid.*, pp. 197–98. (Italics mine.)

[71] *Ibid.*, p. 164.   [72] *Ibid.*, p. 166.

and show the mind its former shape." Feuchtersleben believed that in pathological states of the mind "the old Adam appears, and is in every sense interesting to the psychological physician."[73] He considered such glimpses into the patient's emotional past especially revealing in the transitory states of hysteria and hypochondriasis.

Feuchtersleben was strikingly in advance of his day. Most of his contemporaries still thought of dreams in terms of fortune-telling and superstition.[74] Where he praised the art of doing nothing, his colleagues drugged and purged. Above all, he had the courage to speak of hysteria and, indeed, of all mental aberrations, as transitory stages between health and disease, while the others of his period established rigid classifications that allowed little leeway for recovery or change. Gentle and humorous though he was, he could not help criticizing his predecessors and colleagues for having made "excursions for pleasure, rather than voyages of discovery in the domain of medical psychology."

Feuchtersleben's most famous German colleague was Wilhelm Griesinger (1817–68), whose book entitled *Mental Pathology and Therapeutics* was also published in 1845.[75] The two men shared the same interests, but their beliefs were worlds apart—the worlds of Berlin and Vienna. Although both were exposed to similar intellectual influences, Griesinger severed his ties with philosophy, and Kant played no part in his evolving ideas of psychic disorders. To students of psychiatry, Griesinger represented science, Feuchtersleben literature. The former was diligently read; the latter was scanned for enjoyment and perhaps was not taken quite seriously.

Griesinger was the embodiment of the new German science which was to blossom so luxuriantly. The nineteenth century is recognized as the period of the most rapid development in the history of the medical sciences; and the un-

[73] *Ibid.*

[74] C. G. Carus in his *Vorlesungen über Psychologie* (Leipzig: Gerhard Fleischer, 1831), however, was on the verge of a deeper understanding.

[75] This work was also published in English translation by the Sydenham Society, yet after a more customary and conservative passage of time and period of appraisal, twenty-two years after its first appearance.

precedented acceleration of progress in our time is but a continuation of the powerful thrusts that began over 150 years ago.

Two other famous German professors, both dedicated to the emerging belief in the scientific basis of medicine, shaped Griesinger's orientation. Johann Lukas Schönlein (1793–1864) was among the first to turn from romantic natural philosophy to the scientific school of natural history. As professor of medicine at the University of Berlin, he introduced clinical teaching into Germany and with it the use of the vernacular in 1840. Carl R. A. Wunderlich (1815–77), under whom Griesinger worker as an assistant, displayed his scientific bent by introducing clinical thermometry as an integral part of medicine.[76] Griesinger extended this approach to psychiatry when he succeeded to the professorship of clinical medicine and of mental science at the University of Berlin.

Griesinger's *magnum opus* on the pathology and therapy of mental illness bears witness to his scientific convictions. Even hysteria, the most unclassifiable and multiform of all afflictions, found a neat place in his scheme as one form and cause of insanity. Although this arrangement reveals some of his bias—he thought of hysteria largely in somatic terms—his assumption was not entirely rigid, nor did he believe that hysteria must necessarily lead to insanity. At any rate, he discussed all aspects of the disease in one chapter, compactly and precisely, without wandering into the realms of hypothesis or philosophy.

In spite of its conciseness and positive wording, Griesinger's work lacks the clarity and the modern pertinence of Feuchtersleben's writings. He saw hysteria as a non-specific affliction of the nervous system with variable manifestations arising in different parts of the "nervous apparatus" and almost always accompanied by psychological disturbances. He attributed these disturbances to a conglomeration of causes, including the ancient implication of the uterus, some superficially understood neurological and psychological concepts, and congenital emotional predisposition.

[76] Wunderlich's famous work on the relationship of animal heat on disease, *Das Verhalten der Eigenwärme in Krankheiten* (Leipzig, 1868), formed the foundation of our present clinical thermometry.

THE INVIDIOUS PATIENT

Griesinger maintained that in the majority of the ordinary mild cases, hysteria could not *as yet* be considered a mental disease. He listed as traits which he had come to consider characteristic of hysteria and which were generally exhibited in these light forms and sometimes accompanied by sensory-motor anomalies, "immoderate sensitiveness, especially to the slightest reproach [in which there is a] tendency to refer everything to themselves, great irritability, great change of disposition on the least, or even from no, external motive."[77] Other marks of these patients were their volatile humor and their many apparently senseless caprices. He stated that hysterical women often exhibit unusually active intelligence and "tender sympathy" for other females.

He suggested that hysteria also carried with it a great many negative traits, such as inclination towards deception and prevarication, jealousy, malice, and other sorts of misbehavior. Sydenham's compassion and Feuchtersleben's empathy are completely lacking in Griesinger's writings; his patients were censurable for these unattractive traits. Soon many other voices were heard charging that the behavioral aberrations of hysteria were wilful misdemeanors. Griesinger actually differentiated these mild forms from the "serious hysterical mental disorders" by such presumed conscious and deliberate misbehavior, which was sometimes attributed to an inborn character defect. The more serious cases took the form of episodes of maniacal behavior, sometimes observed in very young girls, which "manifest themselves by vociferation, singing, cursing, aimless wandering; occasionally by more formal delirium, attempts at suicide, nymphomaniacal excitement; occasionally by delirium of a religious or demoniacal character; or there are attacks of all kinds of noisy and perverse, but still coherent, actions. In either case they retain but slight remembrance of what took place during the disorder."[78]

[77] Wilhelm Griesinger, *Mental Pathology and Therapeutics*, trans. C. Lockhart Robertson and James Rutherford (London: New Sydenham Society, 1867), p. 179.

[78] *Ibid.*, p. 180.

Griesinger identified a further variation of the disease as a chronic form of hysterical insanity. This variation begins with a gradual increase in the severity of the habitual manifestations. The symptoms become more persistent and more intense and the patient becomes progressively less able to exert self-control. Although Griesinger did not offer a reason for this aggravation, he noted that it often followed violent emotional disturbances, weakness from a variety of acute diseases, or menstrual irregularities. The first signs were behavioral changes, "greater seriousness, egotism, great care of the health is manifested—indecision and absence of will, impatience, violence, tendency to anger."[79] Then the patient's physical appearance begins to change, she loses weight and suffers from constipation, indigestion, and disordered menstruation. The latter symptom is one of the many inconsistencies in Griesinger's writings in that he, like a number of his less scientifically inclined predecessors, considered menstrual irregularities a cause as well as a result of hysteria. Griesinger also noted an erotic element as both manifesting and predisposing causes in these patients. Increasingly frequent exacerbations were accompanied by "marked cerebral congestion," swelling of the upper lip, violent headache, or diarrhea. Again menstruation is mentioned, for the symptoms become aggravated at the periods, which were generally believed to augment emotional tensions even in normal women. In the words of Griesinger, it was "well known that most females are very sensitive, very peevish and nervous, at the menstrual periods."[80]

The diagnosis, according to Griesinger, was based on three factors: an hereditary disposition; the patient's earlier history of *globus hystericus,* convulsive attacks, local anesthesias and hyperesthesias, or paralyses; and the presence of local diseases of the genital organs, which were "of the

[79] *Ibid.*

[80] It was a belief of the time that menstruation and all its disorders exercised great influence on the development and course of mental diseases. The most simple but also the most rare cases were hitherto healthy persons who experienced, after sudden cessation or suppression of the menses followed by acute violent hyperaemia of the brain and immediately therewith, an outbreak of mental disorder, generally mania with active cerebral congestion. *Ibid.,* p. 200.

greatest importance in regard to prognosis and treatment."[81]

Griesinger insisted that all local diseases of the uterus, ovaries, and vagina were likely to be followed by hysteria, which then may gradually progress into insanity.[82] Obviously, therefore, the possibility of such local disease should be uppermost in mind when hysterical patients were studied. An adequate pelvic examination was imperative. He deplored the fact that many of his colleagues in Germany, France, and England displayed a "truly childish delicacy" about vaginal examinations and using the speculum because they were afraid of arousing or increasing sexual desires in their patients. He considered this danger negligible when balanced against the benefit of making a correct diagnosis, which would then lead to proper treatment. He spoke of "the light which we gain by the speculum, and which so frequently elucidates hysteria,"[83] and he asserted that in his private practice he had observed many cases of hysterical insanity relieved by local treatment of the genital organs after all other means had failed.

Griesinger's reversion to a somatic explanation for hysterical disturbances by implicating the sexual organs almost to the exclusion of everything else must be looked upon as a regression from the psychiatric concepts of Pinel and Feuchtersleben. His writings reveal a gross lack of logic and an obtuseness which probably represented an inability to see and comprehend whatever was not consonant with his preconceived ideas. This is evident also in the nature of the arguments he used to deny the hysterogenic role of ungratified sexual desires and needs: "Some cases may doubtless be attributable to nonsatisfaction of the sexual appetite; but this is, as a rule, much overrated, as the existence of hysteria in girls who have not reached the age of puberty, its great frequency amongst married women—the frequent injurious influence of marriage, pregnancy, and childbirth, and the frequency of the affection amongst prostitutes, show."[84]

He did not merely take exception to those who uncritically ascribed all cases of hysteria to involuntary sexual abstinence. Rather, he revealed a blind spot towards very spe-

[81] *Ibid.*, p. 181.
[82] *Ibid.*, p. 201.
[83] *Ibid.*, p. 202.
[84] *Ibid.*, p. 181.

cific aspects of sexual frustration which were already stirring in the thoughts of his contemporaries and which were to be formulated by Freud a generation later. Repression of erotic thoughts, inadequate gratification in uxorial relations, and even prepubescent (though not infantile) sexuality were accepted topics in the contemporary medical literature. But Griesinger, thinking of himself as a spokesman of the new scientific era, would deal only with demonstrable factors beyond which he refused to speculate. Perhaps, less consciously, he was an adumbration of the exaggerated morality and prudery to come in the later Victorian era.

Paradoxical, too, in light of Griesinger's uncritical acceptance of female pelvic disease as the almost exclusive cause of hysteria, was his recognition of its occasional occurrence in young men. He reported having seen many such cases and having "recently observed one with distinct globus and convulsions in a young married, very anaemic man whose wife was pregnant."[85] Regrettably he did not elaborate on this brief history, which suggests a wealth of interpretations. Nor did he offer any etiological explanations for hysteria in men. His discussion of male hysteria was very brief. Nevertheless, its existence being recognized by a most important and widely read German psychiatrist evoked no hostility, whereas less than thirty years later a comparable statement subjected Freud to a torrent of ridicule and abuse.

So rich was the ferment of intellectual and scientific activity in the mid-portion of the nineteenth century that within the span of a single lifetime ideas bridged the gap between antiquity and today. René Théophile Laennec (1781–1826), for example, whose doctoral dissertation dealt with the pertinence of Hippocratic medicine to the medical practice of his day, also invented the stethoscope, which introduced physical examination into medicine. Only slightly later Rudolf Virchow (1821–1902), building on the labors of his immediate predecessors, proclaimed the doctrine of cellular pathology and thereby established the true nature of physical disease. And with respect to mental disease, the groundwork for Freud's discoveries had been consolidated.

[85] *Ibid.*

CHAPTER IX

The Victorian Era

WITHIN A SHORT TIME in the nineteenth century psychiatry took a greater stride forward than all the advances made since the beginning of its history. One British physician, Robert Brudenell Carter (1828–1918), a contemporary of Griesinger whose professional activities encompassed a wide range of medical subject matter, wrote on mental disease in general and on hysteria in particular with ideas on psychodynamics so strikingly similar to those of Freud—before the latter was even born—that mere coincidence of their ideas seems startling indeed.

Robert Carter belongs to that strange category of creative men whose indirect influence may have been enormous but who had so little impact upon their immediate successors that their names are scarcely known to historians. Although his books are to be found in any well-stocked medical library, even the *Dictionary of National Biography* fails to mention his name. And yet Carter's career was particularly interesting. He was born at Little Wittenham in 1828, the son of a major in the Royal Marines, and was educated at private schools. He began his medical studies as an apprentice to a general practitioner and later entered the London Hospital as a medical student. In 1851 he became a member of the Royal College of Surgeons but, lacking the funds to complete his training for a fellowship, he returned to the country to make his living as a general practitioner. During the subsequent twelve years he not only retained his knowledge of anatomy, but also kept so fully abreast of developments in surgery that he was able to pass his fellowship examination "without either rest for study or coaching."

During his career as a general practitioner, which lasted until his fortieth year, Carter established himself as a medical author. At the early age of twenty-five he wrote a significant work entitled *On the Pathology and Treatment of Hysteria* (1853). Two years later, he published a second book, *The Influence of Education and Training in Preventing Diseases of the Nervous System*. In the same year he joined the army in the Crimea as a staff surgeon and there apparently developed the interest in ophthalmological surgery which dominated the rest of his professional life and brought him considerable renown. Upon his return to civilian life, he helped found several ophthalmological hospitals and eventually became a Fellow of the Royal College of Surgeons in 1864. Four years later he moved to London, where he was elected a member of the staff of the Royal South London Hospital (now Royal Eye Hospital), and in 1870 he received an important appointment in ophthalmic surgery at St. George's Hospital. This amazing career from general practice to eye surgery extended even further. Carter's literary talents were discovered during the Crimean War by W. H. Russel, a famous war correspondent, who urged him to describe his experiences at the front in a series of letters to be published in the *Times*. They evoked such response from readers that soon after he moved to London, Carter was invited to join the staffs of both the *Times* and *Lancet*. He wrote lead articles for both publications for nearly fifty years.

When Carter is mentioned in today's medical or medico-historical literature, it is almost exclusively for his ophthalmological work; little attention is paid to his writings from the country towns where he was engaged in general practice. And yet it is in the two psychiatric works that his clarity of style and depth of perception were first manifest. It may have been that they were largely ignored because they were too embarrassingly perceptive for his Victorian compatriots. One can but marvel at his penetration and lucidity and wonder whence this knowledge came, since these books were written when Carter's training and experience, particularly in the fields of psychology and psychotherapy, was very limited. He clearly integrated hysteria with the emotions and skilfully dissected the emotional patterns of human beings in relation to predisposition to and manifestations of hysterical phenomena. Strong emotion, he insisted, "will not be found to remain as a matter of mere intellectual consciousness; but, on the contrary, always to manifest itself by the production of certain effects, either upon the intellect and will, or upon the physical organism."

THE FIRST THEORY OF REPRESSION

He implicated three main factors in the etiology of hysteria: the temperament of the individual, the event or situations which trigger the initial attack, and the degree to which the affected person is compelled to conceal or "repress" the exciting causes. "Sexual passion," though not the only factor that may give rise to hysteria in an emotionally labile person, is far the most frequent and important of all immediate etiological agents.

And, therefore, it is reasonable to expect that an emotion, which is strongly felt by great numbers of people, but whose natural manifestations are constantly repressed in compliance with the usages of society, will be the one whose morbid effects are most frequently witnessed. This anticipation is abundantly borne out by facts; the sexual passion in women being that which most accurately fulfills the prescribed conditions, and whose injurious influence upon the organism is most common and familiar. Next after it in power, may be placed those emotions of a permanent character, which are usually concealed, because disgraceful or unamiable, as hatred or envy; after them others equally permanent, such as grief or care, but which, not being discreditable, are not so liable to be repressed.[1]

Because women were by nature more sensitive in their emotional structure than men and being compelled by convention to repress sexual needs, they were therefore far more susceptible to hysteria.

If the relative power of emotion against the sexes be compared in the present day, even without including the erotic passion, it is seen to be considerably greater in the woman than in the man,

[1] Robert Brudenell Carter, *On the Pathology and Treatment of Hysteria* (London: John Churchill, 1853), p. 21.

partly from that natural conformation which causes the former to feel, under circumstances where the latter thinks; and partly because the woman is more often under the necessity of endeavouring to conceal her feelings. But when sexual desire is taken into the account, it will add immensely to the forces bearing upon the female, who is often much under its dominion; and who, if unmarried and chaste, is compelled to restrain every manifestation of its sway. Man, on the contrary, has such facilities for its gratification, that as a source of disease it is almost inert against him, and when powerfully excited, it is pretty sure to be speedily exhausted through the proper channel. It may, however, be remarked, that in many cases of hysteria in the male, the sufferers are recorded to have been "continent," a circumstance which may have simulated the effects of amativeness upon them to those which are constantly witnessed in the female.[2]

Why some women had a greater tendency towards hysterical response than others under quite similar environmental conditions, Carter explained as variations in sexual drive. He quoted an ancient maxim to the effect that the greater the salaciousness, the stronger the proclivities to hysteria.[3] He went on to argue:

If the aphorism above quoted may be supposed to have been substantially correct at the time of its enunciation, there is no adequate reason for thinking that it does not apply to the present state of society. For while the advance of civilization and the ever-increasing complications of social intercourse tend to call forth new feelings, and by their means to throw amativeness somewhat into the shade, as one powerful emotion among many others; still its absolute intensity is in no way lessened, and from the modern necessity for its entire concealment, it is likely to produce hysteria in a larger number of the women subject to its influence, than it would do if the state of society permitted its free expression. It may, therefore, be inferred, as a matter of reasoning, that the sexual emotions are those most concerned in the production of the disease.[4]

It is important to recognize the fact that Carter limited the role of sex in the causation of hysteria to repression of sexuality and erotic desires and strongly excluded organic disease or dysfunction of the reproductive organs. Herein lies the essence of his advanced position compared with all

2 *Ibid.,* pp. 32–33.

3 *"Salacitas major, major ad hysteriam proclivitas." Ibid.,* p. 34.

4 *Ibid.,* pp. 34–35.

his predecessors. He graphically described the chain of frustrations that leads into hysteria:

> The emotions likely to be secretly dwelt upon as a consequence of the pleasures derived from them are thus reduced to a very small number; and it is evident that a young woman whose chief enjoyment rests either upon a complacent contemplation of her own perfections, mingled with an angry sense of the neglect shown to them by her associates, or else upon an imagined gratification of her sexual desires, is not in the best possible frame of mind for withstanding the pressure of a new temptation; such as is held out by the discovery that she can, at will, produce an apparently serious illness, and thus make herself an object of great attention to all around her, and possibly, among others, to the individual who has been uppermost in her thoughts.[5]

Carter emphasized the diagnostic importance of an initial convulsive paroxysm. To this he applied the term "primary" and stated that it may or may not recur. Subsequent attacks, following induced or spontaneous recall of the emotions to which the primary fit was due, he called "secondary." A "tertiary" form was an attack designedly excited by the patient herself by means of voluntary recollection and with perfect knowledge of her own power to produce them.

> Attacks of this kind may be distinguished from primary hysteria by the frequency with which they occur in the absence of any exciting cause; by their never being produced under circumstances which would expose the patient to serious discomfort or real danger, but at a time and place discreetly chosen for the purpose; and by observing many little arrangements contrived in order to add to their effect. Thus the hair will often be so fastened as to fall at the slightest touch, in most "admired disorder"; and many analogous devices will be had recourse to, their number and variety depending upon the ingenuity of the performer, and the extent of her resources.[6]

The patient likely to develop the tertiary form was more often, according to Carter, the one who felt herself neglected and uncared for rather than a victim of sexual frustration. Logically, therefore, her efforts are designed to bring her sympathy and solicitous attention. In this campaign, which he calls a "moral state," she displays "selfishness and deceptivity allied in order to indulge that desire for sympathy which is the chief motive for action." In such cases

[5] *Ibid.*, p. 52.   [6] *Ibid.*, p. 46.

the paroxysm is altogether discontinued and the sufferings
of the invalid are limited to her knee joint or her spine, as
the seat of substantive disease, and to innumerable accessory
aches and pains, which are useful in warding off too close
scrutiny from each other."[7]

The "complications" of hysterical states can be both real
and simulative. Carter described the former as ideo-motor,[8]
resulting in local convulsions; opisthotonos (more frequently observed in the secondary stage); frequent vomiting after
meals, possibly injurious if it became habitual; and coughing,
which often became chronic. All ideo-motor acts, Carter
maintained, differed from those dictated by the will in the
rapidity and force with which they were performed and the
length of time they were sustained. Further complications,
real or simulative, or tertiary hysteria often took the form of
illnesses that the patient may have previously experienced or
witnessed in other people.

Simulative complications, Carter had discovered, were the
products of amazing ingenuity. Leeches carried inside the
mouth induced hemorrhage convincingly resembling he-
moptysis and hematemesis; tight bandages caused swelling of
the joints; deliberate delaying of the act of micturition resulted in manifestations of urinary suppression; constipation
could likewise be achieved by artificial withholding; and
cutaneous lesions were produced by scratching and chafing.
Carter advised that physicians should never ask leading or
suggestive questions, particularly those concerning uterine
disorders. If vaginal symptoms were present, they were often
self-inflicted by means of local irritants in an attempt to
attract the physician's attention and thus to make necessary
a pelvic examination.

In contrast to Griesinger, who, as mentioned earlier,
recommended such examination in each case of hysteria,
Carter deplored the abuse of the speculum, which he believed was avidly sought by women of all ages and situations
as a means of sexual gratification. He severely criticized his
unscrupulous or undiscerning colleagues for doing serious

[7] See also William Benjamin Carpenter, *Principles of Human Physiology* (4th ed.; London: J. Churchill, 1844), chap. 14; and *British and
Foreign Medical Review*, XXII (1846), 488.

[8] Carter, *op. cit.*, p. 48.

damage by indiscriminate use of the speculum. He wrote that

no one who has realized the amount of moral evil wrought in girls . . . whose prurient desires have been increased by Indian hemp and partially gratified by medical manipulations, can deny that remedy is worse than disease. I have . . . seen young un-married women, of the middle-class of society, reduced by the constant use of the speculum, to the mental and moral condition of prostitutes; seeking to give themselves the same indulgence by the practice of solitary vice; and asking every medical practi-tioner . . . to institute an examination of the sexual organs.[9]

MORAL TREATMENT

Concerning the management of hysteria, Carter had definite ideas that logically evolved from his etiological concepts. He denied that fumigations, smelling salts, odors, or vapors had any healing effects. Coexistent pathological conditions, such as struma and anemia, he believed, increased the tendency to hysteria and should therefore be treated by medicines, such as iron filings and cod-liver oil, which were thought to strengthen the body and render it more resistant to the pres-sure of emotional influences. But he thought that even such measures must often be withheld because it is in the nature of hysteria that patients develop an insatiable desire for remedies of all sorts. Thus even therapeutic infliction of pain was quite useless, since "the patient herself often inflicts upon herself much more pain than any medical attendant could possibly propose."[10]

Much more effective than physical treatment, in Carter's experience, was "moral treatment," as psychotherapy was then still called. Here, too, he distinguished between the three stages of hysteria and recommended a different regi-men for each stage. Thus, in primary cases, nothing should be done beyond removing all causes of excitement, and at-tempting to substitute incentives for intellectual exercises. After the paroxysm has spent itself the patient should be left in her room with but a single attendant and allowed to fall into the deep sleep that invariably follows. When she awakens, attempts should immediately be made to ascertain

[9] *Ibid.*, p. 69.   [10] *Ibid.*, p. 96.

the events that gave rise to the illness and to prevent further
seizures. These should entail a physical examination, with a
view to finding and correcting debilitating conditions such
as illness or anemia.

Much more important in the management, he thought,
was an investigation of the emotions. According to Carter,
these rarely lay on the surface, being usually deeply hidden;
and the deeper the emotions, the greater the importance of
disclosing them.[11] Physical and intellectual exercise, he held,
functioned to reduce surface emotions only, such as fright
and anger, which the writings of Willis and Whytt had elevated to disproportionate importance in the medical literature. The significantly harmful emotions were unconfessed
or repressed and generally "of an amatory or envious character." Any attempt to counter them was useless, unless the
patient was ready and willing to lend assistance. Since secondary, or chronic, hysteria often followed the initial attack,
determination of the etiology and after-treatment of the
original paroxysm to prevent repetition were of extreme
importance.

But despite all such prophylactic measures, attacks of secondary hysteria frequently ensued, initiated by voluntary or
suggested recall of the original emotional insult. It was Carter's belief that when the secondary paroxysm was produced
by sexual feelings, most parents would do well to arrange a
marriage, even a relatively undesirable one.[12] This was time-
honored advice but did not reflect as enlightened an attitude
as that of Bernard de Mandeville, who pitied the prospective
husband and children.

Carter's tertiary form of hysteria, it must be remembered,
differed from the other two in that it was deliberate and designed for whatever emotional gratification the patient might
hope to gain from it. Its management, therefore, had to be
comparably different in approach as well as technique and
aim "to remove the motives of the patient, by defeating the
ends which she proposes to herself for attainment."[13] Medicines were obviously useless but, as in earlier stages of the
disease, might have a place in the symptomatic control of
subsequent disorders of function, and they may also possibly

11 *Ibid.*, p. 101.   12 *Ibid.*   13 *Ibid.*, p. 96.

PLATE XI. Franz Anton
Mesmer (1734–1815).

PLATE XII. S. Weir Mitchell (1829–1914)

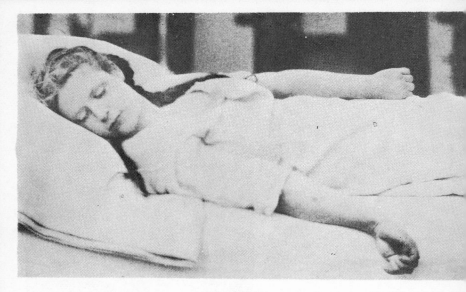

PLATE XIII. Hystero-epileptic attack: *Tétanisme*

PLATE XIV. Hysteria: facial contracture

(Plates XIII and XIV are from Bourneville and P. Regnard, *Iconographie photographique de la Salpêtrière* [Paris: Progrès Médical, 1878].)

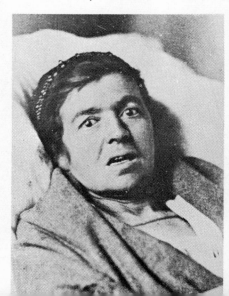

improve the patient's physical status and so make her less reliant on her illness for subjective well-being. Moral, or psychiatric, treatment, Carter believed, could not be effectively carried out so long as the patient remained in her accustomed setting because of the constant interference of solicitous family and friends, and also removal from familiar surroundings was all the more necessary because when the various feigned diseases were unmasked, the disclosure of the imposture would be embarrassing and therefore detrimental. For the same reason, he found it highly conducive to the future health of the patient that she should never suspect that her family and her friends had been aware of her deception.

The first step in systematic treatment was the diligent search for the psychological needs of the patient which motivated her assuming the pseudo-illnesses. This necessitated close observation by the physician and constant encouragement to have her speak freely of past and present ailments, pursuits, tastes, accomplishments, and feelings. During this exploratory period all of the patient's whims should be indulged in order to gain her full confidence. Memoranda should be made of all conversations and observations and progress notes added regularly.

Should major manifestations of the disease occur during this early period of treatment, the patient should be isolated and no reference made to them until she was once again calm and amenable to reason. The chief objective was to evoke the firm conviction on the part of the patient, without ever giving it verbal expression, that her physician fully understood her case and knew not only how many of her symptoms and ailments were self-produced, "but also the exact manner or train of thought by which they are set going." Carter intimated that he had seen numerous patients of this type but "of such analyses no two will be quite alike, except only in their general features."[14]

Carter cautioned against suggesting motives for their behavior to patients but considered it much more salutary to induce them "to fill the outline." In this manner he had found it often possible to gain important information from

[14] *Ibid.*, p. 107.

the patient herself "pregnant, as they will generally be, with
hint of her real motives."[15] Should, as it often happened,
lameness or other physical infirmities occur during this stage
of treatment, they should be made light of and not mentioned in any context other than with regret that they might
possibly exclude the patient from pleasant pastimes, such as
dances or picnics. Above all, he advised casualness in all relations with the patient, "for it often happens, that she may
herself take pleasure in what is thus recommended for her;
and that the treatment itself may become a matter of indulgence, to be prolonged as much as possible. . . . The hysterical desire will be most dangerously gratified by any strict
law."[16] The primary indication of this type of treatment
Carter characterized as "complete moral restoration."[17] If it
destroys the old personality, "the demon will return." The
management must also be constructive so as to leave the
patient morally, that is, psychologically and intellectually,
improved.

Unlike many of his predecessors who considered hysteria
an upper-class ailment, Carter recognized its occurrence
among the poor. He devoted an entire chapter to this aspect,
stating that it occurred frequently, and chiefly among the
more respectable poor who "resisting the normal effects of
passion fall victim to the abnormal."[18] Obviously, these patients were unable to afford intensive treatment by private
physicians and the constant care by attendants that Carter
recommended as essential. The only recourse for indigents
was hospitalization for the concomitant somatic complaints.
However, his experience had convinced him that cure in a
hospital environment was extremely difficult if not actually
impossible.

As will be remembered, Carter published his observations
On the Pathology and Treatment of Hysteria in 1853, when
he was only twenty-five years old. His youth alone, to say
nothing of the precocity of his understanding of the dynam-
ics of the disease, and his suggestions for treatment are indeed
remarkable. It is not surprising, therefore, that he attempted
to forestall the almost inevitable questions about where he

[15] *Ibid.*, p. 115.   [17] *Ibid.*, p. 107.
[16] *Ibid.*, p. 131.   [18] *Ibid.*, pp. 152 ff.

had gained this experience by referring to the works of other authors on which he had drawn.[19] Yet he was actually far more original than he himself thought prudent to admit. In fact, there were few writers in the middle of the nineteenth century who had his clear insight into the psychopathology of hysteria. Underlying his perceptiveness one senses an antipathy towards his hysterical patients, perhaps the expression of his youthful impatience with the whims and foibles of women and their "moral obliquity." At an age when maturity might have mellowed his attitude, Carter was gaining fame as an ophthalmological surgeon; and when he died in 1918, a nonagenarian, few, if any, remembered that he had started his career as a medical author in the field of psychiatry.

It must be apparent from this brief chronological review of hysteria that the manifestations of this disease tended to change from era to era quite as much as did the beliefs as to etiology and the methods of treatment. The symptoms, it seems, were conditioned by social expectancy, tastes, mores, and religion, and were further shaped by the state of medicine in general and the knowledge of the public about medical matters. The more detailed such knowledge became the greater was the variety of symptoms. Thus we have seen departures from and returns to the generalized convulsion, the *globus hystericus*, the loss of consciousness, the cessation of breathing. We have watched the acting-out of demonic possession and the vast variety of physical and mental delusions related to it. Furthermore, throughout history the symptoms were modified by the prevailing concept of the feminine ideal. In the nineteenth century, especially young women and girls were expected to be delicate and vulnerable both physically and emotionally, and this image was reflected in their disposition to hysteria and the nature of its symptoms. The delicacy was enhanced by their illness and as a result, the incidence of overt manifestations was further increased.

Perhaps because of this emotional vulnerability there was a striking rise in the prevalence of hysteria throughout Europe at this time. This is made clear by the vast increase

[19] Carter mentioned his indebtedness to Mr. Stephen Mackenzie, who was then recently deceased but on whose opinions and experiences he had drawn.

in literature concerning this disease brought out during that portion of the nineteenth century that coincides with the reign of Queen Victoria. Concurrent with its proliferation, which reached almost epidemic proportions, the malady exhibited a diminution in severity, and the disabling symptoms gave way to the faintings, whims, and tempers so elegantly designated as vapors.

The less dramatic and spectacular exhibitions made up in chronicity for their lack of severity. In the earlier centuries the physician of a hysterical patient had the frequent and highly satisfying experience of returning his patient to normalcy with almost miraculous speed. The later literature gave evidence of a great variety of persistent physical ailments of a lesser form. These paralyses, aphasias, neuralgias, etc., not only lacked the element of gravity but also made much greater demands on the diagnostic and therapeutic astuteness of the physician. Carter was still convinced that the initial presenting paroxysm was an essential feature of primary hysteria, but he also stressed the fact that it had become so ephemeral and mild that it often escaped notice.

With this altered profile of hysteria, the misanthropic attitude of Carter became more prevalent and found expression by authors in many countries. In Germany this aversion led to drastic reactions that do not seem to be free of a punitive element. The aspersion of "moral obliquity," together with the lingering belief in the genital origin of the disease, induced the famous gynecologist Alfred Hegar (1830–1914) and his pupils to perform ovariectomies in cases of intractable hysteria. Another group followed the renowned neurologist Nikolaus Friedreich (1825–82) in cauterizing the clitorises of those patients whose sexual needs and demands they deemed immoderate.

A less violent but hardly less contemptuous attitude towards women suffering from chronic hysteria appears in the writings of Jules Falret, psychiatrist at the Salpêtrière Hospital and one-time president of the medico-psychological society of Paris. He was the gifted son of the more versatile widely known pioneer in the field of psychiatry, Jean-Pierre Falret. One of Jules's essays, "Folie raisonnante ou folie morale" (1866), suggests that true hysteria constitutes one of the most common varieties of "moral" or psychogenic insanity.[20] In his definition of this disease, Falret's repugnance for its victims becomes quite evident. Indeed, it is so strong that it deprives him of his scientific objectivity. He states that "all physicians who have the occasion to observe many hysterical women, and all other persons who have had the misfortune of sharing their lives with such women, have come to know perfectly well that their character and mind is typified by a moral configuration that is theirs alone and that permits their disease to be recognized even before any physical symptoms have become manifest."[21]

Having described the hysterical patients' emotional volatility, their extraordinary sensitivity, and their proneness to contradiction and controversy, Falret comes to their main characteristic, which he calls the spirit of duplicity and falsehood:

These patients are veritable actresses; they do not know of a greater pleasure than to deceive . . . all those with whom they come in touch. The hysterics who exaggerate their convulsive movement . . . make an equal travesty and exaggeration of the movements of their soul, their ideas and their acts. . . . In one word, the life of the hysteric is nothing but one perpetual falsehood; they affect the airs of piety and devotion and let themselves be taken for saints while at the same time secretly abandoning themselves to the most shameful actions; and at home, before their husbands and children, making the most violent scenes in which they employ the coarsest and often most obscene language and give themselves up to the most disorderly actions.[22]

It is only necessary, Falret repeats, to have received the pitiable confidences of the husbands of hysterical women in order to gain an idea of what life is with these patients. All their passions, including the sexual, are exaggerated, he warns. Some are so dominated by erotic impulses that, unable to find satisfaction with their husbands, they turn to every kind of immoral conduct. Others, carried away by senseless jealousy, ruin their domestic life; and yet another group derive distorted pleasure from tyrannizing over their husbands in public. Physicians, unfamiliar with these emo-

[20] It was originally presented before the Société médico-psychologique and appears in Jules Falret, *Études cliniques sur les maladies mentales et nerveuses* (Paris: Librairie Baillière et Fils, 1890).

[21] *Ibid.*, p. 500. [22] *Ibid.*, p. 502.

tional debauches, might mistake them for simple viciousness. The very immensity of treachery and perversity is in itself diagnostic and indicates beyond question that such hysterical women are truly deranged, despite the appearance of reason they maintain before society.

WOMAN'S ENDEARING FRAILTY

One country of this abnormally oriented world failed to share the otherwise prevalent antipathetic reaction to hysteria in the latter part of the nineteenth century. During the decades in which the rapidly changing views on hysteria were being recorded more or less simultaneously throughout the Old World, a new voice was beginning to make itself heard. The American Colonies had given way to the Republic and the frontier was rapidly being pushed westward. Significant and even revolutionary discoveries, such as anesthesia, emanated from this infant nation, and important contributions were also made in the neuropsychiatric field. The names of Cotton Mather and Benjamin Rush have already been mentioned in connection with hysteria. But the event which triggered renewed interest in this field was the Civil War, the large number of casualties of which imposed upon its physicians the challenge of differentiating between actual nerve injury, shell shock, hysteria, and malingering. The doctors had the particularly difficult task of exposing the wilful misrepresentations for what they were. All other categories of neuropsychiatric casualties had to be treated.

Outstanding among those who accepted this double challenge and met it with comprehension and success was Silas Weir Mitchell (1829–1914), who was Queen Victoria's junior by ten years and a contemporary of Robert B. Carter. Mitchell has been hailed as one of the founders of American neurology and neurophysiology, and his merits in the field of psychiatry were as widely acclaimed as was his fame as a physician as well as a popular author of novels and poems.

S. Weir Mitchell was born in 1829, the son and grandson of prominent and well-born Philadelphia physicians. Graduated from Jefferson Medical College in 1850, he spent the following year in further study in Paris, where he was deeply influenced by the work of the microscopist Charles Robin and by Claude Bernard's personality and lectures. He became personally acquainted with this great French physiologist and throughout his life frequently quoted Bernard's Hunterian admonition: "Why think, when you can experiment? Exhaust experiment and then think."

On his return to Philadelphia in 1852, he joined his father in medical practice, but the idea of scientific research, implanted in Paris, never left him. With the microscope he had acquired abroad, he started a laboratory from which emanated in rapid succession a number of toxicological investigations dealing importantly with the neurological injuries induced by snake venoms and other poisons which presaged his subsequent leadership in the new field of neurology. Among his collaborators was William A. Hammond, who was later to become surgeon-general of the United States during the Civil War; and with him Mitchell produced in 1859 the first of many important toxicological studies. During the following half-century of his life, he published over 240 papers and monographs in the field of experimental and clinical medicine, many of which were concerned with neurological problems. Among these, his study on "Reflex Paralysis" (1864) and his superb "Researches on the Physiology of the Cerebellum" (1869) deserve special mention. These researches were among the earliest on the localization of brain function and were later elaborated by his younger co-workers, W. W. Keen and Charles K. Mills. Throughout his life Mitchell exhibited a genius for attracting young scientists and imbuing them with the desire to carry his own studies forward. His early interest in snake venom persisted for many decades, and in his seventies he inspired both Simon Flexner and his protégé, Hideyo Noguchi, to take up the work he had begun so much earlier.

S. Weir Mitchell's interest in clinical neurology, aroused by the large number of Civil War casualties, so occupied his energies that his researches, perforce, had to be put aside. Assigned to the army hospitals that had been established in and about Philadelphia with facilities to take care of as many as twenty-six thousand sick and wounded soldiers, Mitchell found vast numbers suffering with nerve injuries and their sequelae. Because of his earlier concern with neurology, he eagerly assumed responsibility for the care of these patients that his colleagues were glad to relinquish in light of the prevailing ignorance about such problems. Mitchell's competence "so pleased the surgeon-general [William A. Hammond] that finally . . . a hospital for neural disorders was created at Turner's Lane, near Philadelphia, in August 1862 and pavillions were built for four hundred men." It became the model for the concentration of certain types of injuries in specific centers which was so very effectively made use of by both Great Britain and the United States in World War II. The selected material assigned to Mitchell and his colleagues included cases of tremendous variety and interest. At one time, he reported, there were "eighty epileptics, every kind of nerve wound, palsies, singular choreas, and stump disorders."

The neurological work of Mitchell is given such prominence in this account because of the close relationship between organic nerve injuries, hysteria, and malingering. His paper "On Malingering, Especially in Regard to Simulation of Diseases of the Nervous System" represents one of the significant studies on the tenuous distinction between assumed and genuine disability.[23] Closely allied to malingering was "nostalgia," a frequently identified cause of disability among the soldiers, about which Mitchell wrote with interest and sympathy:

> Cases of nostalgia, homesickness, were serious additions to the perils of wounds and disease, and a disorder we rarely see nowadays. I regret that no careful study was made of what was in some instances an interesting psychic malady, making men hysteric and incurable except by discharge. To-day, aided by German perplexities, we would ask the victim a hundred and twenty-one questions, consult their subconscious mind and their dreams, as to why they wanted to go home and do no better than let them go as hopeless.[24]

These reminiscences expressed in 1913 reflect Mitchell's excellent memory of the war, which had ended nearly half

[23] William W. Keen, S. W. Mitchell, and G. R. Morehouse, in *American Journal of the Medical Sciences*, N.S., XLVIII (1864), 367–94.

[24] From a lecture, "The Medical Department of the Civil War," delivered before the Physicians Club of Chicago in February, 1913.

a century earlier, and they throw light on the preoccupation with psychiatry that filled a great part of his later life. Alert and active until his death in 1914 at the age of eighty-five, he lived long enough to span the teachings of Benjamin Rush, whom he never ceased to admire, and those of Sigmund Freud, who was just then becoming known in the United States. Mitchell's ironical attitude towards the "German perplexities" of psychoanalysis is well portrayed in his words on "nostalgia."

The psychiatric phase of his long and productive professional life derives special interest from its concurrence with the initial period of the Freudian era. While the careers of these two eminent men overlapped for a brief time only, it was long enough for Mitchell to evaluate psychoanalysis and to reject it. Freud, on the other hand, adopted at least one major concept of his older colleague—that of the role of rest in the management of neuroses—and incorporated it into his own therapeutic regimen. Despite the differences in their basic approaches to the problems of mental disease, Mitchell and Freud shared one important aim, namely, to prevent neurotic patients from becoming increasingly disturbed and to work towards their early restoration to society.

The complete survival of Freud's ideas is in striking contrast to the almost total oblivion into which those of Mitchell have fallen, although they were immensely influential in their day. Also, in spite of Mitchell's negative attitude towards psychoanalysis, he helped in no small measure, though quite inadvertently, to pave the way for its ready acceptance in the United States by his initiation of non-institutional treatment of neuroses.

Most of Mitchell's neurotic patients, like many of Freud's, were women suffering from hysteria: it was for their management that he wrote his first psychiatric treatise, *Fat and Blood* (1877).[25] This strange title was an expression of the then not uncommon belief that "moral" or psychiatric treatment could be effective only in persons in good physical health. The cases he thus treated were "chiefly women of the clan well known to every physician,—nervous women,

[25] S. Weir Mitchell, *Fat and Blood: And How To Make Them* (Philadelphia: J. B. Lippincott & Co., 1877).

who as a rule are thin, and lack blood." Most of them had
previously "run the gauntlet of nerve-doctors, gynaecolo-
gists, plaster jackets, braces, water-treatment, and all the
phantastic variety of other cures" and still remained invalids
"unable to attend the duties of life and sources alike of discomfort to themselves and anxiety to others." He saw the
general development of the disease as follows:

> The woman grows pale and thin, eats little, or if she eats does
> not profit by it. Everything wearies her,—to sew, to write, to
> read, to walk,—and by and by the sofa or the bed is her only
> comfort. Every effort is paid for dearly, and she describes herself
> as aching and sore, as sleeping ill, and as needing constant stimu-
> lus and endless tonics. Then comes the mischievous rôle of bro-
> mides, opium, chloral, and brandy. If the case did not begin with
> uterine troubles they soon appear, and are usually treated in vain
> if the general means employed to build up the bodily health fail,
> as in many of these cases they do fail. The same remark applies
> to the dyspepsias and constipation which further annoy the pa-
> tient and embarrass the treatment. If such a person is emotional
> she does not fail to become more so, and even the firmest
> women lose self-control at last under incessant feebleness.[26]

If these events were not interrupted, these women were
destined to become permanently bed-ridden and to furnish
the most lamentable examples of all the strange phenomena
of hysteria. Mitchell saw "the self-sacrificing love and over-
careful sympathy of a mother, a sister, or some other devoted relative" as a further aggravation of the burden that
tended to destroy the patient. He applauded Oliver Wendell
Holmes's incisive description of a hysterical girl as "a vam-
pire who sucks the blood of the healthy people around her."
For this reason Mitchell introduced his famous "rest cure,"
which entailed a specified period of bed rest away from the
influence of the oversolicitous families, believing, as did
Carter, that "once [you] separate the patient from the moral
and physical surroundings which have become part of her
life of sickness, and you will have made a change which will
be in itself beneficial, and will enormously aid in the treatment which is to follow."

Although Mitchell's book was entitled *Fat and Blood*, he
was fully aware that fat itself was not synonymous with
health and that obesity was frequently a symptom of a pro-

[26] *Ibid.*, pp. 27–28.

found disturbance. But he reasoned that since great exertion, periods of prolonged emotional strain, and physical illness frequently resulted in rapid loss of weight, a slight surplus of fat should be possessed by every individual. Many of his patients suffered from "nervous exhaustion" or were emaciated and anemic from continuous dyspepsia and were therefore already depleted of fat resources. For these in particular he prescribed the rest cure—not the pleasurable escape that was often sought by neurotic patients. He said "to lie abed half the day, and sew a little and read a little, and be interesting and excite sympathy, is all very well, but when they are bidden to stay in bed a month, and neither to read, write, nor sew, and to have one nurse,—who is not a relative,—then rest becomes for some women a rather bitter medicine, and they are glad enough to accept the order to rise and go about when the doctor issues a mandate which has become pleasantly welcome and eagerly looked for."[27]

Although Mitchell realized that some patients might take to such treatment with "morbid delight," he felt that they could be handled by a discerning physician. To forestall the weakening of the body by enforced bed rest, he prescribed a great deal of passive exercise in the form of massage and electrical stimulation. He observed that this regimen accompanied by a light but nutritious diet generally evoked a sense of immediate relief and often an abrupt disappearance of all the earlier symptoms. However, rest, isolation from former harmful influences, diet, and passive exercise furnished only the frame for the actual treatment; the substance was supplied by the physician in the form of "moral medication," or psychotherapy. This consisted largely of long conversations with the patient, eliciting, often in writing, her life history and the circumstances preceding the onset of the hysterical state.

In a somewhat later study, he stated "I make use of some of the curious self-analyses which patients who have recovered have placed at my disposal. Both for what they betray and what they conceal these histories are valuable, and especially so when they come from women of educated intelligence. The elements out of which these disorders arise

27 *Ibid.*, p. 41.

are deeply human, and exist in all of us, in varying amount"[28] It is interesting that these statements preceded Freud's publications by several years.

Mitchell was extremely resourceful in his moral therapy. He "urged and scolded, and teased and bribed, and decoyed along the road to health; but this is what it means to treat hysteria. There is no short cut; no royal road." He was an extraordinarily charming man, erudite and entertaining, and doubtless most attractive to his female patients. His resourcefulness in dealing with them was almost boundless. One of his most astounding approaches is related by his biographer A. B. Burr and concerns one of his patients who refused to obey Mitchell's order that she leave her bed. When all arguments and orders proved futile, he finally threatened: "If you are not out of bed in five minutes—I'll get into it with you!" Even this threat proved to be without effect and Mitchell began to undress; but when he was about to remove his trousers the patient left her bed in haste. While this story may be apocryphal, since Mitchell does not relate it himself, it was well known during his lifetime and apparently was never denied by him.

It is strange indeed that with all his intimate contact and understanding of his female patients, he was so little impressed with the etiological role of sexual deprivation, unlike so many other students of hysteria. Although he spoke of the "false relationships with husbands" that could cause neuroses, he nevertheless categorically rejected all sexual implications. He described Freud's writings as "filthy things" that should be consigned to the fire. On one occasion, however, speaking before the American Neurological Association in Philadelphia on May 21, 1908, in a somewhat mellower mood, he admitted an "intellectual welcome" and an open mind to "psychopathic analysis." And he went on to say: "I most gladly read the elaborate and novel studies in psychologic diagnosis, the laboratory aids, the association test, the mind probing examinations. They are interesting and even fascinating, although at times men do seem to me to

[28] *Lectures on Diseases of the Nervous System, Especially in Women* (Philadelphia: Henry C. Lea's Son & Co., 1881), pp. 50–51.

reach by wandering ways facts of individual history more simply to be discovered by less cumbersome methods."

The similarities between the views of Mitchell and Carter on hysteria, although independently arrived at, are obvious. Two important differences, however, have a distinct bearing on the problem. One is Mitchell's rejection of sexual factors as the essential cause of hysterical disturbances. The other is their diametrically opposed attitudes towards the hysterical female, Carter and most of his colleagues being critical and hostile and Mitchell entertaining a sympathy and even fondness for these unfortunate women. They constituted his primary psychiatric interest, particularly the female neurotic patient of the "leisure class." In a later treatise, he even took for granted a similar attitude on the part of his colleagues: "With all her weakness, her unstable emotionality, her tendency to morally warp when long nervously ill, she is then far easier to deal with, far more amenable to reason, far more sure to be comfortable as a patient, than the man who is relatively in a like position. The reasons for this are too obvious to delay me here, and physicians accustomed to deal with both sexes as sick people will be apt to justify my position."[29]

Mitchell admitted that he had often been asked whether his constant contact "with the nervous weaknesses, the petty moral deformities" of his female patients had not lessened his esteem for women. He answered with an emphatic denial: "The largest knowledge finds the largest excuses"; and the physician aware of the many possible educational errors and the marital difficulties will not condemn the patient but understand and help her.

The priest hears the crime or folly of the hour, but to the physician are oftener told the long, sad tales of a whole life, its far-away mistakes, its failures, and its faults. None may be quite foreign to his purpose or needs. The causes of breakdowns and nervous disaster, and consequent emotional disturbances and their bitter fruit, are often to be sought in the remote past. He may dislike the quest, but he cannot avoid it. If he be a student of character, it will have for him a personal interest as well as the relative value of its applicative side. The moral world of the

29 *Doctor and Patient* (Philadelphia: J. B. Lippincott & Co., 1888), p. 11.

sick-bed explains in a measure some of the things that are strange in daily life, and the man who does not know sick women does not know women.[30]

The women of Mitchell's day cherished this special concern and thrived under his benevolent protection. But Mitchell's day ended on the eve of World War I, and at its close women had renounced all the special frailties and privileges that Mitchell had found so endearing and that had provided the basis for his therapy. The last vestiges of Victorian reticence had also disappeared, and the new climate of thought, thoroughly receptive to Freudian views, had little interest in Mitchell's tranquil methods or in his efforts to put "wholesome fat" on women who were rigorously dieting to achieve the figures of young boys.

[30] *Ibid.*, p. 10.

CHAPTER X

From Mesmerism
to Hypnotism

The EVOLUTIONARY PATTERN followed in this study of hysteria explains only part of the basis for modern ideas. Another, and a more tangible, bridge between eighteenth-century concepts and our own was being synchronously erected. In order to trace this second sequence of ideas—which actually bear more directly on present-day thinking—it is necessary to go back to the last quarter of the eighteenth century and pick up the strand where it first became noticeable, namely, with mesmerism, animal magnetism, and the genesis of hypnotism.

The enigma of Franz Anton Mesmer (1734–1815) remains as unexplained as ever. Starting from a traditional origin as a graduate in medicine of the University of Vienna, he became the innovator and promulgator of what he called animal magnetism, which became almost a religion and seriously affected social and medical life all over Europe. He has successively been hailed as a genius and denounced as an imposter. But his ideas took firm root and are discernible indirectly as a constituent of Freudianism and directly in their application to medicine, surgery, and dentistry today.

Far from beginning as a charlatan—a role in which we are now wont to cast him—Mesmer's early motivations were highly ethical. Soon after being graduated from the University of Vienna in 1766, he began to be increasingly aware that the therapeutic limitations of the medicine of his day compared unfavorably with the widened knowledge of hu-

man physiology and pathology. His search for a more effective therapeutic approach turned to the ancient idea of astral
influences upon the world; he theorized that by means of an
invisible and impalpable "universal fluid" a cosmic influence
might even extend to the organism of the human individual.
The nature of the connection between man and the universe
resembled to him the attraction between the magnet and
metallic objects. Disease, he thought, was due to an imbalance of the universal fluid and cure could be effected by
bringing the patient into contact with its source. Man, like
the magnet, is bipolar and, therefore, the magnet appeared
to be the logical instrument by which the cosmic powers
could be conveyed to the patient. When his early experiments proved dramatically successful, he found that the
human hand was equally effective, and, from this as well as
its application to living beings, he derived the concept of
"animal magnetism."

Mesmer's first results with his method of treatment in
Vienna were so impressive that patients came to him from
all over Europe. The initially disinterested medical profession became increasingly hostile to the point that in 1778
Mesmer felt it advisable to shift his scene of operation to
Paris, where innovations always found a more hospitable
environment.

In Vienna he had complied with the medical customs of
his day by restricting his ministrations to individual patients.
In Paris, however, he developed the theory that the healing
power of the magnetic fluid would be greatly enhanced if it
were passed from him through, and to, many patients simultaneously. This "group practice" was attended by elaborate
ceremony, which strongly appealed to the jaded tastes of his
well-born patients in the French capital. The healing rituals
took place in a heavily curtained room occupied by a large,
covered wooden tub in the center. This tub, or *baquet,* was
filled with water and magnetized iron filings. Jointed iron
rods protruding through the pierced lid were directed by
the patients to the ailing parts of their bodies. Mesmer made
his appearance with the accompaniment of soft mournful
music. He slowly passed among his patients, draped in a
lavender-colored silken robe or suit, fixing his eyes upon
each in turn and touching them with his hands or with a long

magnetized iron wand, which he always carried with him. Occasionally the healing ceremonies were held out-of-doors under previously "magnetized" oak trees or on the banks of "magnetized" fountains or brooks. Beguiled by this impressive ritual, the participants, predominantly women, fell into a somnolent trance or mesmeric sleep, from which they awoke refreshed and healed. The suggestion that the state of well-being may have been sexual gratification that was perhaps not entirely elicited by astral influence has often been raised.

The obvious charlatanry thoroughly justified his medical colleagues' hostile criticism and after a few years they succeeded in putting an end to Mesmer's séances. The public, however, clamored so vociferously that in 1784 Louis XVI appointed a Royal Commission to examine the validity of "animal magnetism." This illustrious body was composed of the leading scientific personalities of the day, including such men as Benjamin Franklin and chemist Lavoisier and astronomer Bailly. Restricting their investigation to determining the existence of "animal magnetism," which was their mandate, they reported that there was no such thing and that Mesmer's cures were entirely due to imagination.

THE MESMERISTS

Mesmer was so disheartened by this verdict, and the consequent interdiction of his practices by the medical faculty of the University of Paris that he withdrew into obscurity for the rest of his life. The doctrine of animal magnetism survived, however. It found numerous adherents in Paris and throughout France and in many other countries, including the United States. Among the persons most responsible for its continuation in France was Mesmer's student, the Marquis de Puységur, whose *Mémoirs pour servir à l'histoire de l'établissement du magnetism en France* appeared in 1784, the very year the practice of mesmerism was forbidden by the University of Paris. On his country estate at Buzancy, Puységur, emulating Mesmer, magnetized persons who came to him for help. The most important of these from the standpoint of further developments was Victor, a simple young shepherd in whom Puységur believed he had induced a complete change in personality. In the state of magnetized sleep, the usually taciturn and ignorant subject became an animated, eloquent, and intelligent conversationalist. Moreover, some of his utterances appeared to the Marquis to be clairvoyant. Upon awakening, Victor resumed his former ignorance and was completely unaware of his behavior under magnetism.

Puységur and his colleagues thought that personality changes such as were observed in Victor and others during magnetic sleep bordered on the miraculous. This aspect of magnetism appeared to them of even greater interest and significance than the therapeutic results obtained by Mesmer. Thus the "somnambulistic sleep" displaced in their investigations the "salutary crisis," or the post-magnetic physical and vocal contortions that Mesmer had believed to have brought about the cure of his patients.

Inducing in subjects states of mental acuity entirely beyond and foreign to their normal condition, suggesting even clairvoyance, was sensational indeed; it appealed strongly to the showmanship of itinerant magnetizers whose aims were entertainment for profit. But Puységur's group, genuinely interested in the scientific possibilities of these new discoveries, continued their investigations. They concentrated on studying the sleep-wake state of the mesmerized subjects, whom they called "lucid somnambulists," and consequently probed into the normal and pathological nervous and mental phenomena of other spontaneous conditions similar to the one they evoked. They were thus among the early investigators of neurologic and psychological disorders and actually prepared the way for modern psychology.

The magnetizers, both theoretical and practical, created tremendous enthusiasm and attracted countless followers, many of whom were physicians of great repute and scientific integrity. But their unlimited hopes were the undoing of the movement. Their scientific ambition extended to the search for a complete understanding of the physiology of the nervous system, and their therapeutic aim was to find the answer to all forms of disease. Again, as in the case of Mesmer, learned French committees were convened, and in

1840 a verdict adverse to the entire movement was issued. The consequent disrepute of magnetism was so intense that those physicians who wished to pursue the study of somnambulism had to do so in secrecy.

In the meantime, a particularly vigorous movement developed in England under the ardent leadership of John Elliotson. Here, too, the mesmerists were excluded from the regular hospitals and were compelled to establish their own institutions; the most important, the London Mesmeric Infirmary, was opened in 1850. But Elliotson and his fellow magnetizers never deviated from Mesmer's methods, nor did it ever occur to them to question or to analyze the phenomenon of mesmeric sleep.

NERVOUS SLEEP

James Braid was finally impelled to do so because his initial violent skepticism towards mesmerism was shaken by closer acquaintance with the actual phenomenon. Born in 1795 in Fifeshire, Scotland, he was educated in Great Britain's leading medical school, the University of Edinburgh, then settled in Manchester, where he practiced surgery. In 1841 he attended several séances of an itinerant mesmerist "as a complete sceptic . . . [and] fully inclined to join with those who considered the whole to be a system of collusion or delusion, or of excited imagination, sympathy or imitation." Yet, on the contrary, he became profoundly interested in the phenomenon.

Braid subsequently devoted a great deal of time to studying artificially induced sleep. He soon developed an entirely new and scientific vocabulary, which was to him more representative of the phenomenon than the previous mesmeric terminology and by which he intended to save his work from any taint of charlatanism. He summarized the results of his labors in 1843 in a small, highly readable volume entitled *Neurypnology; or the Rationale of Nervous Sleep, Considered in Relation with Animal Magnetism*. It introduced the terms "neuro-hypnotism," or hypnosis, and proved conclusively that hypnotic "phenomena are induced solely by an impression made on the nervous centers" without any "mystical universal fluid" or other substance passing from operator to patient.

The first part of Braid's book is devoted to the separation of hypnotism from the mesmeric approach and to methods of hypnosis and similar general consideration. He attempted to disprove some of the sensational claims that had made mesmerism so odious to the medical profession. The most striking and a still unresolved and debated question was the assumption that patients in a hypnotic trance could be exploited to perform criminal or obscene acts. Braid had firm opinions on this matter:

> I am aware great prejudice has been raised against mesmerism, from the idea that it might be turned to immoral purposes. In respect to the Neuro-Hypnotic state, induced by the method explained in this treatise, I am quite certain that *it* deserves no such censure. I have proved by experiments, both in public and in private, that during the state of excitement, the judgment is sufficiently active to make the patients, if possible, even *more* fastidious as regards propriety of conduct, than in the waking condition; and from the state of rigidity and insensibility, they can be roused to a state of mobility, and exalted sensibility, either by being rudely handled, or even by a breath of air. Nor is it requisite this should be done by the person who put them into the Hypnotic state. It will follow equally from the manipulations of any one else, or a current of air impinging against the body, from any mechanical contrivance whatever. And, finally, the state cannot be induced, in any stage, unless with the knowledge and consent of the party operated on.[1]

In view of the generous prescriptions of opium then in vogue among the physicians, Braid's argument concerning the harmlessness of hypnosis in contrast to "a great number of our most valuable medicines" is quite to the point.

> There are many [drugs] which we are in the daily habit of using, with the best advantage in the relief and cure of disease, which may be, and have been rendered most potent for the furtherance of the ends of the vicious and cruel; and which can be administered without the knowledge of the intended victims. It ought never to be lost sight of, that there is the *use* and *abuse* of every thing in nature. It is the *use,* and only the *judicious use* of Hypnotism, which I advocate.[2]

[1] *Neurypnology; or the Rationale of Nervous Sleep, Considered in Relation with Animal Magnetism* (London: J. Churchill, 1843), p. 10.
[2] *Ibid.,* pp. 10–11.

The second part of the book contains specific case histories with extensive commentaries. In these Braid reported successful treatment of tic douloureux, paralysis, aphasia, deafness, rheumatism, headache, palpitation, skin diseases, and other organic and functional diseases. He also used hypnotism with signal success in his surgical operations to eliminate pain, since anesthesia was not yet available. Braid was, however, by no means uncritically confident of the lasting effects of all cures and often realized that, although temporary alleviations could be obtained, the extent of organic impairment rendered some diseases incurable.

Braid completely separated animal magnetism from hypnosis, but he was still attacked by the foes of mesmerism, who felt that the findings of the French commission should have ended the subject once and for all. He answered them by pointing out that a similar learned body had been appointed two hundred years earlier "to investigate and to report on Harvey's discovery of the circulation of the blood, and that this most important discovery was rejected by them as a fallacy." He felt that a fair hearing should be given to the cause of hypnotism and particularly to his own experiences and experiments in this matter, but he was emphatic in disclaiming hypnosis as a universal panacea; "I feel quite confident we have acquired in this process a valuable addition to our curative means; but I repudiate the idea of holding it up as a universal remedy; nor do I even pretend to understand, as yet, the *whole range of diseases* in which it may be useful. Time and experience alone can determine this question, as is the case with all other new remedies."[3]

Apart from its role as a pain-killer in surgical operations, Braid stressed the therapeutic value of hypnosis in functional disorders particularly. He was among the first to emphasize the distinction between functional and organic diseases and to recognize the value of suggestion in the former: "By the impression which hypnotism induces on the nervous system, we acquire a power of rapidly curing many functional disorders, most intractable, or altogether incurable, by ordinary remedies, and also many of those distressing affections which, as in most cases they evince no pathological change of structure, have been presumed to depend on some pecul-

[3] *Ibid.*, p. 5.

iar condition of the nervous system, and have therefore, by
universal consent, been denominated 'nervous complaints.' "[4]
Here we find the definitive separation of behavioral disorders
from organic disease of the nervous system.

THE GREAT CHARCOT

Braid never had the satisfaction of finding acceptance for his
views in his own country. And when the movement was
revived, decades later, primarily in France, in spite of Braid's
work the thought lingered that an intangible fluid, activated
in the process of hypnotism and transmitted by an inanimate
instrument, was the effective agent in the procedure. It is remarkable that one of those who shared this view was Jean-
Martin Charcot, the most precise neurological scientist of his
day.

The tragedy of the story of Charcot, who was so vitally
important in the history of hysteria and psychiatry in general, rests largely on his exaggerated confidence in certain
aspects of hypnotism. The collapse of these hypotheses cost
him much of the fame and respect which his earlier labors
had brought him.

Jean-Martin Charcot was born in Paris in 1825, a contemporary of Griesinger, Carter, and Mitchell.[5] Medicine was
his choice as a career, and he began his studies at the University of Paris at the age of nineteen. During internship he
completed his inaugural thesis on chronic progressive rheumatism, which he was the first in France to differentiate
from gout. After successfully defending his thesis in 1853,
he received the appointment of *Chef de Clinique* of the Faculty of Medicine, which he held for two years. He was
fortunate to have the sponsorship of Professor Pierre François Rayer, an influential friend of France's leading medical
figures. When Charcot began his private practice, Rayer
immediately referred to him an extremely wealthy patient

---

[4] *Ibid.*, p. 15.

[5] The bibliographical account is taken from Georges Guillain, *J.-M. Charcot, 1825–1893, Sa vie–son oeuvre* (Paris: Masson, 1955). This book was edited and translated by Pearce Bailey, *J.-M. Charcot, 1825–1893: His Life–His Work* (New York: Paul Hoeber, 1959).

whom he accompanied as a medical attendant on a trip through Italy. He began to draw and paint on this journey, an avocation that he pursued throughout the remainder of his life. He applied this talent to his professional work also and often sketched the expressions and postures of unusually interesting patients.

As Charcot passed through the various stages of a French academic career, he had shown signs of great promise, publishing widely on different medical subjects, but he evinced little interest in the pathology and clinical correlation of diseases of the nervous system. At the age of thirty-seven he was made physician to the Salpêtrière Hospital, which attained its first major publicity in connection with Pinel's work. It usually housed some five thousand neurotic indigents, epileptics, and insane patients, many of whom were deemed incurable. With this extraordinary number and variety of patient material, his orientation changed; "it was during a period of only eight years, between 1862 and 1870, that Charcot structured his magnificent masterpieces by his descriptions of multiple sclerosis, the tabetic arthropathies, amyotrophic lateral sclerosis, and the localization of lesions of the spinal cord."[6] These studies established his fame as a scientist and provided a magnificent beginning for his additional contributions to neurology and neuropathology. He also proved to be a superb teacher and later attracted students from all parts of the world.

Charcot's enormous popularity is all the more astonishing in view of the calm aloofness that struck all those about him, an aloofness maintained even during the last stages of the Prussian siege of Paris in 1871. He was described as arriving for work promptly every morning, "looking very calm, and very cold as usual with his thin cleanly shaved face, long black hair, and his Napoleonic profile."[7] Much later, Havelock Ellis used almost the same terms when he said of Charcot: "Anyone who was privileged to observe his methods of work at the Salpêtrière will easily recall the great master's towering figure; the disdainful expression, sometimes even, it seemed, a little sour; the lofty bearing which enthusiastic

---

[6] *Ibid.*, p. 10.   [7] *Ibid.*, p. 12.

admirers called Napoleonic."[8] The sheer number and variety of patients at the Salpêtrière that he studied so effectively might have defeated many other men, particularly those warmer personalities who had a closer kinship with their fellow beings. Charcot saw these patients as a huge neurological laboratory of material for his experiments, his famous clinical lectures, and his subsequent publications.

After ten years as chief of the medical services at the Salpêtrière, Charcot was nominated to the professorship of pathological anatomy at the University of Paris. He occupied this chair until 1882, when he was appointed to the newly established professorship in diseases of the nervous system at the same institution. Although he maintained an interest in organic neurologic disorders throughout his teaching career, in his later years he was chiefly concerned with investigation of the neuroses, hysteria, and hypnotism.

This interest logically grew out of his life at the Salpêtrière; but his shift from organic neurological and neuropathological studies to hysteria was the accidental result of an administrative arrangement at that hospital. As related by Pierre Marie, one of Charcot's students, certain parts of the ancient buildings that composed the Salpêtrière had become so decrepit that they had to be abandoned. The inmates were transferred to other divisions and the non-psychotic epileptics and the hysterics were separated from the insane. Since the first two groups manifested episodic behavior, it was considered logical to house them together and to establish a special section, called the *quartier des épileptiques simples,* or the "division of simple epileptics."[9] This service was assigned to Charcot as the senior physician, who suddenly found himself surrounded by the problems of hysteria.

Pierre Marie went on to explain the results of this anomalous condition. Whereas in this new situation the seizures of the epileptics remained unchanged in frequency and severity, the hysterics were greatly affected by their constant exposure to epileptic patients. Because of their neurotic tendency to mimic, especially the young hysterics began to imi-

[8] Quoted by Fielding H. Garrison, *An Introduction to the History of Medicine,* p. 640.

[9] J.-M. Charcot, *Leçons du mardi à la Salpêtrière, policlinique du 19 mars, 1889* (Paris: Félix Alcan, 1889), II, 424.

tate every phase of epileptic seizures, the tonic and the clonic convulsions, the subsequent hallucinations, and finally Charcot's "bizarre postures."

Unfortunately Charcot failed to recognize this imitation at first and believed that a new entity was manifest, which he termed "hystero-epilepsy." Only much later did he realize the absurdity of this designation, and he called attention to the great difference between the clinical form as well as the substratum of a true epileptic attack which have been classed under the name of epileptiform hysteria.[10]

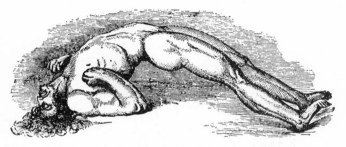

Fig. 8. Opisthotonos. In Charcot's clinic this *arc en cercle* was described as follows: "The body is bent in a bow-like curve and is supported only by the neck and the feet; the hair is disshevelled; the extremities are agitated by clonic '*grands mouvements*' of flexion and extension and the mouth is opened widely." (From Charles Bell, *The Anatomy and Philosophy of Expression* [London, 1806].)

In the meantime, having immersed himself specifically in the study of hysteria, he noted that the *grandes* paroxysms, which to him represented "hysteria major," always occurred in an identical manner in the same patient. As mentioned earlier, such convulsive attacks had become rare in his day but, as mimicked epileptic fits, they appeared to occur frequently in the Salpêtrière. Charcot distinguished these seizures of "hystero-epilepsy," from the veiled manifestations that he called "hysteria minor." He noted narrowing of the field of vision as well as disturbances of skin sensitivity,

[10] J.-M. Charcot, *Lectures on the Diseases of the Nervous System*, trans. George Sigerson (London: New Sydenham Society, 1877), p. 304.

which included hemianesthesia. When these two somatic manifestations occurred simultaneously, they were characterized as the physical stigmata of hysteria. Thus he defined hysteria as a specific neurosis that manifests itself by periodic attacks and permanent stigmata.

Charcot was among those who knew that the same symptoms could be found in men as well as women. He wrote in one of his lectures: "Keep it well in mind and this should not require a great effort, that the word 'hysteria' means nothing, and little by little you will acquire the habit of

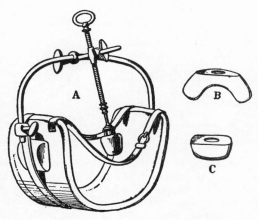

Fig. 9. "Ovary compressor" used by Charcot. (From Bourneville and P. Regnard, *Iconographie photographique de la Salpêtrière* [Paris: Progrès Médical, 1878].)

speaking of hysteria in man without thinking in any way of the uterus."[11] But since the Salpêtrière was a hospital for female patients, most of Charcot's patients were women, and among them he found symptoms that had not previously been recorded, namely, spontaneous pains in the region of the ovaries and the mammary glands. This suggested to Charcot that these regions were "hysterogenic zones." Because of this idea a peculiar device was developed, an "ovary compressor," and was frequently used in the Salpêtrière in an attempt to avert major paroxysms after the prodromata had become evident.

[11] *Ibid.*, p. 37.

Contrary to all previous observers, Charcot described the attacks as being quite uniform in all his patients. The paroxysm itself, he said, consisted of the four stages that he had described in hystero-epilepsy. With a similar attempt at systematization, he arranged the stigmata in three categories: (1) the sensory disturbances, which included the anesthesias

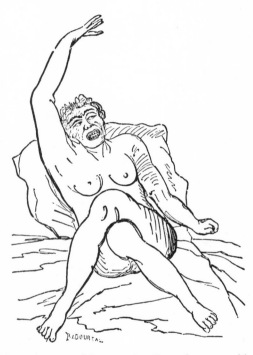

Fig. 10. Hysteria: convulsive attack. (From *Iconographie photographique de la Salpêtrière.*)

and hyperesthesias; (2) the disturbances of the special senses, such as deafness and narrowing of the field of vision, and (3) the motor disturbances. He was aware, of course, that all these impairments were functional, but that they mimicked organic disease. Charcot never doubted that the paroxysm would invariably unfold into the major hysteric crisis with its four well-defined phases. It seems never to have

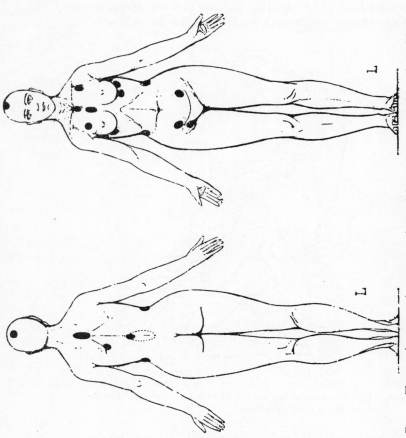

Fig. 11. Twenty hysterogenic zones as observed in a twenty-year-old patient. (From *Iconographie photographique de la Salpêtrière* (Paris: Progrès Médical, 1879–80.)

occurred to him that the patients might be acting out what they knew was expected of them; or that the repetition of these dramatic crises at the precise time of lectures and demonstrations before an appreciative audience of physicians and medical students may have been engineered by his assistants as a misguided expression of helpfulness. The means by which it is believed this was achieved will be described later.

Charcot is popularly credited with recognizing the role of the emotions in the production of hysteria. Although it has been shown above that he was far from the first to do so, his pronouncements, coming as they did from the leading figure in neuropsychiatry, were not only more acceptable but also spread to a much wider medical public. Among his observations was the role of suggestion in creating certain symptoms, such as artificially induced paralysis, and he stated that "in the matter of suggestion, what is done can be undone." Charcot also knew of the narrow and often barely perceptible line that seems to divide hysteria from malingering, which often evaporated to amalgamate the two states. He expressed his admiration for "the ruse, the sagacity, and the unyielding tenacity that especially the women, who are under the influence of a severe neurosis, display in order to deceive . . . particularly when the victim of the deceit happens to be a physician."[12]

Even more than his predecessors, Charcot attributed a major significance to psychic trauma in the production of hysterical attacks and, for this reason, urged the removal of patients from the psychopathogenic environment:

It would not be possible for me to insist too much on the capital importance which attaches to Isolation in the treatment of hysteria. Without doubt, the psychic element plays a very important part in most of the cases of this malady, even when it is not the predominating feature. I have held firmly to this doctrine for nearly fifteen years, and all that I have seen during that time—everything that I have observed day by day—tends only to confirm me in that opinion. Yes, it is necessary to separate both children and adults from their father and their mother, whose influence, as experience teaches, is particularly pernicious.

Experience shows repeatedly, though it is not always easy to understand the reason, that it is the mothers whose influence is so

12 J.-M. Charcot, "Isolation in the Treatment of Hysteria," in *Clinical Lectures on Diseases of the Nervous System*, trans. Thomas Savill (London: New Sydenham Society, 1889), III, 368.

deleterious, who will hear no argument, and will only yield in general to the last extremity.[13]

The validity of the observations in terms of the position held today is obvious. Again, they were more acceptable coming from Charcot than from Carter, the relatively unknown practitioner in the English countryside, or from the Americans, Mitchell and Holmes, though all these men were prominent in their own countries. Similarly, the phenomenon of hysterical contagion, first noted by Baglivi and afterwards observed by so many others, was described by Charcot as explaining some of the mass hysterias in the convents of the Middle Ages and the Renaissance. He prescribed "the breaking up or scattering of a group . . . [as] the most certain method, under these circumstances, that can be devised to check further propagation of the illness."

Charcot's formula for treatment of hysteria was largely limited to symptomatic therapy. It consisted of two approaches. The first was psychological and was directed towards the neutralizing of the original psychic trauma and assuring patients that their afflictions were curable. He insisted on a change of their "moral environment," i.e., their separation from parents and from other hysterical patients, and he demanded submission to a certain amount of discipline. His second approach was the traditional effort directed towards the reinvigorating of organs and extremities and stimulating the muscles to alleviate concurrent symptomatic impairment.

On the whole, however, it appears that Charcot was far less intensely concerned with therapy than with scientific analysis of the disease. This has been elaborated by Thomas Szasz, who suggested that Charcot's primary role as a professor of neurology was to increase knowledge of the diseases of the nervous system and to teach students and physicians.[14] But more significant than this, perhaps, was his aloof personality, which could not identify itself with the miseries of his patients, particularly since the dregs of society com-

13 *Ibid.*, p. 210.

14 Thomas S. Szasz, *The Myth of Mental Illness: Foundations of a Theory of Personal Conduct* (London: Secker & Warburg, 1961), p. 21.

FIG. 12. Hypnotic production of catalepsy in a hysterical patient. (From *Iconographie photographique de la Salpêtrière* [Paris: Progrès Médical, 1878].)

prised the inmates of the Salpêtrière. For these reasons, he
more easily differed in his physician-patient relationships
than had Mitchell whose nervous ladies were part of his own
social milieu.

This image of Charcot is further portrayed by some of his
colleagues and acquaintances. Thus he has been described as
"magnificent like a god of Mount Olympus, . . . severe, with
the head of an antique Jupiter . . . a somewhat sad expression
. . . soft eyes which scrutinized slowly but profoundly, a
profile of an old cameo." Havelock Ellis further remarked:
"For purely psychological investigation he had no liking and
probably no aptitude. . . . The questions addressed to the
patient were cold, distant, sometimes impatient." Nevertheless, in his rather impersonal fashion, Charcot contributed to
the welfare of the hysterical patients as much as Mitchell
had helped them with his warm, individualized concern. Just
as Mitchell had removed the stigma from the neurotic patient and made her again acceptable in society, so Charcot
made sick people of the apparently wilfully misbehaving,
disagreeable women who had, in the nineteenth century,
been suspected of malingering. To both these eminent neu-
ropsychiatrists, even the person who pretended an emotional
illness was not entirely a pure malingerer but was suffering
from a neurotic state.

That Charcot, the most scientific and productive of all
neurologists of his day, should ever be actively involved
with hypnotism is astounding. It can only be explained as
the result of his broad interest in all aspects of brain function, including the new field of psychology. The study of
mental function had been up to his time almost exclusively
in the hands of scholars and philosophers. Charcot felt that
such knowledge could add a new dimension to understanding diseases of the nervous system, and he therefore invited
several psychologists to join in his researches as part of his
effort to combine all elements that had any bearing on mental processes, which naturally also extended to hypnotism.
His interest awakened, he made a systematic study of the
subject beginning with the writings of Braid and then introduced hypnotism into his own program at the Salpêtrière in
1878. At the outset "a prudent and conservative orientation
was developed and applied to these investigations." But soon

this caution gave way to uncritical and enthusiastic reports of spectacular findings that were totally unsupported by scientific proof. Thus, as intimated above, Charcot's concern with hypnotism led him into error that proved to have catastrophic repercussions. It would appear that Charcot first visualized hypnotism primarily as a diagnostic agent rather than an important therapeutic tool. In fact, in the beginning he became convinced that mere susceptibility to hypnotism indicated that the subject was potentially hysterical, and he never deviated from this view.

Significantly, Charcot never induced the trance state himself but relegated this duty to his assistants. It has been assumed that unbeknown to Charcot these men conditioned the patients to perform according to their chief's expectations. Thus the eminent neuroscientist was led into serious error by the well-meaning efforts of his faithful associates. The regular responses to implanted suggestion, of which he was unaware, gave him reason to believe that the hysterical patients' uniform reactions to hypnotism were characteristic of the disease; and on these convictions he staked his scientific reputation.

Charcot concluded from these studies that "major hypnotism" could only be induced in grave hysterics and that the manifestations of "major hypnotism" were always a reenactment of a typical grand paroxysm. In the paralyses that so often followed the attack, Charcot reported an exaggerated patellar tendon reflex on the side that was paralyzed. He also claimed to be able to transfer analgesia or anesthesia from the affected side to the opposite side by means of magnets. To him, this constituted a diagnostic tool far more reliable than any previous one for recognizing this confusing disease and differentiating it from such states as epilepsy or malingering, which it so closely resembled. And this Charcot proclaimed with the full authority of his fame and official position.

Although the French Academy of Sciences had repeatedly condemned all work on magnetism, it could not ignore serious pronouncements by the world's leading neurologist. Despite the fact that its approval in 1882 was grudging and partial, it was nevertheless sufficient to lift the onus from hypnotism and make possible further research concerning it.

This new freedom was taken advantage of just two years later by a group of investigators who came to be known as the "Nancy School," which was to rival and challenge Charcot's work at the Salpêtrière until his death in 1892. The challengers were A. A. Liébault, a local medical practitioner, and Hyppolyte Bernheim (1837–1919), a professor at the University of Nancy. Their approach to hypnosis differed radically from Charcot's. They hypnotized patients themselves, were unconcerned with the reflexes and contractures brought about by hypnosis, and operated with words alone, without recourse to instruments and magnets. Moreover, they were decidedly interested in the therapeutic uses of hypnotism, and Bernheim recorded a great number of speedy cures of hysterical disorders. Like Braid, they altogether denied the existence of any fluid passing from hypnotizer to patient and strongly maintained that whatever influence was exerted was entirely psychological.

Bernheim insisted that the hypnotic state was nothing more than sleep brought about by suggestion and that it accentuated the effects of suggestion by removing intellectual control. Both Liébault and Bernheim found that susceptibility to hypnosis was not restricted to neuropaths and that, although impressionability varied from person to person, "the majority of persons can be readily inclined towards it." Bernheim postulated that hysteria was not actually a disease at all and that everyone was potentially more or less hysterical.[15] According to his definition, hysteria consisted simply of attacks occurring in persons whose psychological reaction to emotional traumata was exaggerated or distorted. Bernheim coined the expression *hystérisables* for such persons, and a series of attacks he called "hysterical diathesis." This tendency towards hysteria could be corrected through emotional education or guidance, which was in reality a form of suggestion. Bernheim himself readily admitted that hysterics were especially suggestible, but he emphatically denied that suggestibility in itself was a pathological condition.

The question of augmented suggestibility in connection with hypnosis led to a re-examination of the problem of

15 This view was independently pronounced by Bernheim's younger German contemporary, the Leipzig neurologist Paul Julius Moebius (1853–1907).

criminal suggestion, and, contrary to Braid, Maudsley, and Charcot, the followers of the Nancy School agreed that hypnosis might constitute a definite danger. This was but one aspect of the Nancy School's difference from Charcot, the totality of which was directed towards attempting to invalidate completely the work of Charcot as it related to hysteria.

Bernheim's initial pronouncements were restrained, but they became violent after Charcot's pupils attacked his work as unscientific and published their own extraordinary claims, such as their ability to transfer diseases to hysterics by way of magnets. Bernheim, in turn, openly expressed his doubts about the soundness of Charcot's observations of exaggerated reflexes[16] and finally suggested that the patients had been subjected to specialized training before being studied by Charcot, that they had not undergone natural hypnosis but were "suffering from a suggestive hysterical neurosis."

As the battle waxed, the confines of scholarly scientific publications were transcended and a bitter public polemic ensued. Bernheim, presenting his case in 1891 in a leading newspaper, *Le Temps*, said that "the hypnotism of the Salpêtrière is an artificial product, the outcome of training." Babinski, one of a group of prominent neurologists who supported Charcot, replied in an article in the *Gazette Hebdomadaire* criticizing the vagueness of the psychological notions of the Nancy School and their overemphasis on suggestion without any attempt at its definition. But the Nancy School gradually gained adherents and Charcot's position became increasingly untenable. Eventually the few voices raised in his behalf also fell silent, and, at the time of his death in 1892, the Nancy School claimed full victory.

Without the stimulus of a running battle with their strong adversary, the Nancy School lost much of its momentum, and the medical world at large became indifferent to the subject of hypnotism. Publications on hypnotism, which had

[16] Much earlier, while Charcot was at the very height of his fame, S. Weir Mitchell admitted his own frustration with the healing success of the magnetic "metal cure" and said that he had "never once witnessed the phenomenon of transfer of the analgesia or anaesthesia to the opposite side—a phenomenon which seems to be undeniably frequent in the hands of as admirable an observer as Charcot." S. Weir Mitchell, *Lectures on the Diseases . . .*, p. 24.

TABLE OF DIAGNOSIS

	NEURASTHENIA.	HYSTERIA.	HYPOCHONDRIASIS.
Sex	BOTH SEXES ALMOST EQUALLY.	FEMALE SEX ALMOST EXCLUSIVELY.	MALE SEX ALMOST EXCLUSIVELY.
Age	ANY AGE—YOUNG MALE ADULTS SLIGHTLY PREDISPOSED.	THE FIRST ACTUAL MANIFESTATIONS ALWAYS APPEAR BEFORE 30.	VERY RARE UNDER 30.
Mental Peculiarities	Intellectual weakness; memory defective; deficient power of attention.	Deficient will power (i.e. vacillation, indecision). Want of control over the emotions.	Great determination and perseverance towards one end, viz. cure of an imaginary disease.
Causes	Overwork; dyspepsia; other causes of malnutrition; autotoxemia; traumatic or nervous shock.	A patient is born with the hysterical diathesis. The determining cause of its active manifestations is generally an emotional upset or shock.	Solitary, sedentary life.
Onset and Course	Starts somewhat gradually and runs a fairly even course.	HYSTERIA ESSENTIALLY A PAROXYSMAL DISORDER. All phenomena (healthy or morbid) vary from hour to hour, day to day, and paroxysmal outbreaks are frequent.	Starts very gradually and runs a very even course of most indefinite duration.
Mental Symptoms	MENTAL EXHAUSTION and inability to think or study. Inattention. Memory deficient. Restlessness. Temper irritable. Prostration and sadness. Not equal to the exertion of amusement. Sometimes suicidal.	Wayward, hard to please, EMOTIONAL, restless. No introspection, nor living by rule, nor study of medical works. If sad, it is transient (excepting in the male). Fond of gaiety and amusement. Usually joyous, but laughter and tears may alternate with great rapidity. No tendency to suicide.	INTROSPECTIVE habit. Close study of medical books. Observing all accessible organs and secretions. Habitual sadness. No taste for amusement. But little tendency to suicide.

Somatic and General Symptoms .	Occasionally attacks of vertigo. Convulsions rare. Syncope never. Attacks of flushing and other sensations after meals.	SEIZURES OF DIFFERENT KINDS frequently arise. Always flush very readily at any time. Convulsive attacks in 75% of the cases (Briquet). Syncope very frequent. A great variety of symptoms occurring IN PAROXYSMS.	No attacks of any kind.
	Easily tired, easily startled. State of DEBILITY AND EXHAUSTION. Constant headache. Restlessness. Sleeplessness. Long-drawn sighs.	Between the attacks no symptoms usually present. But symptoms referable to the nervous and neuro-muscular systems may be present.	The digestion is often deranged, but in the patient's belief he has some grave disease either of the alimentary tract, abdominal, or other viscera.
	Hemianæsthesia never. General hyperaesthesia and dysesthesia common. Pain in the back and sometimes in limbs. Reflexes may be increased, or normal.	Hemianæsthesia common (though may be undiscovered). "Ovarie," tender spots around the mammæ, and in other positions. Reflexes usually increased. Borborygmi, globus, and other spasms of the voluntary and involuntary muscles are frequent.	Small and insignificant symptoms, or even normal sensations, are endowed with great and perhaps lethal significance. Patient tries an endless succession of remedies and doctors; always striving for a cure (which distinguishes hypochondriasis from the hopeless and suicidal tendencies of neurasthenia and melancholia).
Termination .	Lasts many weeks or months. CURABLE.	The DIATHESIS lasts a lifetime; but the active manifestations come on suddenly, and after lasting a short time, usually disappear. TEMPORARILY CURABLE.	Once established, the condition is very difficult to ameliorate, impossible to eradicate, and therefore— INCURABLE.

FIG. 13. Table of differential diagnoses of the most frequent nervous disorders at the beginning of this century. (From Thomas D. Savill, Lectures on Hysteria [New York: William Wood & Co., 1909].)

numbered in the thousands in the seventies and the eighties dwindled to a small trickle at the turn of the century and soon ceased altogether. Contemplating this rapid decay, Pierre Janet wrote: "No one repudiated hypnotism, no one denied the power of suggestion; people simply ceased to talk about [them]."[17]

Nevertheless, an indirect though important relationship has linked modern psychiatry, particularly psychoanalysis, to the work of the two rival schools, and hypnotism played a significant part in the early stages of Freud's work.

It is clear that Charcot's peculiar misconceptions in his studies of hysteria in no way affected his enormous contributions to the field of neurology, or his status as one of the world's leading neurologists. But since they seemed to become more and more fixed towards the end of his life, these lapses and misconceptions tended to loom large in the minds of his contemporaries. His colleagues were also unable to appreciate fully one of his most interesting contributions, namely, his study *Les démoniques dans l'art*, which was done in collaboration with Paul Richer and published in 1887. This work had grown out of Charcot's own great talent and interests in drawing and painting and was the first to attempt a psychological interpretation of the artistic self-expression of the mental patient. This type of investigation has since become an important and almost indispensable adjunct to all aspects of the study of behavior. Charcot's study, however, had the additional significance of pointing to the demoniacal element that often becomes uppermost in minds that are unbalanced. In calling attention to the affinity of demonism and mental derangement, he gave a logical and rational interpretation of most of the supernatural phenomena, the presumably "possessed," the exorcist, and the witch hunter.

One of Charcot's greatest assets was, of course, his ability to attract extremely promising students and to give them superb training. From his school there came Pierre Marie (1853–1940), the most brilliant of his pupils in neurology, who described many hitherto unknown forms of nervous system disease. There was Charcot's Polish assistant, Joseph

17 Pierre Janet, *Psychological Healing: A Historical and Clinical Study*, trans. Eden and Cedar Paul (New York: Macmillan Co., 1925), p. 200.

Babinski (1857–1932), who is known for the great-toe reflex that bears his name (1896) and for his contributions to the knowledge of cerebellar disorders. There were also the great psychologist Pierre Janet and Sigmund Freud who was but briefly under Charcot's tutelage but was decisively influenced by him. These are the leading and best-known from among dozens of distinguished neurologists who flocked to the lectures of Charcot from all over the world. He left an indelible mark upon his pupils, who were fiercely proud of their teacher even if they could not always defend his mistakes. The extent of his influence is most evident when we realize that three of his most outstanding pupils, Janet, Babinski, and Freud, devoted years of their lives to that very subject that had occupied their teacher so intently during his last decade. Pierre Marie, the fourth of this distinguished quartet, who himself had never been involved in Charcot's studies on hysteria, gently spoke of the unfortunate experiments with hypnotism as his teacher's "slight failing."[18]

There is evidence that shortly before his death, Charcot had begun to reconsider his theories on hysteria. The first sign of a different and fresh point of view can be detected in his article "La foi qui guérit" ("Faith Healing"), which was published simultaneously in London and Paris.[19] He was encouraged to write this article by the editors of the *New Review*, who, after publishing the experiences of a famous explorer when visiting a religious sanctuary, consulted Charcot concerning his own views on miraculous healing. These he set forth in a most interesting manner, for the subject had long been of concern to him as, he thought, it should be to every physician—"the goal of medicine being the cure of patients without distinction as to what curative process is used."[20] For this reason the ability to heal by faith appeared to him a most valuable attainment because it is often effective when all other means have failed.

Charcot further states: "The cure of a particular symptom directly produced by faith healing, which is commonly called a miracle cure, is as one can show in the majority of

[18] Guillain, *op. cit.*, p. 174.
[19] *New Review* and *Revue Hebdomadaire* (December, 1892), pp. 112–32.
[20] Quoted in Guillain, *op. cit.*, p. 177.

cases a natural phenomenon that has occurred in all ages, among the most varied civilizations and religions, and even a phenomenon that is actually observed in all geographic regions."[21] He then stressed that faith healing should be limited to diseases that do not require any other tangible intervention beyond the power of the mind over the body. This subject was debated by many of Charcot's colleagues with whose writings he was conversant. He quoted Hack Tuke's small treatise on the influence of the mind upon the body,[22] and he agreed with Russel Reynolds, who spoke of "paralysis dependent upon an idea."[23] Yet his article was far from a summary of the contemporary literature on the subject. The depth of his personal involvement with the topic is evident from his references to the pilgrimages to the Christian shrines, to the sanctuaries of Egypt, and to the temples of Aesculapius in all of which he recognized three common elements: anticipation of the cure, autosuggestion, and the contagiousness of shared belief in recovery. But most significant, in view of his earlier opinions on hysteria, was his final paragraph:

In summary, I believe that for those who wish to practice it, faith healing requires a special patience and special kinds of disease which are susceptible to the influence that the mind possesses over the body. Hysteric patients possess an eminently favorable mental picture for the cultivation of faith healing, because they are in the first place suggestible, either through suggestions coming from without or more especially because they possess of themselves a very powerful element of autosuggestion. Among these individuals, both men and women, the influence of the mind over the body is sufficiently effective to precipitate a recovery from some diseases which, because of our past ignorance, were considered incurable. Does this mean that from now on we know everything about faith healing and that every day we shall see its frontiers retract under the influence of scientific discoveries? Certainly not. We must always search into everything, we must know how to be patient. I am still among the first to admit:

21 *Ibid.*, p. 178.

22 Daniel Hack Tuke, *Illustrations of the Influence of the Mind upon the Body in Health and Disease, Designed To Elucidate the Action of the Imagination* (London, 1872).

23 Russel Reynolds, "Remarks on Paralysis and Other Disorders of Motion and Sensation Department on Idea" in "Medical Section of the British Medical Association," *British Medical Journal* (July, 1869).

"There are more things in heaven and earth than are dreamed of in your philosophy."[24]

This paragraph reveals that he did not cling to preconceived notions of the nature of hysteria, and disputes the frequently voiced criticism that Charcot's orientation was purely organic. That this is so is also borne out by the notes of Georges Guinon, Charcot's last private secretary, who described some of the conversations he had had with the master shortly before the latter's death. These indicate that Charcot had planned to revise his entire work on the pathology of the nervous system because he had come to the conclusion "that his concept of hysteria had become decadent . . . [that he] had foreseen the need of dismembering his theory on hysteria and was preparing to dynamite the edifice to which he had personally contributed so much in building."[25] In offering this revelation, Guinon was conscious of the incongruity that he, a secretary, apparently alone knew of Charcot's contemplated changes and that only he was aware of the critical turn of mind that the master had directed against himself.

CHARCOT'S DISCIPLES

Just when Charcot must have been contemplating these radical changes in his own thinking on hysteria, his pupil Pierre Janet completed a book entitled *The Mental State of Hystericals* (1893).[26] This work was based on Janet's doctoral dissertation for the Doctor of Medicine degree. The degree was awarded to him in 1893, when he was thirty-four years old and after he had made a name for himself as a philosopher and author of studies on Bacon and Malebranche. In his brief and somewhat contradictory preface to this publication, Charcot generously recommended it to the medical public. He emphasized not only that Janet had been his pupil but

---

[24] Guillain, *op. cit.*, p. 179.

[25] Georges Guinon, "Charcot Intime," *Paris Médical*, May 23, 1925, pp. 511–26; quoted in Guillain, *op. cit.*, p. 176.

[26] Pierre Janet, *The Mental State of Hystericals: A Study of Mental Stigmata and Mental Accidents*, trans. C. R. Carson (New York: Putnam & Sons, 1901).

also that the studies upon which the text was based had been conducted during his service at the Salpêtrière and merely confirmed a thought often expressed in his own lectures "that hysteria is largely a *mental* malady,"[27] and that it could be understood and treated only if this feature was constantly borne in mind.

Janet, in turn, frequently and gratefully referred to the inspiration he had derived from his "eminent master," but he made it clear that the book was the result of his own studies and researches, and that "the largest portion of these observations are new."[28]

In the definition of hysteria, Janet agreed with Paul Briquet (1796–1881), the author of another monumental treatise on hysteria, that "hysteria is a general disease which modifies the whole organism"[29] and, for this reason, the interrelations of the psychological and the physiological phenomena should be minutely investigated. "It is thus only," Janet stated, "that medicine will be able to acquire the knowledge of the whole man and understand the diseases that affect the whole organism."

His method of research was limited to close and careful observation, for he thoroughly distrusted psychological experimentation. The statement he made to this effect is significant and has lost little of its validity in the intervening three-quarters of a century.

We must distrust complicated experiments on the mind, which are not easy to make; they are often sufficient to upset the mental state we wish to study. Psychology is not yet advanced enough to admit of many precise measures. The general nature of the phenomena, their thousand variations, their changeable conditions, are not sufficiently known for us to boast of measuring any one isolated fact. It is useless and even dangerous to take a microscope and engage in rough anatomy; we expose ourselves thus in not knowing what we look at. We believe that we should, before all, know well our subject in his life, his education, his disposition, his ideas, and that we should be convinced that we can never know him enough. We must then place this person in simple and well-determined circumstances and note exactly and on the spur of the moment what he will do and say. To examine

[27] *Ibid.*, p. v. (Italics mine.)   [28] *Ibid.*, p. xv.

[29] Paul Briquet, *Traité clinique et thérapeutique de l'hystérie* (Paris: J. B. Baillière, 1859), p. 517; quoted by Janet, *op. cit.*, p. xiii.

his acts and words is as yet the best means of knowing men, and we find it neither useless nor wearisome to write down the wandering speeches of a lunatic.[30]

He thus prepared the reader for the detailed case histories and the circumstantial descriptions of actions, words, and phrases spoken or written by the patients. These he saw as "instructive documents" and as the "graphics of pathological psychology," which naturally had to be interpreted but which must never be ignored.

The small group of patients presented in such detail were called from the vast numbers he had treated. The sum of his observations led him to the conclusion that hysterical symptoms fall into two different forms: they are either essential and temporary, or they are permanent, i.e., they persist as long as the last indications of the disease have disappeared. This difference, less clearly analyzed, had been characterized by earlier writers by the terms "stigmata" and "accidents." Although Janet found this terminology not entirely satisfactory, he retained it and simply focused attention on the mental aspects of both. In so doing he introduced a new and extremely interesting insight into the disease whose apparently protean manifestations and infinite variety of symptoms had baffled untold generations of physicians. The analysis of the *mental* aspects of the disease completely altered the picture. What initially appeared to be varied and disconnected fell into a consistent and coherent pattern when subjected to the analysis of their psychological counterparts. In this way Janet differentiated hysteria from all other mental disturbances.

Janet recognized five groups of *mental stigmata:* anesthesia, amnesia, abulia,[31] motor disturbance, and modifications of the character. The last-mentioned was divided into two components, the intelligence and the emotions. In the former he generally noted a deterioration; in the latter, exaggerated reactions to a diminished number of emotions owing to the fact that "these patients are in general very indifferent, at least to all that is not directly connected with a small number of fixed ideas."

[30] Janet, *op. cit.*, pp. xiv–xv.

[31] *Abulia:* loss or marked diminution of will power.

The mental accidents he divided among suggestion and subconscious acts, fixed ideas, convulsive attacks, somnambulisms, and deliria. There is little doubt that among his patients who provided him with this detailed symptomatology there were—as there had been among Charcot's patients—many who suffered from severe psychoses and whose hysteria, if it existed at all, was superimposed upon an even more serious disease. But although he was unable, or unwilling, always to make a differential diagnosis, he nevertheless presented a novel and penetrating picture of the psychology of hysteria. Indeed the book is so rich and original that a summary of it can hardly be given; a discussion of a few of the highlights must suffice. Of special interest here is Janet's opinion concerning the behavioral peculiarities of the hysterical patients. "It is impossible to enter into this description, which would come nearer a romance of morals and manners than a medical clinique, but hysterics, having attracted attention these many years, have a reputation and a legend."[32]

Convention had come to attribute to hysterics a certain characteristic mode of conduct that he wished to analyze. He was interested primarily in their alleged sexual proclivities, for "after having accused hystericals of all crimes of witchcraft, and having reproached them with cohabiting every Saturday with the devil, disguised as a he-goat, people have long preserved a vague remembrance of these superstitions, and have maintained that these patients had an eminently erotic disposition."[33] He was so convinced of the absurdity of this notion, which he considered a relic of the uterine theory, that he ignored the possibility that that theory might have been formulated from the erotic disposition.

Dismissing, then, as absurd the role of the uterus, Janet claimed that the time had now come to investigate the reputed hypereroticism of hysterical patients. From his study of hundreds of cases, he found that such erotic disposition does exist in hysteria but only to the same degree as do all other fixed ideas. In 120 patients so studied there were but four in which sexuality played an altogether prominent role. And even in this manifestation, he felt, there was nothing

32 Janet, *op. cit.*, pp. 214–15.   33 *Ibid.*, p. 215.

strange or pathological. Amorous passions and sexual desires simply were normal to the younger inmates of the Salpêtrière as they were among all groups of young women. Hysterical patients were as disposed to talk of love, to see its evidence, and to read descriptions of it as were all other elements in the population. "Why should their minds, so ready to receive impressions, so docile to all influences, resist this one?" In their hysterical delirium he had often heard patients speak of love, of husbands, of men, of rape, and of pregnancy. These, he believed, must be paramount in the patients' thoughts, for "you cannot put into your delirium what is not in your mind." The same is true also for the contents of dreams.

But Janet simply could not accept the traditional beliefs of exaggerated sexual preoccupation in hysteria and stated flatly that, with a very few exceptions, "the hystericals are, in general, not any more erotic than normal persons." On the contrary, he maintained that they are rather more frequently frigid than sensual, and they are more likely to forget their former attachments than to increase them. The reason for this, Janet believed, was simply due to the shrinking of their emotional radius, to their increasing egocentricity, their preoccupation with their own concerns, and their indifference to demands and expectations from others. Even the tendency towards simulation and mendacity he attributed simply to their forgetfulness or to lack of interest in their own earlier statements, promises, or facts of life, rather than to character defects.

It is for this reason also, according to Janet, that hysteria, which was formerly considered a most variable and protean malady, was actually extraordinarily predictable and repetitious in each individual patient. He observed that early in the course of the disease patients organized their fixed ideas and their resulting manifestations; they tended to organize their emotional patterns, their movements, and their ideas— whether borrowed or their own—and to weave them all together to "transform them more or less through a kind of subconscious meditation." But the exacerbations in illnesses of longer standing were systematized and uniform and could not be altered. Thus, far from being too labile, the hysterical patient was not sufficiently so. Absorbed in their preoccupation with their fixed ideas, the patients retained a constant emotional climate that was unaffected by and unadaptable to all external influences.

The *idée fixe* that characterizes hysteria is developed "below consciousness" and remains "outside of normal consciousness. . . . The subconscious character of the fixed ideas . . . plays an important part in the therapeutics of these affections."[34] Referring to an earlier work, Janet stated: "We formerly showed that it was necessary to look up, so to say, these subconscious phenomena in order to attack them, and that one could not treat the hysterical accident before having reached those deep layers of thought within which the fixed idea was concealed."[35]

This thought is undoubtedly what modern psychology has come to consider "Freudian," and it is regrettable for historical reasons that Janet failed to cite the place where his earlier demonstrations were made and documented. He referred to the work of his Austrian colleagues gently, but firmly claimed priority, viz.: "We are happy to see to-day MM. Breuer and Freud express the same idea . . . . [when they say that] it is necessary to make the patient conscious of the provocative event, and to bring it out into full light. As soon as the subject recognizes his fixed ideas, the [hysterical] accidents are bound to disappear."[36] Despite his pleasure with Breuer and Freud's verification of his already "somewhat old" interpretations of subconsciously fixed ideas in hystericals, he scouted their claims of easy cure.[37] In concluding these deliberations, he said, "in any case, it is certain that this discovery of the subconscious phenomena is an indispensable preliminary."[38] Whether this statement is intentionally enigmatic concerning the priority of the discovery of the subconscious phenomena in hysteria, or whether Janet simply took it for granted that it was his, will remain unresolved.

[34] *Ibid.*, pp. 411–12.   [35] *Ibid.*, p. 412.

[36] Joseph Breuer and Sigmund Freud, "Über den psychischen Mechanismus hysterischer Phaenomene?" *Neurologisches Centralblatt*, 1893, Nos. 1–2, p. 4.

[37] Janet, *op. cit.*, p. 290.

[38] Breuer and Freud, *op. cit.*, pp. 4–6.

Freud, too, seems to have been troubled by this question, for he stated somewhat curiously, "I always treated Janet with respect, since his discoveries coincided to a considerable extent with those of Breuer, which were made earlier but were published later than his."[39] Later, this respect dwindled when Janet became less than enthusiastic about the importation of psychoanalytical ideas into France. On that occasion, Freud reports in his autobiography: "Janet behaved ill, showed ignorance of the facts and used ugly arguments. And finally he revealed himself to my eyes and destroyed the value of his own work by declaring that when he had spoken of 'unconscious' mental acts he had meant nothing by the phrase—it had been no more than a *façon de parler*."[40] This was but a part of Freud's polemic, to which further reference will be made in a later section.

In Zilboorg's opinion, Freud was somewhat unfair in accusing Janet of such total lack of comprehension. The latter's definition of "unconscious" also included the sense of "automatic" actions, and indeed, he was the first to have brought out fully the significance of the automatic behavior of the hysterical patient. Nor was his use of the word "subconscious" actually entirely lacking in its present dynamic connotation, as the following brief excerpts quite clearly show: "The subconscious act may influence consciousness even before its execution; it may call forth vague impulses which the patient calls 'desires,' the origin of which he does not understand. . . . Let us take a step further; subconscious ideas, before any kind of manifestation, may through the association of images, create real hallucinations which will suddenly invade the consciousness."[41]

The real weaknesses in Janet's position were his etiological theories. He believed in "provocative agents" of hysterical accidents; but these were mostly of a physical nature and included hemorrhages, chronic diseases, localized infections, typhoid fever, auto-intoxication, organic diseases of the

[39] Sigmund Freud, *Die Medizin der Gegenwart in Selbstdarstellungen Sonderdruck* (Leipzig: Verlag von Felix Meiner [n.d.]), p. 19. Also, Sigmund Freud, *An Autobiographical Study,* trans. James Strachey (2d ed.; London: Hogarth Press, 1946), p. 55.

[40] *Autobiographical Study,* p. 55.

[41] Janet, *op. cit.,* p. 26.

nervous system, and various alcoholic and other intoxica-
tions. He did admit a few psychological alternatives, such as
"physical or moral shocks, overwork . . . painful emotions,
and especially a succession of that sort of emotions the
effects of which are cumulative."[42]

All these provocative agents appeared to Janet to have one
feature in common, namely, "they weaken the organism and
increase the depression of the nervous system." The vulnerability to their injurious effect was particularly great during
the state of "moral" or emotional puberty that follows physical pubescence and occurs at a different age in various countries and climates. The many problems typical of this period
of life can bring about a condition which Janet termed "psychological insufficiency." If this happens in minds already in-
stable because of hereditary influences, the resulting damage
generally takes the form of hysteria.

Janet devoted little space to the treatment of hysteria. It is
clear, however, that he utilized both suggestion and the
manipulation of environment. In the former he thought himself in full agreement with Bernheim of the Nancy School;[43]
in the latter he followed the pattern of his teacher Charcot
in separating his patients from their earlier influences and
environments. In his apparent indifference to the therapy of
hysteria, Janet also followed in Charcot's footsteps, by concerning himself primarily with the control of manifestations
of the disease and its predisposing factors. Bernheim, who
was more clinically inclined, spoke logically of "de-sugges-
tion" as the true therapy of hysteria, a subtle difference not
mentioned by Janet.

Hysteria was a dominant interest in Janet's professional
life and even towards the term "hysteria" he displayed a
rather sentimental attachment: "The word 'hysteria' should
be preserved, although its primitive meaning has much
changed. It would be very difficult to modify it nowadays,
and truly it has so great and beautiful a history that it would
be painful to give it up."[44] This remained his attitude
throughout the succeeding decades of his rising fame and

[42] *Ibid.*, p. 526.

[43] Hippolyte Bernheim, *Suggestive Therapeutics*, trans. Christian A.
Herter (Westport: Associated Booksellers, 1957), p. 262.

[44] Janet, *op. cit.*, p. 527.

mounting success during which he continued to lecture and write on the subject. In an impressive series of lectures delivered at Harvard University in 1906, on the occasion of the inauguration of the new medical school buildings, he devoted fifteen sessions to the subject of hysteria. Similar presentations were given at the Johns Hopkins and Columbia universities. These lectures were subsequently published under the title *The Major Symptoms of Hysteria* (1907).[45] But apart from minor changes and refinements, this book is similar in content to that of *The Mental State of Hystericals* published in 1892.[46]

Janet's devotion to the word hysteria, and his desire to preserve it even though it had become etymologically meaningless, was not shared by all of Charcot's disciples. Babinski created a new term, "pithiatisme," which to him expressed its most important features, since it combined the Greek words *peithō*, I persuade, and *iatos*, curable, believing that amenability to cure by persuasion was not only the most important characteristic of hysteria but also of diagnostic importance. Although the term still lingers in the current medical dictionaries, it failed to become part of the general medical vocabulary.

Babinski's great number of publications on hysteria beginning in the early nineties of the past century had made him an authority on the subject. Soon after the outbreak of the First World War, concern with hysteria became of enormous practical importance, since this was one of the totally disabling diseases among the soldiers of all armies. Moreover, the problem of distinguishing the malingerer from the hysteric that had faced S. Weir Mitchell and W. W. Keen in the Civil War had become even more pressing in this much larger international conflict. Actually, it is hard to see how Babinski's "pithiasmic" concept could have been very helpful in this dilemma, although his discussion of treatment is a very positive and optimistic one.

[45] Pierre Janet, *The Major Symptoms of Hysteria, Fifteen Lectures given in the Medical School of Harvard University* (2d ed.; New York: Macmillan Co., 1920).

[46] The most recent, exhaustive, and laudatory study of Janet's work was written by Leonhard Schwartz, *Die Neurosen und die dynamische Psychologie von Pierre Janet* (Basel: Benno Schwabe, 1951).

The physician's task he saw simply as (*a*) the prevention of pithiatic disorders by means of hygiene and prophylaxis, and (*b*) the cure of these disorders once they have developed. Since they were caused by autosuggestion as well as by hetero-suggestion, the best prophylaxis was for physicians, nurses, and visiting friends always to weigh their statements when visiting patients so as to avoid suggesting hysterical conditions. Therapeusis, in turn, demanded persuasion and countersuggestion and, above all, an atmosphere of confidence and faith. The confidence in the physician should also extend to his ability to distinguish organic disease from hysterical disorders and to treat it accordingly.[47]

Needless to say, this point of view struck some of Babinski's contemporaries, even those who greatly admired his neurological acumen as somewhat naïve, and it failed to stir the medical imagination.

[47] For a listing of Babinski's numerous publications on hysteria see J. Babinski and J. Froment, *Hysteria or Pithiasm and Reflex Nervous Disorders in the Neurology of War* (London: University of London Press, 1918), pp. 290–304.

CHAPTER XI

Hysteria and the Evolution
of Psychoanalysis

F ROM THE PRECEDING ACCOUNTS, it can be seen that Charcot's influence extended to a group of brilliant pupils who
inherited their master's interest in hysteria. They included
Janet and Babinski in France and, especially, Freud in
Austria. Beyond this, however, Charcot's tremendous renown gave the subject of hysteria a dignity that resulted in
the publication of voluminous treatises not only by Charcot's disciples but also by such famous authorities as Kraepelin, Moebius, and Kretschmer in Germany, Daniel Hack
Tuke in England, and the Swiss C. G. Jung. While their ideas
quite naturally varied to a considerable degree, there is recognizable a consistent pattern that marks the further evolution
of the theories of Charcot. This unifying belief lies in the
acceptance of suggestion as the governing aspect of hysteria
at this phase of its history, both in its etiology and, in reverse,
in its treatment.

VIENNESE STUDIES ON HYSTERIA

This, then, was the status of world thought on hysteria when
Freud burst upon the awareness of his contemporaries. The
revolution created by him in psychiatry, in particular, and in
Western thought as a whole, had been anticipated in certain
fragments by many of his predecessors, some of whom have

been quoted in this book.[1] Nevertheless, his role in establishing current concepts of mental function and its disturbances is beyond challenge. Noteworthy in relation to this book is that it was specifically his interest in and study of hysteria that formed the starting point of psychoanalysis and led to the formulation of those final new ideas on the illness which have as yet not been superseded. It is for this reason also that a summary of Freud's concern with hysteria should form the conclusion of this book.

In the preceding pages we have traced the introduction and development of the word and concept of neurosis that evolved in Freud's writings from their initial somatic to a psychological interpretation, so that today the word "psychoneurosis" as applied to hysteria is self-descriptive and hardly requires any explanation. Although Freud's *Autobiographical Study* and his contribution *On the History of the Psychoanalytic Movement* and Ernest Jones's *Life of Freud* have made the beginnings of psychoanalysis a familiar story, a very brief reiteration of it is necessary here to bring out the supremely important role played by hysteria in its development.

It was hysteria that brought Freud in touch with Josef Breuer, one of the most distinguished Viennese internists, whose large and busy practice included patients suffering from hysteria; among them was Miss Anna O., whose treatment lasted two years and whose case is one of the most famous in the annals of psychoanalysis. It was the history of Miss Anna O. that Breuer related to Freud in the course of the therapy during the years 1880–82. Freud's intense interest was aroused by it, particularly since he greatly admired Breuer, who was his senior by fourteen years, and he spoke of him as a man of superior intelligence, to whom he was soon bound by ties of close friendship.

Breuer's approach to Miss Anna O.'s hysteria was a completely novel one and provided both physicians a much more profound insight into the causes and meaning of hysterical symptoms than had ever been gained before. Quite accidentally Breuer had observed that the symptoms could be

---

[1] See Walter Riese, "The Pre-Freudian Origins of Psychoanalysis," *Science and Psychoanalysis* (New York: Grune & Stratton, 1958), pp. 29–72.

corrected if she could be induced, while under hypnosis, to put into words the fantasy from which she suffered at the moment. This one experience with a single patient suggested to Breuer his method of treatment, although the patient when awake was unable to trace any connection between her illness and any previous experience of her life. Through hypnosis Breuer was readily able to produce the missing links. When listening to Breuer's notes of the case, Freud became convinced that this man was coming closer to an understanding of the nature of psychoneurosis than anyone had before.

Freud's involvement with hysteria and his friendship with Breuer occurred early in his medical career, even before he had decided to devote all his energies to psychiatry, although in his original decision to study medicine he had been motivated by a "curiosity which was . . . directed . . . towards human concerns." This led him first towards neurology. He became intensely involved in the field of neuroanatomy and while still a junior resident he began to publish short papers on various neuroanatomical subjects. Indeed he was so successful a diagnostician that "the fame of his diagnoses and their postmortem confirmation" brought him large audiences of admiring American physicians.[2] Yet, in spite of his serious interest in neurology and neuroanatomy at the University of Vienna, he said that he felt himself drawn elsewhere and "in the distance glimmered the great name of Charcot."[3] Freud received his appointment as lecturer in neuropathology in the spring of 1885 and shortly thereafter, with the help of his mentor Professor Brücke, he was awarded a very generous travel fellowship for his studies with Charcot at the Salpêtrière.

Initially, Charcot paid no personal attention to Freud, who was simply one of a large number of foreigners attending the famous clinical demonstrations. But when one day in Freud's hearing Charcot expressed his regret that his work had as yet not found a German translator, Freud offered to undertake this task. Charcot accepted gratefully and henceforth admitted Freud to the circle of his personal acquaintances and to all the work that was conducted at the Salpêtrière.

In contrast to many other more critical visitors, Freud was

[2] *An Autobiographical Study*, p. 19.   [3] *Ibid.*

deeply impressed with Charcot's work on hysteria and said that "Charcot had proved, for instance, the genuineness of hysterical phenomena and their conformity to laws, . . . the frequent occurrence of hysteria in men"; and furthermore, that artificially (i.e., hypnotically) produced hysteria closely resembled the spontaneous attacks. However, in spite of his hero worship of Charcot, Freud confessed that many of the demonstrations provoked in him and in other visitors a sense of astonishment and an inclination to skepticism,[4] and he therefore decided to tell Charcot of his impressions of Breuer's work but " 'the master' showed no interest in my first outline of the subject, so that I never returned to it and allowed it to pass from my mind."[5]

Freud's receptivity to Charcot's methods can be explained by the fact that he was intellectually prepared to favor the therapeutic use of hypnotic suggestion. For, following Breuer's example, Freud himself had used hypnosis for the purpose of eliciting from patients their own stories about the origin of their symptoms, which, when awake, they would have been unable to recall or unwilling to divulge.

On his return to Vienna in 1886, Freud was even more convinced of the universal relevance of Breuer's theories. He said that "the state of things which he [Breuer] had discovered seemed to me to be of so fundamental a nature that I could not believe it could fail to be present in any case of hysteria if it had been proved to occur in a single one."[6] Yet only a great deal of experience could confirm this supposition. In order to test Breuer's theory and to prove his own belief in it, Freud began to repeat Breuer's methods on his own patients with the eventual exclusion of all other therapeutic approaches.

Freud recorded his own observations and case histories minutely and then suggested to Breuer that they jointly publish their combined experiences with this new therapy of hysteria. Initially, Breuer objected strongly to the plan of a

[4] See also Axel Munthe, *The Story of San Michele* (New York: E. P. Dutton & Co., 1930), pp. 300–303, 320–21.

[5] *Autobiographical Study*, p. 22. The German edition uses the expression *der Meister* translated as "the great man" in the English edition, pp. 33–34.

[6] *Ibid.*, p. 36.

joint publication, but he consented after he had become aware that Pierre Janet's book had meanwhile anticipated some of his own important findings, namely, the need to trace hysterical symptoms back to the causative events in the patient's life, and to remove these symptoms by means of a re-creation under hypnosis of the original situation.

The first joint publication of Breuer and Freud was brief; it was entitled "On the Psychical Mechanism of Hysterical Phenomena" (1893).[7] In this preliminary article the authors submitted the opinion that in hysteria the patients re-experience the original psychic trauma. Their physical symptoms that heretofore had been regarded as spontaneous random manifestations were thus closely related to the original causal event. This publication was succeeded in 1895 by a larger jointly authored volume entitled *Studien über Hysterie*. Although this now appears as part of Freud's *Collected Works*, he emphasized that it was largely the product of Breuer's practical experience, while his contribution was the formulation of the theory. At any rate, the major object of this book was less the definition of the nature of hysteria than the elucidation of its symptoms. In the case of Miss Anna O., the first patient Breuer treated by hypnotic suggestion to recall the precipitating event, it was revealed that her symptoms could be traced back to a severe illness of her father, whom she had been nursing with affectionate devotion. From these revelations Breuer interpreted the meaning of all her symptoms, i.e., that they were converted reminiscences of those stressful situations she had then experienced. After complete recall of these situations under hypnosis and unreserved expression of those emotions she had originally suppressed, the symptoms gradually disappeared and their return was prevented.

HYSTERIA AND CATHARSIS

For this therapeutic method Breuer had found the designation *catharsis*, the results of which were highly satisfactory. The theory of catharsis was in no way involved with the

[7] Sigmund Freud in collaboration with Josef Breuer, in Sigmund Freud, *Collected Papers* (London: Hogarth Press, 1950), I, 24–41.

subject of sexuality as an etiological agent. This was to a
much greater extent Freud's contribution, for the case histories that he contributed to their first volume were characterized by sexual factors, whereas Breuer wrote of Miss
Anna O. that her "sexual side was extraordinarily underdeveloped."[8]

The subsequent stages of Freud's work were devoted to
the gradual transition from catharsis to psychoanalysis. In
the course of this evolution, Breuer withdrew from the collaboration and left Freud as "the sole administrator of his
legacy."[9] The reasons for Breuer's withdrawal were not so
much of an ideological nature but rather owing to the fact
that his medical practice did not permit him the time for
intensive involvement with psychiatric patients, whereas
Freud, upon his return from Paris, had devoted his professional life solely to the practice of psychiatry. His reasoning
for giving up neurology ran as follows:

This implied, of course, that I abandoned the treatment of organic nervous diseases; but that was of little importance. For on
the one hand the prospects in the treatment of such disorders
were in any case never promising, while on the other hand, in
the private practice of a physician working in a large town, the
quantity of such patients was nothing compared to the crowds
of neurotics, whose number seemed further multiplied by the
manner in which they hurried, with their troubles unsolved,
from one physician to another. And apart from this, there was
something positively seductive in working with hypnotism. For
the first time there was a sense of having overcome one's help-
lessness, and it was highly flattering to enjoy the reputation of
being a miracle-worker.[10]

Freud's favorable inclination towards the use of hypnotism evolved in a fashion similar to that of Braid; it originated while he was still a medical student. He had attended
a public exhibition by a well-known "magnetist" and, on
noticing that one of the subjects turned deathly pale under
hypnosis, he became convinced of the genuineness of the
phenomenon. Although a scientific explanation of this observation was soon forthcoming, the professors of psychiatry
in Austria and Germany remained convinced that hypnotism
was dangerous as well as fraudulent and that all those em-
ploying it in their practice should be treated with contempt.

8 *Ibid.*, p. 39.   9 *Ibid.*   10 *Ibid.*, pp. 28–29.

During his stay with Charcot, Freud had seen Europe's most prominent and gifted neurologists make use of hypnotism at the Salpêtrière in the production of symptoms and in their removal. Soon after his return from Paris he became aware of the use of suggestion by the school at Nancy where two physicians, Liébault and Bernheim, made extensive and remarkably successful use of suggestion for therapeutic purposes, with or without hypnosis. It was under these influences that in the first years of his activity in private practice Freud employed hypnotic suggestion almost as the sole psychotherapeutic method. To his chagrin, however, he found himself unable to induce deep hypnosis in every patient, a disadvantage inherent in all hypnotic treatment. In order to perfect himself in his hypnotic technique, he decided in 1889 to go to Nancy to observe the work of the two physicians of that school. There he "received the profoundest impression of the possibility that there could be powerful mental processes which nevertheless remained hidden from the consciousness of men."[11] It is interesting that at the time when Freud journeyed to Nancy a stereotyped image of the hysteric must have been in existence, so that beyond the designation "the hysteric" there was no need for any further description. This is evident in Freud's statement: "Thinking it would be instructive, I had persuaded one of my patients to follow me to Nancy. She was a very highly gifted hysteric, a woman of good birth, who had been handed over to me because no one knew what to do with her."[12]

Freud felt obliged to show his appreciation for the travel grant from the university that had made his study trip possible by giving a report before the Viennese Medical Society on his impressions during his stay in Paris. His talk was badly received and some of those present bluntly declared that much of it was incredible.[13] This adverse reaction referred particularly to his reports on having seen hysteria in *men* at the Salpêtrière; and one of the physicians in his audience, "an old surgeon, actually broke out with the exclamation: 'But my dear Sir, how can you talk such nonsense? Hysteron . . . means the uterus, so how can a man be hysterical?' "[14]

[11] *Ibid.*, p. 29.
[12] *Ibid.*, pp. 29–30.
[13] *Autobiographical Study*, p. 25.
[14] *Ibid.*

Freud's Viennese colleagues also made it impossible for him
to demonstrate his findings; they refused him permission to
work with or observe their patients. Only once was he
applauded—when outside the hospital he accidentally came
upon a man suffering from an obvious hysterical hemianesthesia and succeeded in presenting him to the same Medical
Society; but in spite of their approbation on this occasion,
Freud failed to arouse his colleagues' interest in his work.
Their persistent denial of his observations extended to include the production of hysterical paralyses by suggestion, at
that time a phenomenon accepted all over the world as one
of the most frequent etiologic agencies.

The general, persistent, and unconcealed rejection of his
ideas became increasingly irritating to Freud. He was excluded from the laboratory of cerebral anatomy and was
thus deprived of the opportunity to lecture to students.
Therefore he decided to withdraw from academic life altogether and from participation in the work of the local medical society; in fact, he completely discontinued the treatment of organic nervous diseases and limited his practice to
the treatment of psychoneurotic disorders. In an interesting
observation of the reversal of current evaluations, Karl Menninger calls attention to the greater scientific potential of
Freud's clinical practice in contrast to his research work. "It
was with neurological studies of sensation that Freud began
his scientific career and his research work led to the discovery of the local obliteration of sensation through injected
chemicals (cocaine, etc.). When he then turned to clinical
work, the phenomena of blocked sensation were of particular interest to him, as they appeared in 'hysterical' patients,
and in experiments with hypnosis."[15]

THE REDISCOVERY OF SEXUALITY

In reminiscing in his *Autobiographical Study* about the writing of the *Studies on Hysteria,* Freud wrote: "It would have
been difficult to guess what an importance sexuality has in
the aetiology of the neuroses." This importance he began to
appreciate later in his own increasing practice, when he

[15] Karl Menninger, *The Vital Balance*, p. 109.

learned what had been suggested over and over again by other physicians for nearly two thousand years, "that it was not *any* kind of emotional excitation that was in action behind the phenomena of the neurosis, but habitually one of a sexual nature, whether it was current sexual conflict or the effect of earlier sexual experiences." Only many years later did he realize that in associating hysteria with sexuality, he "was going back to the very beginnings of medicine and reviving a thought of Plato's."[16]

The discovery of the importance of sexual factors in the etiology of hysteria induced Freud to examine the sexual life of his many neurasthenic patients. "This experiment cost me, it is true, my popularity as a doctor, but it brought me convictions which today, almost thirty years later, have lost none of their force."[17] Eventually, Freud came to regard *all* the neuroses as being the results of disturbed sexual functions, i.e., that "*actual*" neuroses being the direct morbid expression of such disturbances and the psychoneuroses their mental expression. The mechanism by which he visualized the physical act to exert its influence is quite obscure and very difficult to comprehend in the light of the terms which he used. "It [sexuality] had a somatic side as well, and it was possible to assign chemical processes to it and to attribute sexual excitement to the presence of some particular, though at present unknown, substances."[18] In coming to these conclusions, Freud thought that he had proved sexuality to be a physical phenomenon and not something purely mental as had hitherto been believed. Freud held that its somatic side was responsible for the production of certain chemical processes producing specific substances. That these hypotheses are vaguely reminiscent of the theories underlying the "vapors," and those of Galen concerning the hysterogenic effect of retained sperm owing to unaccustomed sexual continence, is all the more striking because Freud appeared totally unaware of the historical background and earlier humoral theories. Indeed, far from

---

[16] *Autobiographical Study*, pp. 41–42. It was the above-mentioned statement from Plato's *Timaeus* (917c): "The womb is an animal which longs to generate children. When it remains barren too long after puberty, it is distressed and sorely disturbed."

[17] *Ibid.*, p. 42.   [18] *Ibid.*, p. 44.

believing he had proved the veracity of old historical beliefs, Freud was pleased to have found a way of relating psychiatry to modern science and the burgeoning field of chemistry, and hence considered his own hypotheses of distinct scientific merit. His preoccupation with psychotherapy left him no time to pursue further the chemical alterations behind those neuroses which he termed "actual," nor was anyone else sufficiently interested in taking up this aspect of Freud's work. Even thirty years later, when composing his *Autobiographical Study,* he proudly spoke of these "early findings," saying, "They strike me as being the first rough outlines of what is probably a far more complicated subject. But on the whole they seem to me still to hold good." A rather startling comment regarding the role of sexual disturbances reads: "All that I am asserting is that the symptoms of these patients are not mentally determined or removable by analysis, but that they must be regarded as direct toxic consequences of disturbed sexual chemical processes."[19] Perhaps if the term "endocrinological" were substituted for "chemical," his views might not strike us now as quite so bizarre, even though the physico-chemical effects of sexual intercourse are not prominently encountered in modern writings on normal or morbid sexuality.

In spite of his earlier determination to withdraw from an academic career and from participipation in the work of learned societies, Freud used the years that followed the publication of the *Studies on Hysteria* to read papers dealing with the role of sexuality in the production of neuroses before a number of medical societies outside Vienna, "but was only met with incredulity and contradiction."[20]

For some time after the publication of their joint work, Breuer continued to express his support of Freud's theories without, however, materially improving the general medical reaction to them. But, however, Breuer's loyalty stopped short of fully accepting Freud's concept of the sexual etiology of neuroses. The reason for Breuer's adverse reaction to these theories was perhaps his own experience with his first famous patient, Miss Anna O., whose case history he had been reluctant to detail fully to Freud and about

[19] *Ibid.*, p. 46.   [20] *Ibid.*

whom he later said that her sexual feelings were remarkably underdeveloped. Long after the conclusion of Miss Anna O.'s treatment, Freud was able to reconstruct the final events, which accounted for Breuer's silence on the subject. Her reaction appears to have been the first recorded "transference love,"[21] becoming manifest after catharsis had been accomplished. This is one of the earliest mentions of "transference," a factor, Freud stated, which is allowed to play the decisive part in analysis in determining the therapeutic results. In his transference the patient, initially quite unconsciously, acts out upon the analyst those emotional experiences that had their origin in his earliest attachments during the repressed period of his childhood.[22] Miss Anna O.'s expressions of her transference had been so embarrassing to Breuer and the memory of this event so painful to him that Freud's continued emphasis on sexual factors in hysteria served as a permanent reminder of his own awkwardness in the face of such manifestation. It seems to have been for this reason that he dissociated himself generally from Freud's etiological speculations. Nevertheless, he too appreciated the effect of the sexual drives on mental stability and said: "The sexual instinct is undoubtedly the most powerful source of persisting increases of excitation (and consequently of neuroses)."[23] And, later on, "*I do not think I am exaggerating when I assert that the great majority of severe neuroses in women have their origin in the marriage bed.*"[24] In view of the frequent assertion that the emphasis on sexuality was a preoccupation peculiar to Freud and his special contribution to psychoanalysis, it may be of interest to present Breuer's footnote to the above-quoted italicized statement.

It is a most unfortunate thing that clinical medicine ignores one of the most important of all the pathogenic factors or at least only hints at it delicately. This is certainly a subject in which the acquired knowledge of experienced physicians should be communicated to their juniors, who as a rule blindly overlook sexuality—at all events so far as their patients are concerned.[25]

[21] *Ibid.*   [22] *Ibid.*, p. 77.

[23] Josef Breuer's "Theoretical Section" in Breuer and Freud, *Studies on Hysteria* (London: Hogarth Press, 1957), p. 200.

[24] *Ibid.*, p. 246.   [25] *Ibid.*

In spite of this positive statement, there must have remained in Breuer's mind reservations and qualifications of his belief in the sexual etiology of neuroses. Breuer's doubts about the all-importance of sexuality became evident in a letter from Freud to his friend Fliess, written in 1895, the year of the publication of *Studies on Hysteria.* At that time in a formal address to the Physicians' Collegium, Breuer spontaneously declared his own belief in the sexual etiology of neuroses. However, when Freud later on approached him to thank him for this public testimony, Breuer strangely remarked, "All the same, I don't believe it." Breuer's lack of concurrence with all the theories of his co-author was matched by Freud's gradual departure from the use of hypnosis and his evolution of the psychoanalytic method that was solely Freud's contribution to psychiatry. The reasons for this shift arose from Freud's growing belief in the possibility of exploring the patient's unconscious and repressed memories without altering his mental state by inducing hypnosis. This rationalization was superimposed upon his failure mentioned above, to induce hypnosis in some of his patients. Instead, he attempted to put them into a state of deep "concentration," aided by a mild pressure of his hand and having the patient lie down and close his eyes. This method, which was described by him as "pressure technique," initiated Freud's use of the recumbent position during psychoanalysis, a position he maintained even after he had given up the method of "concentration" and laying-on of hands.[26]

PSYCHOANALYSIS

The omission of hypnosis was in keeping with Bernheim's demonstration that events recalled in a hypnotic trance are only apparently forgotten by the patient when awake and can be rather easily recalled by a mild word of command and pressure with the hand.[27] Instead of losing depth of insight into his patient's psyche by abandoning hypnotism, Freud's new approach actually broadened his understanding of mental processes. In this fashion he came to learn of

[26] *Ibid.*, p. 110 n.   [27] *Ibid.*, pp. 107 ff.

some patients' resistance to therapy and of their unwilling-ness to collaborate in their own restoration to health. Indeed it was the patients' resistance of the physician's effort to at-tain recall that often brought attention to the repressed event and the traumatic memory. Without hypnotic sug-gestion there was no immediate way of overcoming the re-luctance of these resistant patients to delve into their own unconscious mental processes and to produce their old and unpleasant memories. For this reason, he refrained more and more from active interference by suggestion with the pa-tient's trends of thought and began to encourage a constant flow of "free associations," which practice, in turn, even-tually directed his attention to dream analysis. Moreover, additional reasons for his abandonment of hypnotism, and for his replacing it with his own methods, were that he was anxious not to be restricted to treating hysteriform condi-tions so that he could devote himself to nervous disorders in general.[28]

Freud's psychotherapy was based on three concepts which became the fundamental pillars of psychoanalysis: *repres-sion*, the *unconscious*, and, finally, *infantile sexuality*. The last-named was an extension of the role of sexuality in general as a predisposing factor towards neurosis. By making sexuality into a concept, i.e., by freely making use of this word, which in his day was still more or less taboo, Freud referred to patients' early conflicts between their sexual impulses and their resistance to sexuality. In seeking the pathogenic events in his patients' lives, namely, the occa-sion when the repression of their sexuality had been first experienced, he found himself pushing them further and further back into their lives and often reaching the earliest years of their childhood.

To his astonishment he found that these experiences of childhood were always concerned with sexual excitations and were reactions against them, and therefore he found himself faced by what he called "the fact of infantile sexuality—which was once again a novelty and a contradic-tion of one of the strongest of human 'prejudices.' "[29] In his day childhood was looked upon as innocent and free

---

[28] *Ibid.*, p. 59.   [29] *Ibid.*

from the lusts of sex, and the fight with the demon of
sensuality was not thought to begin until "the troubled age
of puberty."[30] A very similar statement was recently made
by Philippe Ariès in *Centuries of Childhood*, in which he
dispels the idea of the permanence of the sexual mores that
the twentieth century has come to assume as the only valid
ones.

One of the unwritten laws of contemporary morality, the strict-
est and best respected of all, requires adults to avoid any reference, above all any humorous reference, to sexual matters in the
presence of children. This notion was entirely foreign to the society of old. The modern reader of the diary in which Henry
IV's physician, Heroard, recorded the details of young Louis
XIII's life is astonished by the liberties which people took with
children, by the coarseness of the jokes they made, and by the
indecency of gestures made in public which shocked nobody and
which were regarded as perfectly natural.[31]

As might have been expected, infantile sexuality was the
one finding of psychoanalysis that was universally con-
tradicted and aroused fierce hostility and indignation and
caused Freud's complete social and professional isolation.
But when the adverse reaction had become nearly irrepara-
ble, Freud realized that his "third pillar" of psychoanalysis
rested upon a colossal error on his part. This error was his
belief in the veracity of his patients' repressed memories of
having been seduced by an adult in early infancy, his female patients generally naming their fathers or other elder
male relatives in the role of the seducer. Later, and with
regret, Freud told that so reluctant had he been to believe
these stories that he intentionally kept his critical faculties
in abeyance so as to preserve an unprejudiced and receptive
attitude towards the many novelties that were daily coming
to his notice.[32] Eventually, however, he was shocked to
realize that his deliberate open-mindedness had served him
ill; he began to recognize that these scenes of seduction
had never occurred at all and were revoked by the patients

[30] *Autobiographical Study*, p. 59.

[31] Philippe Ariès, *Centuries of Childhood: A Social History of
Family Life*, trans. Robert Baldick (New York: Alfred A. Knopf,
1962), p. 100.

[32] *Autobiographical Study*, p. 60.

as entirely imaginary on their part. This discovery was a severe blow to his self-confidence, particularly when he began to suspect that these false and disturbing confessions might possibly have been the fault of his own technique inasmuch as his line of questioning might have impelled his patients to fabricate these memories. The realization of this enormous mistake seriously interfered with the progress of Freud's work, but eventually he succeeded in mastering his discouragement and in "pulling himself together," and he arrived at the rationalization that his discovery disclosed "that the neurotic symptoms, while not related directly to actual events but to fantasies embodying wishes must be explored for their important hidden meaning, and that as far as the neurosis was concerned psychical reality was of more importance than material reality."[33] Even later when he described his error in his *Autobiographical Study*, he expressed his certainty that he had suggested rather than *forced* these seduction-fantasies upon his patients; he further realized that these disagreeable events had made him unknowingly "stumble for the first time upon the *Oedipus Complex*" which was later to play such a large part in the framework of psychoanalysis but which under the mask of fantasy he failed to recognize.[34]

Freud then came to appreciate the pitfalls that had threatened every historian since the days of Livy, namely, that historical truths and actual fact are generally difficult to recognize and that the historian as well as the analyst has to contend with the narrator's reaction against the memory of times and circumstances that to him were insignificant and occasionally, perhaps, inglorious. Freud felt that the way to the study of the sexual life of children was opened up as soon as he had understood and elucidated his own mistake, and, in his *Three Contributions to the Theory of Sexuality*, he brought together all the thoughts and conclusions on the subject that he had reached during more than a decade.

So far as hysteria was concerned, it seemed surprising to both Breuer and Freud that events experienced so long ago continued to operate with such intensity that their recol-

[33] *Ibid.*, p. 61.

[34] "The Psychical Mechanism of Hysterical Phenomena" (1893) in *Studies on Hysteria*, pp. 7 ff.

lection should not be subject to the process of wearing
away to which most memories succumb. The state of in-
tactness of the memory, they felt, depended on the extent
of the reaction to the event that had originally produced
the affect. The concept "reaction" included such reflexes as
tears, rage, anger, and acts of revenge. Both Breuer and
Freud suggested that a sufficiently strong reaction discharged the affect completely, i.e., it leads to the abreaction
of the affect of the event. Breuer and Freud retained the old
distinction between chronic hysteria and (acute) hysterical
attacks and called attention to Charcot's schematic description of the four phases that were believed to characterize
all major hysterical attacks. Freud's loyal reference to
Charcot's favorite theory was made in 1893, the year after
Charcot's death and long after French medicine had dis-
credited as fictitious his theories on the four phases of
hysteria.

In enumerating Charcot's four phases of hysteria—the
epileptoid phase, the phase of large movements, the hallucinatory phase (*attitudes passionelles*), and the phase of
terminal delirium—Freud, speaking of Charcot as though he
were still alive, said that "Charcot derives all those forms
of hysterical attack which are in practice met with more
often than the complete grande attaque."[35] Freud's and
Breuer's own observations tended to confirm the existence
of Charcot's third phase, i.e., the *attitudes passionelles;* they
said, "Where this is present in a well-marked form, it exhibits the hallucinatory reproduction of a memory which
was important in bringing about the onset of the hysteria—
the memory either of a single major trauma or of a series
of interconnected part-traumas (such as underlie common
hysteria)."[36] Then they suggested that the symptom is always a symbol of a repressed traumatic memory. Similarly,
they found that an attack could be provoked under hypnosis
and that such artificially provoked seizures would then
serve an ancient need, namely, the establishment of a differential diagnosis of hysteria and epilepsy. And on this
occasion they gave a description of the usual manifestations

[35] *Ibid.*, p. 13.   [36] *Ibid.*, p. 14.

of hysteria which would also serve to explain the symptoms
of Freud's patient who accompanied him to Nancy.

The motor phenomena of hysterical attacks can be interpreted
partly as universal forms of reaction appropriate to the affect
accompanying the memory (such as kicking about and waving
the arms and legs, which even young babies do), partly as a
direct expression of these memories; but in part, like the hysterical stigmata found among the chronic symptoms, they cannot be
explained in this way.[37]

It is this description of the hysterical patient's extraordinary behavior that helps, in a way, to explain why hysteria
has become an apparently infrequent illness. In this century
behavior that includes "kicking about" and "waving the
arms and legs" is met with distaste and lack of sympathy
and is tolerated at best only among shrieking mobs of teen-
aged girls in response to their current idols. Whether it is
true or not, it has been suggested that, unlike the psychotic
patient, the person suffering from hysteria retains a sense
of reality in the course of the seizure and is thus able to
control his manifestations and to keep them within the limits
permissible in his ambient setting. Unacceptable today
would be the fainting ladies of the Victorian period, partly
because they would altogether fail to evoke any sympathetic
response in their social environment and partly because the
skill of fainting gracefully has almost disappeared. With the
increasing awareness of conversion reactions and the popularization of psychiatric literature, the "old-fashioned"
somatic expressions of hysteria have become suspect among
the more sophisticated classes, and hence most physicians
observe that obvious conversion symptoms are now rarely
encountered and, if at all, only among the uneducated of the
lower social strata. Thus hysteria has become subjectively
unrewarding. The helpful concern that was shown for hysterical women throughout the ages up to early in this
century has given way to uncomprehending indifference.

From the above it can be seen that Freud's studies on
hysteria, instead of endowing this illness with greater significance, actually divested it of much of the mystical importance it had held for more than two millennia. With

[37] *Ibid.*, p. 15.

much of the Freudian terminology having become part of sophisticated language, expressions such as "psychosomatic," "flight into illness," and "secondary gain" are understood by the potentially hysterical and by many others who are unwilling to make the hysteric a focus of attention. If, as has been stated, hysteria is primarily a means of achieving ego-satisfaction, this lack of attention could easily account for the nearly total disappearance of the illness. Thus, it may not be too paradoxical to state that it was the intensified understanding of the cause of hysteria by leading psychiatrists during this century that contributed to the near-disappearance of the disease. The newly gained insight into therapy finds its application in the severe psychoneuroses in general within which the potential hysterics of today are presumably included.

Bibliography

ABRICOSSOFF, G. *L'hystérie aux XVIIᵉ et XVIIIᵉ siècles.* Paris, 1897.

ALBUTT, CLIFFORD, *Greek Medicine in Rome.* London: Macmillan & Co., 1921.

ALEXANDER, FRANZ. *Fundamentals of Psychoanalysis.* New York: Norton & Co., 1948.

———. *The Scope of Psychoanalysis.* New York: Basic Books, 1961.

ALEXANDER, FRANZ, and ROSS, HELEN (eds.). *Dynamic Psychiatry.* Chicago: University of Chicago Press, 1952.

AMSELLE, GASTON. *Conception de l'hystérie. Étude historique et clinique.* Paris, 1907.

ARETAEUS. *The Extant Works of Aretaeus the Cappadocian.* Edited and translated by FRANCIS ADAMS. London: Sydenham Society, 1856.

ARIÈS, PHILIPPE. *Centuries of Childhood: A Social History of Family Life.* Translated by ROBERT BALDICK. New York: Alfred A. Knopf, 1962.

ARIETI, SILVANO. *American Handbook of Psychiatry.* New York: Basic Books, 1959.

ARNALDI VILLANOVI. *Philosophi et medici opera omnium.* Basel: Conrad Waldkirch, 1585.

ASTRUC, JEAN. *Traité des maladies des femmes.* Vol. VI. Paris, 1761–65.

AUGUSTINUS, ST. AURELIUS. *Writings of Saint Augustine.* Vol. VIII: *The City of God.* Translated by GERALD J. WALSH and DANIEL J. HONAN. New York: Fathers of the Church, 1954.

———. *The City of God against the Pagans.* Translated by GEORGE E. McCRACKEN. Cambridge, Mass.: Harvard University Press, 1957 (Loeb Classical Library).

———. *The Confessions of St. Augustine.* Translated by E. B. PUSEY. Rev. ed. Oxford: John Henry Parker, 1843.

BABINSKI, J. "Définition de l'hystérie," *Société de Neurologie* (Paris), November 7, 1901.

BABINSKI, J. "Démembrement de l'hystérie traditionelle. Pithiatisme," *Semaine médicale* (Paris), January 6, 1909.

———. "Hypnotisme et hystérie. Du rôle de l'hypnotisme en thérapeutique," *Gazette hebdomadaire* (Paris), July, 1891.

BABINSKI, J., and FROMENT, J. *Hysteria or Pithiatism and Reflex Nervous Disorders in the Neurology of War.* London: University of London Press, 1918.

BÄLZ, E. "Über Bessessenheit und religiöse Extase in Japan," *Mitteilungen der Gesellschaft für Natur- und Völkerkunde Ostasiens* (Tokyo), VI (1893–97), 293–397.

———. "Zur Psychologie der Japaner," *Globus*, LXXXIV, Part 20 (1903), 311–19.

BAGLIVI, GEORGE [GIORGIO]. *The Practice of Physic, reduc'd to the ancient Way of Observations, containing a just Parallel between the Wisdom of the Ancients and the Hypothesis's of Modern Physicians.* 2d ed. London: Midwinter, Linton, Strahan, etc., 1723.

BEALL, JR., OTHO, and SHRYOK, RICHARD H. *Cotton Mather: First Significant Figure in American Medicine.* Baltimore: Johns Hopkins Press, 1954.

BEKKER, BALTHASAR. *Die bezauberte Welt, oder eine gründliche Untersuchung allgemeinen Aberglaubens, betreffend die Art und das Vermögen, Gewalt und Wirkung des Satans und der bösen Geister über den Menschen und was diese durch derselben Kraft und Gemeinschaft thun.* Amsterdam: Daniel von Dohlen, 1693.

BELL, CHARLES. *The Anatomy and Philosophy of Expression.* London, 1806.

BERNHEIM, HIPPOLYTE. *De la suggestion et ces applications à la thérapeutique.* Paris, 1886.

———. *Suggestive Therapeutics: A Treatise on the Nature and Uses of Hypnotism.* Translated by CHRISTIAN A. HERTER. Westport, Conn.: Associated Booksellers, 1957.

BINZ, CARL. *Doktor Johann Weyer; ein rheinischer Arzt, der erste Bekämpfer des Hexenwahns.* 2d ed. Berlin, 1896.

BJERRE, POUL. *The History and Practice of Psychoanalysis.* Boston: Richard G. Badger, 1920.

BLANDFORD, G. FIELDING. *Insanity and Its Treatment: Lectures on the Treatment, Medical and Legal, of Insane Patients.* Philadelphia: Henry C. Lea, 1871.

BOURNEVILLE and REGNARD, P. *Iconographie photographique de la Salpêtrière, Service de M. Charcot.* Paris: Progrès Médical, 1877–80.

BRACHET, JEAN-LOUIS. *Traité de l'hystérie.* Lyons, 1847.

BRAID, JAMES. *Neurypnology: Or the Rationale of Nervous Sleep, Considered in Relation with Animal Magnetism.* London: J. Churchill, 1843.

Bibliography

BRAIN, LORD RUSSELL. "The Concept of Hysteria in the Time of William Harvey," *Proceedings of the Royal Society of Medicine,* LVI (April, 1963), 321–23.

BRENNER, CHARLES. *An Elementary Textbook of Psychoanalysis.* New York: International University Press, 1955.

BREUER, JOSEF, and FREUD, SIGMUND. *Studies on Hysteria. The Standard Edition of the Complete Psychological Works of Sigmund Freud.* Vol. II. London: Hogarth Press, 1957.

BRIQUET, PAUL. *Traité clinique et thérapeutique de l'hystérie.* Paris: J. B. Baillière, 1859.

BROCK, ARTHUR J. (trans.). *Greek Medicine, Being Abstracts Illustrative of Medical Writers from Hippocrates to Galen.* London: J. M. Dent & Sons, Ltd., 1929.

BROMBERG, WALTER. *Man above Humanity: A History of Psychotherapy.* Philadelphia: J. B. Lippincott Co., 1954.

BROWN, BAKER. *On the Curability of Certain Forms of Insanity, Epilepsy, Catalepsy, and Hysteria in Females.* London, 1866.

BUDBERG, ROGER BARON. "Zur Charakteristik des chinesischen Seelenlebens," *Globus,* XCVII (1910), 111–13.

BURR, G. L. *Narrative of the Witchcraft Cases.* New York: Barnes & Noble, 1959.

BURTON, ROBERT. *The Anatomy of Melancholy.* Edited by Floyd Dell and Paul Jordan-Smith. New York: Tudor Publishing Co., 1948.

CALEF, ROBERT. *More Wonders of the Invisible World.* London, 1700.

CARPENTER, WILLIAM BENJAMIN. *Principles of Human Physiology.* London: J. Churchill, 1844. Also published in *British Foreign Medical Review,* XXII (1846), 488.

CARTER, ROBERT BRUDENELL. *On the Pathology and Treatment of Hysteria.* London: John Churchill, 1853.

CARUS, C. G. *Vorlesungen über Psychologie.* Leipzig: Gerhard Fleischer, 1831.

CELSUS, AULUS CORNELIUS. *Celsus on Medicine, in Eight Books.* Translated from the L. Targa edition by ALEX LEE. London: E. Cox, 1831.

CESBRON, HENRY. *Histoire critique de l'hystérie.* Paris: Asselin et Houzeau, 1909.

CHAMBERLIN, BASIL HALL. *Things Japanese.* Yokohama: Kelly & Walsh, 1902.

CHARCOT, J.-M. "Isolation in the Treatment of Hysteria," *Clinical Lectures on Diseases of the Nervous System.* Translated by THOMAS SAVILL. London: New Sydenham Society, 1889.

———. *Leçons du mardi à la Salpêtrière, policlinique du 19 Mars.* Paris: Félix Alcan, 1889.

———. *Leçons sur les maladies du système nerveux faites à la Salpêtrière.* Paris: Delahaye, 1872–73.

———. *Lectures on the Diseases of the Nervous System.* Translated by GEORGE SIGERSON. London: New Sydenham Society, 1877.

CHARCOT, J.-M., and RICHER, PAUL. *Les démoniaques dans l'art.* Paris: A. Delahaye & E. Lecrosnier, 1887.

CHEYNE, GEORGE. *The Natural Method of Cureing the Disease of the Body and the Disorders of the Mind, Depending on the Body.* London: Strahan & Leake, 1873.

CULLEN, WILLIAM. *First Lines of the Practice of Physic, with practical and explanatory notes by John Rotheram.* Edinburgh: Bell, Bradfute etc., 1796.

D'ARCY, M. C., S.J., ET AL. *St. Augustine.* New York: Meridian Books, 1957.

DE GROOT, J. J. M. *The Religious System of China.* Leyden: E. J. Brill, 1910.

DIEPGEN, PAUL. *Geschichte der Medizin.* Berlin: Walter de Gruyter, 1949.

DORÉ, HENRI. *Manuel des superstitions chinoises.* Shanghai: Imprimerie de la Mission Catholique, 1926.

———. "Recherches sur les superstitions en Chine," *Variétés sinologiques,* Vols. 32–34, 36, 39, 41, 42–46, 49, 51, 61, 62, and 66. Shanghai: Imprimerie de la Mission Catholique, 1911–38.

DUBOIS, E. FRÉDÉRIC. *Histoire philosophique de l'hypochondrie et de l'hystérie.* Paris, 1833.

EDELSTEIN, EMMA J. and LUDWIG. *Asclepios: A Collection and Interpretation of the Testimonies.* Baltimore: Johns Hopkins Press, 1945.

EDWARDS, E. D. *Chinese Prose Literature of the T'ang Period.* London: Arthur Probsthain, 1937.

EHMANN, P. "Volkstümliche Vorstellungen in Japan," *Mitteilungen der Gesellschaft für Natur- und Völkerkunde Ostasiens* (Tokyo), VI, Part 57 (1893–97), 329.

FAIRBAIRN, W. R. D. "Observations on the Nature of Hysterical States." *British Journal of Medical Psychology* (London), Vol. XXVII (1954), 105.

FALRET, JEAN PIERRE. *De l'hypochondrie et du suicide.* Paris, 1882.

FALRET, JULES. *Études cliniques sur les maladies mentales et nerveuses.* Paris: Librairie Baillière et Fils, 1890.

FENICHEL, OTTO. *The Psychoanalytic Theory of Neurosis.* New York: Norton, 1945.

FÉRÉ, CH. *The Pathology of Emotions: Physiological and Clinical Studies.* Translated by ROBERT PARK. London: University Press, Ltd., 1899.

FEUCHTERSLEBEN, ERNST VON. *The Principles of Medical Psychology, being the outlines of a Course of Lectures.* Translated by H. EVANS LLOYD. Revised and edited by B. G. BABINGTON. London: Sydenham Society, 1847. Originally published as *Lehrbuch der ärztlichen Seelenkunde.* Vienna: Gerold, 1845.

FOREL, AUGUST. *Psychotherapy and Suggestion or Hypnotism: A Study of the Psychological, Psycho-physiological and Therapeutic Aspects of Hypnotism.* Translated from the fifth German edition H. W. Armit. New York: Allied Publishing Co., 1927.

Frankfort, Henri. *Kingship and the Gods: A Study of Near Eastern Religions as the Integration of Society and Nature.* Chicago: University of Chicago Press, 1948.

Freud, Sigmund. *An Autobiographical Study.* Translated by James Strachey. London: Hogarth Press, 1946.

———. "General Remarks on Hysterical Attacks." Vol. I. *Collected Papers.* London: Hogarth Press, 1948.

———. *Zur Geschichte der psychoanalytischen Bewegung.* Leipzig: Internationaler Psychoanalytischer Verlag, 1924.

———. *Die Medizin der Gegenwart in Selbstdarstellungen, Sonderdruck.* Leipzig: Felix Meiner, 1925.

Galen. *De locis affectis.* Liber VI. Venice: apud Junta, 1541.

Garinet, Jules. *Histoire de la magie en France.* Paris: Foulon, 1818.

Garrison, Fielding H. *An Introduction to the History of Medicine.* Philadelphia: Saunders Co., 1929.

Glanvil, Joseph. *Saducismus Triumphatus.* London: J. Collins & S. Lownds, 1681.

Glaus, A., and Grünthal, E. *Beiträge zur Geschichte der Psychiatrie und Hirnanatomie.* Basel: S. Karger, 1957.

Goltz, Frhr. von der. "Zauberei und Hexenkünste, Spiritismus und Schamanismus in China," *Mitteilungen der Deutschen Gesellschaft für Natur- und Völkerkunde Ostasiens* (Tokyo), II, Part 51 (1893–97), 17.

Granet, Marcel. *Le religion des Chinois.* Paris: Gauthiers-Villars, 1922.

Gregory, William. *Letters to Candid Inquiry on Animal Magnetism.* London: Taylor, Walton and Maberly, 1851.

Griesinger, Wilhelm. *Mental Pathology and Therapeutics.* Translated by C. Lockhard Robertson and James Rutherford. London: New Sydenham Society, 1867.

Grube, W. "Die chinesische Volksreligion und ihre Beeinflussung durch den Buddhismus," *Globus,* LIII (1893), 297–303.

Guillain, Georges. *J.-M. Charcot, 1825–1893, Sa vie–son oeuvre.* Paris: Masson, 1955. *J.-M. Charcot, 1825–1893, His Life–His Work.* Edited and translated by Pearce Bailey. New York: Paul Hoeber, Inc., 1959.

Guinon, Georges. *Les agents provocateurs de l'hystérie.* Paris, 1889.

Guttmacher, Alan F. "Ambroise Paré Does a Delivery," *Bulletin of the History of Medicine,* IV, No. 9 (1936).

Hammond, William A. *Spiritualism and Allied Causes and Conditions of Nervous Derangement.* London: H. K. Lewis, 1876.

Harvey, William. *On Parturition; in the Works of William Harvey, M.D.* Translated and with "A Life of the Author" by Robert Willis. London: Sydenham Society, 1847.

HELLPACH, WILLY. *Grundlinien einer Psychologie der Hysterie.* Leipzig: Wilhelm Engelmann, 1904.

HENDERSON, SIR DAVID, and BATCHELOR, IVOR R. C. *Textbook of Psychiatry.* London: Oxford University Press, 1962.

HERFELT, H. G. *De affectione hypochondriaca.* Duisburg on Rhine, 1678.

HIGHMORE, NATHANAEL. *De passione hysterica et hypochondriaca, responsio epistolaris ad Doctorem Willis.* London, 1670.

——. *Exercitationes duae quarum prior de passione hysterica; altera de affectione hypochondriaca, pathologia spasmodica vindicata.* . . . Leyden, 1671.

HILLMAN, ROBERT G. "A Scientific Study of Mystery: The Role of the Medical and Popular Press in the Nancy-Salpêtrière Controversy on Hypnotism," *Bulletin of the History of Medicine,* XXXIX, No. 2 (1965), 163–83.

Hippocrates. Vol. II. Translated by W. H. S. JONES. London: William Heineman, 1923 (Loeb Classical Library).

——. *Oeuvres complètes d'Hippocrate.* Vols. I, VII, and VIII. Translated by E. LITTRÉ. Paris: Baillière, 1851.

HOFFMANN, FRIEDRICH. *Opera omnia physico-medica.* Geneva: Fratres de Tournes, 1746.

HUNTER, RICHARD, and MACALPINE, IDA. *Three Hundred Years of Psychiatry, 1535–1860.* London: Oxford University Press, 1963.

HUTCHINSON, FRANCIS. *An Historical Essay concerning Witchcraft.* London: R. Knaplock, 1718.

JAMES VI. *Daemonologie, In Form of a Dialogue divided into three books: written by the high and mighty Prince, James by the grace of God, King of England, Scotland, France and Ireland, Defender of the Faith, etc.* London: Robert Waldgrave, 1603.

JANET, PIERRE. *The Major Symptoms of Hysteria: Fifteen Lectures Given in the Medical School of Harvard University.* 2d ed. New York: Macmillan Co., 1920.

——. *The Mental State of Hystericals: A Study of Mental Stigmata and Mental Accidents.* Translated by R. C. CARSON. New York: Putnam & Sons, 1901.

——. *Les obsessions et la psychasthénie.* Paris: Félix Alcan, 1908.

——. *Psychological Healing: A Historical and Clinical Study.* Translated by EDEN and SEDAR PAUL. New York: Macmillan Co., 1925.

JASPERS, KARL. *General Psychopathology.* Translated by J. HOENIG and MARIA W. HAMILTON. Chicago: University of Chicago Press, 1963.

——. *Plato, Augustin, Kant. Drei Gründer des Philosophierens.* Munich: R. Piper & Co., 1957.

JONES, ERNEST. *The Life and Work of Sigmund Freud.* New York: Basic Books, 1953.

JORDEN, EDWARD. *A Brief Discourse of a Disease called the Suffocation of the Mother.* London: John Windet, 1603.

KAECH, RÉNÉ. "Die Hysterie," *Ciba Zeitschrift* (Basel), X, Part 120 (1950), 4406–36.

KANT, IMMANUEL. *Von der Macht des Gemüts durch den blossen Vorsatz seiner krankhaften Gefühle Meister zu sein.* Edited by C. W. HUFELAND (1824). Leipzig: Philipp Reklam jun., 1929.

KRAEPELIN, EMIL. *One Hundred Years of Psychiatry.* New York: Citadel Press, 1962.

KRETSCHMER, ERNST. *Hysterie, Reflex und Instinkt.* 5th ed. Stuttgart, 1948.

LAIGNEL-LAVASTINE, MAXIME, and VINCHON, JEAN. *Les maladies de l'esprit et leurs médecins du XVIe au XIXe siècles.* Paris, 1930.

LAYCOCK, THOMAS. *An Essay on Hysteria.* Philadelphia, 1840.

LEGRAND DU SAULLE, HENRI. *Les hystériques.* Paris, 1863.

LEIGH, DENIS. *The Historical Development of British Psychiatry.* New York: Pergamon Press, 1961.

LEIPOLDT, JOHANNES, *Von Epidaurus bis Lourdes: Bilder aus der Geschichte Volkstümlicher Frömmigkeit.* Hamburg: Herbert Reich Evangelischer Verlag G.m.b.H., 1957.

LESKY, ERNA. "Wiener Psychiatrie im Vormärz," *Gesnerus,* XIX (1962), 119–29.

LINTON, RALPH. *Culture and Mental Illness.* Springfield, Ill.: Charles C Thomas, 1956.

LOEWENFELD, LEOPOLD. *Pathologie und Therapie der Neurasthenie und Hysterie.* Wiesbaden, 1894.

MACKAY, CHARLES. *Extraordinary Popular Delusions and the Madness of Crowds.* New York: L. C. Page & Co., 1932.

———. *Memoirs of Extraordinary Popular Delusions.* London: Richard Bentley, 1841.

MACKINNEY, LOREN. *Early Medieval Medicine, with Special Reference to France and Chartres.* Baltimore: Johns Hopkins Press, 1937.

MALLEUS MALEFICARUM. Translated and with an Introduction, Bibliography, and Notes by MONTAGUE SUMMERS. London: Pushkin Press, 1951.

MATHER, COTTON. Diary. Edited by W. C. FORD, 1911–12.

———. *History of New England.* 1702.

MAUDSLEY, HENRY. *Body and Will, Metaphysical, Physiological, and Pathological Aspects.* New York: D. Appleton & Co., 1884.

———. *Life in Mind and Conduct.* London: Macmillan & Co., 1902.

MENNINGER, KARL. *The Vital Balance.* New York: Viking Press, 1963.

MILLER, PERRY. *The New England Mind: From Colony to Province.* Cambridge, Mass.: Harvard University Press, 1953.

MITCHELL, S. WEIR. *Doctor and Patient.* Philadelphia: J. B. Lippincott & Co., 1888.

MITCHELL, S. WEIR. *Fat and Blood: and How To Make Them.*
Philadelphia: J. B. Lippincott & Co., 1877.
———. *Lectures on the Diseases of the Nervous System, Especially
in Women.* Philadelphia: Henry C. Lea's Son & Co., 1881.
MOOR, BARTHOLOMEUS DE. *Dissertatio de suffocatione hypochondriaca et hysterica.* Leyden, 1699.
MOORE, GEORGE. *The Power of the Soul over the Body, Consid-
ered in Relation to Health and Moral.* 2d ed. London: Long-
man, Brown, Green and Longmans, 1845.
MÜLLER, F. W. K. "Japanisches Buch, Gespenster-Darstellungen
enthaltend," *Verhandlungen der Berliner Gesellschaft für An-
thropologie, Ethnologie und Urgeschichte,* XXVI (1894), pp.
77–79.
MUNTHE, AXEL. *The Story of San Michele.* New York: E. P. Dut-
ton & Co., 1930.
NEUBURGER, MAX. *History of Medicine.* Translated by ERNEST
PLAYFAIR. London: Oxford University Press, 1910.
NOYES, ARTHUR. *Modern Clinical Psychiatry.* Philadelphia: W. B.
Saunders Co., 1953.
*The Papyri Petri, Hieratic Papyri from Kahun and Gurob.
Principally of the Middle Kingdom.* Vol. I: *Literary, Medical
and Mathematical Papyri from Kahun.* Edited by F. L. I. I.
GRIFFITH. London: Bernard Quaritch, 1897.
The Papyrus Ebers, the Greatest Egyptian Medical Document.
Translated by B. EBBELL. Copenhagen: Levin & Munksgaard,
1937.
PARÉ, AMBROISE. *The Workes of that famous Chirurgion Am-
brose Parey, trans. out of the Latine and compared with the
French* by THOMAS JOHNSON. London: R. Cotes & W. Du-
gard, 1649.
PINEL, PHILIPPE. *Nosographie philosophique ou la méthode de
l'analyse appliquée à la médecine.* 5th ed. Paris: J. A. Brosson,
1813.
———. *A Treatise on Insanity.* Translated by D. D. DAVIS. Lon-
don: Cadell and Davies, 1806.
PISO, C. *Selectiorum observationum et conciliorum de praeteretis.*
Pont-à-Mousson, 1618.
PITRES, A. *Leçons cliniques sur l'hystérie et l'hypnotisme faites
à l'hôpital Saint-André de Bordeaux.* Paris: Octave Doin, 1891.
POMME, PIERRE. *Traité des affections vapoureuses de deux sexes,
ou maladies nerveuses vulgairement appelées maux de nerfs.*
Paris: Imprimerie Royale, 1782.
POPE, HUGH (O.P.). *Saint Augustine of Hippo.* London: Sands
& Co., 1937.
P'U, SUNG-LING. "Die Füchsin," translated by PAUL KÜHNEL, *Geist
des Ostens, Monatsschrift für Asiatische Völkerpsychologie*
(Munich), I, Part 3 (1913), 137–47.
———. *Strange Stories from a Chinese Studio.* Translated and ed-

ited by HERBERT A. GILES. London: Thos. de la Rue & Co., 1880.

RABELAIS, FRANÇOIS. *Pantagruel* in *The Portable Rabelais.* Translated and edited by SAMUEL PUTNAM. New York: Viking Press, 1946.

RAIMANN, EMIL. *Die Hysterischen Geistesstörungen: Eine Klinische Studie.* Leipzig and Vienna: Franz Deuticke, 1904.

RAULIN, JOSEPH. *Traité des affections vaporeuses du sexe avec l'exposition de leurs symptômes, de leurs différentes causes et la méthode de les guérir.* Paris, 1758.

REYNOLDS, RUSSEL. "Remarks on Paralysis and Other Disorders of Motion and Sensation. Department on Idea," *British Medical Journal,* July, 1869.

RICHARDSON, BENJAMIN WARD. *Diseases of Modern Life.* New York: D. Appleton & Co., 1876.

RICHER, PAUL. *Étude descriptive de la grande attaque hystérique ou attaque hystéro-épileptique et de ces principales variétés.* Paris: Adrien Delahaye, 1879.

———. *Études cliniques sur hystéro-épilepsie ou grande hystérie, précédé d'une lettre-préface de M. le professeur J.-M. Charcot.* Paris: Adrien Delahaye, 1884.

RIESE, WALTHER. *Conception of Disease: Its History, Its Versions, and Its Nature.* New York: Philosophical Library, 1953.

———. *A History of Neurology.* New York: MD Publications, Inc., 1959.

———. "History and Principles of Classification of Nervous Diseases," *Bulletin of the History of Medicine,* XVIII (1945), 465.

———. "The History of the Term and Conception of Neurosis" in "Pre-Freudian Origins of Psychoanalysis" in *Science and Psychoanalysis.* New York: Grune & Stratton, 1958.

RIESE, W., and HOFF, E. C. "A History of the Doctrine of Cerebral Localization," *Journal of the History of Medicine and Allied Sciences,* I (1950), 50, and VI (1951), 439.

ROEDER, G. *Urkunden zur Religion des alten Aegyptens.* Jena, 1916.

RUSH, BENJAMIN. "An Account of the Influence . . . of the American Revolution upon the Human Body" in *Medical Inquiries and Observations.* 3d ed. Philadelphia: Hopkins and Earle, 1809.

———. *Medical Inquiries and Observations upon the Diseases of the Mind.* Philadelphia: John Grigg, 1812.

SARTON, GEORGE. *Galen of Pergamon.* Lawrence: University of Kansas Press, 1954.

SAUNDERS, J. B. DE C. M. *The Transitions from Ancient Egyptian to Greek Medicine.* Lawrence: University of Kansas Press, 1963.

SAUVAGES, FRANÇOIS BOISSIER DE. *Nosologia methodica sistens morborum classes.* Amsterdam, 1763.

SAVILL, THOMAS DIXON. *Lectures on Hysteria and Allied Vasomotor Conditions.* New York: William Wood & Co., 1909.

SCHMIDT, R. W. *Der Hexenhammer.* Berlin: H. Barsdorf, 1906.

SCHULTZ, PAUL. *Gehirn und Seele.* Leipzig: Ambrosius Barth, 1903.

SCHWARTZ, LEONHARD. *Die Neurose und die dynamische Psychologie von Pierre Janet.* Basel: Benno Schwabe, 1951.

SELIGMANN, KURT. *The History of Magic.* New York: Pantheon Books (n.d.).

SIGERIST, HENRY E. *Civilization and Disease.* Chicago: University of Chicago Press, 1962.

———. *Four Treatises by Paracelsus.* Translated and with introductory essays by C. LILLIAN TEMKIN, GEORGE ROSEN, GREGORY ZILBOORG, and HENRY E. SIGERIST. Baltimore: Johns Hopkins Press, 1941.

———. *A History of Medicine.* Vol. I. *Primitive and Archaic Medicine.* New York: Oxford University Press, 1951.

SMITH, JACKSON. *Psychiatry: Descriptive and Dynamic.* Baltimore: Williams & Wilkins, 1960.

SMOLLIUS, G. *Trias maritima, proponens per introductionem trium aegrotantium, sororum morbosarum, domesticarum, hypochondriacae spleneticae; hypochondriacae meseraicae; hypochondriacae phantasticae; ortum et interitum.*

SOLLMANN, TORALD. *A Manual of Pharmacology.* Philadelphia, 1918.

Soranus' Gynecology. Translated and with an Introduction by OWSEI TEMKIN. Baltimore: Johns Hopkins Press, 1956.

STRÜMPELL, ADOLF. *A Textbook of Medicine for Students and Practitioners.* New York, 1911.

SWIETEN, GERARD VAN. *The Commentaries upon the Aphorisms of Herman Boerhaave.* Translated. 2d ed. London: Horsfield & Longman, 1765.

The Works of Thomas Sydenham, M.D. Translated from the Latin edition of Dr. Greenhill with a "Life of the Author" by R. G. LATHAM. London, 1848.

SZASZ, THOMAS S. *The Myth of Mental Illness: Foundation of a Theory of Personal Conduct.* London: Secker & Warburg, 1961.

TEMKIN, OWSEI. *The Falling Sickness.* Baltimore: Johns Hopkins Press, 1945.

TEN KATE, H. "Ethno-psychologische Beobachtungen und Betrachtungen," *Geist des Ostens, Monatsschrift für volkstümliche Asienkunde,* I, Part II (1914), 642–63.

———. "Zur Psychologie der Japaner," *Globus,* LXXXII, Part 4 (1902), 53.

Townshend, Chauncey Hare. *Facts in Mesmerism with Reasons for Dispassionate Inquiry into it.* London: Hippolyte Ballière, 1844.

Trotula of Salerno. *The Diseases of Women.* A Translation of *Passionibus Mulierum Curandorum* by Elizabeth Mason-Hohl. Los Angeles: Ward Ritchie Press, 1940.

Tuke, Daniel Hack. *A Dictionary of Psychological Medicine.* London: J. & A. Churchill, 1892.

———. *Illustrations of the Influence of the Mind upon the Body in Health and Disease, Designed to Elucidate the Action of the Imagination.* London, 1872.

Van Diik, C. *De suffocatione hypochondriaca.* Leyden, 1665.

Van Gulik, R. H. *Sexual Life in Ancient China: A Preliminary Survey of Chinese Sex and Society from* ca. *1500 B.C. until 1644 A.D.* Leyden: E. J. Brill, 1961.

Veith, Ilza. "Government Control and Medicine in Eleventh Century China," *Bulletin of the History of Medicine,* XIV, No. 2 (1959), 159–72.

———. "From Mesmerism to Hypnotism," *Modern Medicine,* May 15, 1959, pp. 195–206.

———. "From Hypnotism to Suggestion," *ibid.,* June 15, 1959, pp. 304–14.

———. "Hysteria," *ibid.,* February 15, 1960, pp. 178–83.

———. "On Hysterical and Hypochondriacal Afflictions," *Bulletin of the History of Medicine,* XXX, No. 3 (1956), 233–40.

———. *Some Philosophical Concepts of Early Chinese Medicine.* Transaction No. 4. Basavangudi: Indian Institute of Culture, 1950.

———. "Psychiatric Thought in Chinese Medicine," *Journal of the History of Medicine and Allied Sciences,* X, No. 3 (1955), 263–68.

Visser, M. W. de. "The Dog and Cat in Japanese Folk-lore," *Transactions of the Asiatic Society of Japan* (Yokohama), XXXVII, Part I (1909), 1–84.

———. "Fire and ignes fatui in China," *Mitteilungen des Seminars für orientalische Sprachen zu Berlin* (Berlin), Vol. XXVII, Part I (1914).

———. "The Fox and the Badger in Japanese Folk-lore," *Transactions of the Asiatic Society of Japan* (Yokohama), XXXVI, Part III (1908), 10.

———. "The Snake in Japanese Superstition," *Mitteilungen des Seminars für orientalische Sprachen zu Berlin* (Berlin), XIV, Part I (1911), 267–322.

———. "The Tengu," *Transactions of the Asiatic Society of Japan* (Yokohama), XXXVI, Part II (1908), 25–99.

Voss, Georg. *Klinische Beiträge zur Lehre der Hysterie. Nach*

Beobachtungen aus dem Nordwesten Russlands. Jena: Gustav Fischer, 1909.

WALEY, ARTHUR. *The Way and Its Power: A Study of the Tao Te Ching and Its Place in Chinese Thought.* New York: Grove Press, 1958.

WATTERS, THOMAS. "Chinese Fox Myths," *Journal of the North China Branch of the Royal Asiatic Society* (Shanghai), New Series, VIII (1874), 45–65.

WERNER, E. T. C. *Myths and Legends of China.* London: George Harrap & Co., Ltd., 1958.

WESTHOFF, R. *De affectu hypochondriae.* Argentorati, 1668.

WHYTT, ROBERT. *Observations on the Nature, Causes, and Cure of those Disorders which have been commonly called Nervous, Hypochondriac, or Hysteric: to which are prefixed some Remarks on the Sympathy of the Nerves.* Edinburgh: J. Balfour, 1767.

WIERUS (WEYER), J. *Joannis Wieri illustrissimi Ducis Julioe Clevioe etc., quondam archiatri, Opera omnia. . . . Apud Petrum vanden Berge, sub signo Montis Parnassi.* 1660.

WILLIS, THOMAS. *Affectionum quae dicuntur hystericae et hypochondriacae, vindicata contra responsionem epistolarum Nathanaelis Highmore.* London, 1670.

———. *Cerebri anatome, cui accessit nervorum descriptio et usus.* London, 1664.

———. *An Essay of the Pathology of the Brain and Nervous Stock in which Convulsive Diseases are treated of.* Translated by S. P. CORDAGE. London: Dring, Leigh, and Harper, 1684.

———. *Pathologiae cerebri et nervosi generis in quo agitur de morbis convulsivis.* Oxford, 1667.

WYLIE, A. *Notes on Chinese Literature.* Shanghai: American Presbyterian Mission Press, 1867.

ZILBOORG, GREGORY. *A History of Medical Psychology.* New York: W. W. Norton & Co., 1941.

———. *The Medical Man and the Witch during the Renaissance.* Baltimore: Johns Hopkins Press, 1935.

ZÜRICH, PSYCHOLOGISCHER CLUB. *Die kulturelle Bedeutung der komplexen Psychologie.* Berlin: Julius Springer, 1935.

ZWAAN, J. P. KLEIWEG DE. "Völkerkundliches und Geschichtliches über die Heilkunde der Chinesen und Japaner," *Natuurkundige Verhandelingen van de Hollandsche Maatschappij der Wetenschappen to Haarlem,* 3d Series, Part 7. Harlem: Erven Loosjes, 1917.

Name Index

Subject Index

Abdomen, 10, 13, 39, 63, 115, 116, 129, 135, 141, 157, 162, 164, 168
Abdominal binder, 11, 99, 116, 135, 136, 216
Ablution, 12, 13, 17
Abortives, 26
Abstinence, sexual, 10, 31, 38, 42, 43, 56, 96, 97, 114, 115, 123, 127, 130, 167, 182, 197, 202, 203, 218, 265
Abulia, 249
Academy of Sciences, French, 239
Addiction, 165, 166, 205, 216
Alchemy, 100
Alcohol, 95
Alexandria, 25, 33
Alienation, mental. *See* Disease, mental
Amenorrhea, 13, 97, 98, 111, 118, 119, 123, 172, 181, 182, 183, 196
America, 50, 70, 151, 171, 173, 174, 212, 214, 259
Amnesia, 28, 87, 101, 122, 179, 195, 216, 249, 259
Amusement as therapy, 151, 181, 208
Amyotrophic lateral sclerosis, 229
Analgesia, 227, 239, 241
Analgesics, 165, 227
Anatomy, 11, 27, 28, 32, 33, 39, 51, 108, 112, 113, 131, 132, 133, 176, 187, 199, 248
Ancestral spirits, 76, 81, 83, 90; worship, 80, 83
Anemia, 167, 198, 205, 206
Anesthesia, 61, 65, 67, 114, 120, 121, 122, 129, 196, 227, 239, 241, 249

Anger, 44, 91, 123, 125, 142, 143, 161, 162, 185, 196, 206, 272
Animal faculties, 122, 123; magnetism, 221, 222, 223, 225, 226, 227; spirits, 114, 133, 134, 135, 136, 143, 144, 160, 170
Animism, 55, 75, 83, 84, Pl. V
Anorexia, 39, 98, 116, 148, 149, 179, 181, 216
Antihystericals, 4
Antiquity, 2–42, 49, 60, 94, 102, 115, 119, 141, 156, 198
Antispasmodics, 4, 136
Anxiety. *See* Fear
Aphasia, 18, 23, 24, 98, 101, 120, 126, 181, 182, 183, 210, 237
Aphonia, 10, 12, 29, 69, 98, 129
Aphorisms: Boerhaave's, 167; Hippocratic, 10, 25
Apoplexy, 108
Arabs, 94, 95, 96, 102, 104
Armada (Spanish), 137
Aromatics, 4, 5, 11, 13, 24, 30, 98
Arthropathy, tabetic, 229
Asafetida, 4, 136
Asia, 74–94, 109
Asthma, 164
Astrology, 100, 104, 124
Astronomy, 222
Asylum. *See* Hospitals, mental
Athens, 16
Atoms, 27
Attacks, hysterical. *See* Convulsions
Auscultation, 185
Austria, 167, 185, 252, 257, 262
Automatism, 253
Autopsy, 33, 133, 134, 178, 179, 183, 259